On Linearization

Linguistic Inquiry Monographs
Samuel Jay Keyser, general editor

A complete list of books published in the Linguistic Inquiry Monographs series appears at the back of this book.

On Linearization
Toward a Restrictive Theory

Guglielmo Cinque

The MIT Press
Cambridge, Massachusetts
London, England

The MIT Press would like to thank the anonymous peer reviewers who provided comments on drafts of this book. The generous work of academic experts is essential for establishing the authority and quality of our publications. We acknowledge with gratitude the contributions of these otherwise uncredited readers.

This book was set in Times New Roman by Westchester Publishing Services. Printed and bound in the United States of America.

Library of Congress Cataloging-in-Publication Data

Names: Cinque, Guglielmo, author.
Title: On linearization : toward a restrictive theory / Guglielmo Cinque.
Description: Cambridge, Massachusetts : The MIT Press, 2023. | Series: Linguistic inquiry monographs | Includes bibliographical references and index.
Identifiers: LCCN 2022016358 | ISBN 9780262544955 (paperback) | ISBN 9780262372879 (epub) | ISBN 9780262372862 (pdf)
Subjects: LCSH: Grammar, Comparative and general—Word order.
Classification: LCC P295 .C55 2023 | DDC 415—dc23/eng/20220502
LC record available at https://lccn.loc.gov/2022016358

10 9 8 7 6 5 4 3 2 1

To Cino Renzi and Sandu Niculescu

Contents

Series Foreword

We are pleased to present the eighty-fourth volume in the series *Linguistic Inquiry Monographs.* These monographs present new and original research beyond the scope of the article. We hope they will benefit our field by bringing to it perspectives that will stimulate further research and insight.

Originally published in limited edition, the *Linguistic Inquiry Monographs* are now more widely available. This change is due to the great interest engendered by the series and by the needs of a growing readership. The editors thank the readers for their support and welcome suggestions about future directions for the series.

Samuel Jay Keyser
for the Editorial Board

Acknowledgments

I wish to thank David Adger, Boban Arsenijević, Paola Benincà, Noam Chomsky, Yoshio Endo, Alessandra Giorgi, Alex Grosu, Roland Hinterhölzl, Richard Kayne, Jaklin Kornfilt, Iliyana Krapova, Yuri Lander, Audrey Li, Rita Manzini, David Peter Medeiros, Andrea Moro, Nicola Munaro, Cecilia Poletto, Andrew Radford, Luigi Rizzi, Ian Roberts, Joachim Sabel, Emanuela Sanfelici, Ur Shlonsky, Dominique Sportiche, Stanislao Zompì, and in particular Peter Svenonius and two anonymous referees for their helpful observations in written or oral form. None of them should be taken to share the conclusions reached here. Part of this work was initiated at the University of Connecticut, Storrs, in the spring of 2020. I thank the students of my Problems in Syntax class, where I presented part of this material, and Željko Bošković, Andrea Calabrese, William Snyder, Adrian Stegovec, and Yuta Tatsumi for discussions relating to various parts of this work.

I'm also grateful for the questions and comments I received from the participants of the online reading group seminars of the University of Padua (Cecilia Poletto, Nicola D'Antuono, Tommaso Mattiuzzi, Giacomo Presotto, Emanuela Sanfelici, Yangyu Sun, Caterina Tasinato) and the University of Graz (Boban Arsenijević, Svitlana Antonyuk-Yudina, Predrag Kovačević, Stefan Milosavljević, Petra Mišmaš, Stefano Quaglia, and Marko Simonović), as well as to Aquiles Tescari Neto,

Sandra Quarezemin, and the audience of my online talk in June 2021 at the colloquium series "Zoom na Cartografia," organized by LaCaSa (Cartographic Syntax Laboratory) at the University of Campinas and NEG (Grammar Studies Center) at the Federal University of Santa Catarina, and to the audiences of an online talk on "Cartography and Linear Order" given at the 4th International Workshop on Syntactic Cartography at Beijing Language and Culture University on October 29th 2021, and at the University of Geneva on November 30th 2021.

Abbreviations and Symbols

*	Ungrammatical construction
%	Interspeaker variation
-	Morpheme boundary
=	Clitic boundary
( )	Optional
1, 2, 3	first, second, third person
ABL	Ablative
ABS	Absolutive
ACC	Accusative
Add	Additive
A(dj)	Adjective
Adv(P)	Adverb (Phrase)
AFF	Affix
Agr	Agreement
AN	Adjective Noun
ANIM	Animate
AOR	Aorist (tense)
AP	Adjective Phrase
ART	Article
Asp	Aspect
Ass	Associative (marking possession)
AT	Actor Topic
Aux	Auxiliary (verb)

C	Complementizer
Card	Cardinal (morpheme/Numeral)
CLF	Classifier
CM	Class marker
COMP	Complementizer
COP	Copula
CP	Complementizer Phrase
DE	de (Chinese nominal marker)
DEF	Definite
Deg	Degree
Dem	Demonstrative
Det	Determiner
DIM	Diminutive
DO	Direct Object
DP	Determiner Phrase
DU	Dual
DUR	Durative
ERG	Ergative
EVID	Evidential
EXT	Existential
F	Feminine
FOFC	Final-over-Final Condition
FP	Functional Projection
FUT	Future (tense)
GEN	Genitive
GN	Genitive Noun
Hum	Human
I-Language	Internal, Individual, Intensional Language
IMPF	Imperfect
INF	Infinitive
INTNS	Intensifier
INTR	Intransitive
IO	Indirect Object

IP	Inflectional Phrase
IPP	*Infinitivus Pro Participio*
KP	Case Phrase
LCA	Linear Correspondence Axiom
LF	Logical Form (interface)
Mod	Modal
N	Noun
NA	Noun Adjective
Neg	Negative (morpheme)
NMLZ	Nominalizer
NOM	Nominative
NP	Noun Phrase
Num	Numeral
O(bj)	Object
OP	Object Preposition
Ord	Ordinal (morpheme/Numeral)
OV	Object Verb Order
P	Preposition
Part	Particle
PART	Participle
PERF	Perfect
PERS	Person
PF	Phonetic-Form (interface)
PL	Plural
Po	Postpositional
PO	Preposition Object
POSS	Possessive
PP	Prepositional Phrase
PRES	Present (tense)
PRN	Pronoun
PRFV	Perfective
PROG	Progressive (morpheme)
PROX	Proximate (Demonstrative)

PST	Past (tense)
REFL	Reflexive
REL	Relative Marker/Clause
REP	Reportive (Evidential)
S	Sentence
s	Singular
SG	Singular
SM	Sensory-Motor (interface)
SOV	Subject Object Verb
Spec	Specifier
SR	Subject Relative
Subj	Subject
Subord	Subordinator
SVO	Subject Verb Object
TOP	Topic(alized)
T(P)	Tense (Phrase)
TV	Transitive Verb Suffix
UTAH	Uniformity of Theta Role Assignment
V	Verb
V2	Verb Second
VO	Verb Object
VOS	Verb Object Subject
VP	Verb Phrase
VSO	Verb Subject Object
WALS	World Atlas of Language Structures
WCCFL	West Coast Conference in Formal Linguistics (Proceedings of__)
XP	stands in for NP, VP, AP, . . .

1 Introduction

The derivation of linear order is often taken to be rather trivial as the physics of speech, it is said, leaves just two options (a head either precedes or follows its complements and modifiers). However, this idea falls short of a number of generalizations concerning linear order; among which are the facts that of all the theoretically possible combinations of *n* elements only a specifiable subset is ever attested, and more orders are found to the right of a head than to its left (just one). The physics of speech does not help us understand these generalizations. An account of them and the hope of deriving the orders of all languages from one and the same hierarchical structure via the same basic principles through a restrictive theory of linear order, however, may be attained once we have (i) a precise understanding of the fine-grained hierarchies and subhierarchies that underlie the clause and its phrases, (ii) a restriction on movement whereby only the head of each (sub)hierarchy can move (by itself or in one of the two pied piping modes), and (iii) Kayne's Linear Correspondence Axiom (LCA). Here I will try to delineate a possible first implementation of a restrictive theory of linear order along these lines.

The bewildering variation in word order among the languages of the world should not detain us from researching what, if anything, determines which orders are possible (and attested or attestable) and which orders are impossible (and not attested/

nonattestable), both when they maximally conform to the "head-final" or "head-initial" types and when they depart from them to varying degrees. This quest should be pursued, I think, as some results may be within our reach.

A recent influential position takes word order variation not to be part of I-language (internal, individual, intensional language) but of the sensory-motor (SM), or phonetic-form (PF) interface, in other words, as a product of externalization: "There is mounting evidence that linear ordering is not part of I-language, though it is of course required by the sensory-motor system. The I-language therefore provides the hierarchical structure, but externalization to SM has to fix order" (Chomsky in Boechat de Medeiros 2017: 18).[1]

If the I-Language (specifically, narrow syntax) creates only hierarchical structures via Merge, how are hierarchical structures linearized?

Chomsky's current position of Merge as binary set formation yielding unordered sets that are linearized only at PF (Chomsky 2020: 22) was already discussed in Chomsky (1965: 123–126) given proposals in Curry (1961) and Šaumjan and Soboleva (1963) (cf. Hall [Partee] 1964 and Šaumjan 1965) that rewriting rules should yield unordered sets (as in (1)) rather than the ordered strings widely assumed then (cf. (2)).[2]

(1) a. S → {NP, VP} = {VP, NP}
    b. VP → {V, NP} = {NP, V}

(2) a. S → NP ⁀ VP
    b. VP → V ⁀ NP

At the time Chomsky dismissed that proposal as "no proponents of a set-system has given any indication of how the abstract underlying unordered structures are converted into actual strings with surface structures" (1965: 125).

As also noted in Holmberg (2017: 44), things could now be different because there is one detailed proposal of how hierarchical structures can be converted into actual strings: Kayne's (1994)

LCA. And the following year, this was Chomsky's position: "we take the LCA to be a principle of the phonological component" (1995: 340), which implied that some meaningless movement in narrow syntax had to be assumed for the correct derivation of word order differences within one language and across languages.

However, as this is incompatible with the idea that meaningless movements (just "to yield the proper hierarchies" [Chomsky 2004: 110]) should be eliminated from narrow syntax, and because asymmetric c-command is no longer always ensured in the bare phrase structure approach, things have more recently become less clear as to what mechanisms are responsible for word order differences.

Absence of an explicit theory of linearization/externalization would thus risk taking us back to Chomsky's (1965) dismissal of set systems.

Although it is perfectly possible that some externalization mechanism distinct from the LCA could be found that accounts for the conversion of the universal set–based hierarchical structure to the variety of word orders found within and across languages, the task is anything but trivial. As noted, what is often assumed (see (3) and (4)) seems in any event far from being sufficient:

(3) "The physics of speech demand that linguistic units must be pronounced sequentially in time, giving rise, in this case, to just two options: the head either precedes or follows its complements." (Eguren, Fernández-Soriano, and Mendikoetxea 2016: 12)

(4) "[In Japanese] the VP is linearized with OV order (*John-o sikarta*), whereas a corresponding English VP would surface with VO order (*scolded John*). Interpretation is not affected by this difference, suggesting that the relevant parameter should be a matter of externalization of internally generated expressions alone." (Chomsky, Gallego, and Ott [2017] 2019: 4)

The idea that the linearization of two unordered elements, {XP, Y}, can be trivially obtained by having one to either precede or follow the other (XP > Y or Y > XP) falls short of at least the following generalizations, two of which were already mentioned:

(5) a. Why, out of all the mathematically possible orders of *n* elements, only a subset is ever attested.
  b. Why there are more ordering possibilities to the right of a lexical head than to its left.
  c. Why in the same extended projection a head-initial phrase above a head-final one is attested but a head-final one above a head-initial one is never or extremely rarely found.[3]
  d. Why among the possible, attested, orders some are cross-linguistically frequent and others less frequent, in a decreasing cline.

I assume that a theory of linearization/externalization should be able to say something about these generalizations.

As movement appears to provide a unified answer to them,[4] there may be some reason to retain at least *some* apparently meaningless movement in narrow syntax (see section 5.4), which in turn will allow us to retain the LCA (whether at PF, as in Chomsky [1995: 340, 2020], or in narrow syntax, as in Kayne [2018, 2020a]—also see Willer Gold et al. [2018]). Indeed, as I try to argue, we can attain a restrictive theory of linearization that may also derive the generalizations in (5) once we have a precise understanding of the hierarchies and subhierarchies that constitute the clause and its phrases, Kayne's LCA, and, crucially, a condition on movement whereby only the head of each (sub)hierarchy can move (by itself or in one of the possible ways movement can take place). For example, we know that Internal Merge of a *wh*-phrase can take place in one of three ways: (i) by moving just the *wh*-phrase, the minimal relevant target phrase undergoing Internal Merge (see (6a)); (ii) by moving a larger constituent containing the target and lower nontarget material (which we may call [*whose-pictures*] pied piping) (see (6b)); (iii) by moving a larger constituent containing the target and higher nontarget material (which we may call [*pictures-of-whom*] pied piping) (see (6c)):[5]

(6) a. Aylan, [**who**] you have certainly seen [pictures of [__]],..
b. Aylan, [[**whose**] pictures] you have certainly seen [__],..
c. Aylan, [pictures of [**whom**]] you have certainly seen [__],..

In the nominal extended projection, KP, the targets are the nominal heads (e.g., the Noun, the Determiner, the Case head), which move, just like the *wh*-phrase, by themselves, or, in one of the two pied piping modes, dragging along nontarget material within a larger constituent. In the verbal extended projection, Complementizer Phrase, CP, the relevant targets are the verbal heads (e.g., the Verb, the Aspectual Verbs, the Modal Verbs), which move, by themselves or in one of the two pied piping modes.

As we are going to see later, movements of the [*whose-pictures*] pied piping type, as well as those without pied piping (both of which reverse the original order of Merge), underlie head-initial constructions/languages, while movements of the [*pictures-of-whom*] pied piping type underlie head-final constructions/languages.

Whether the following trees are taken to represent just the hierarchical arrangement of constituents (as in Chomsky's 1995 and subsequent works) or already linearized constituents (as in Kayne 1994 and subsequent works), I will assume, still in compliance with Antisymmetry, that complements, like modifiers, are merged in Specifier positions, to the left of the head if linear order is part of narrow syntax.[6]

(7)

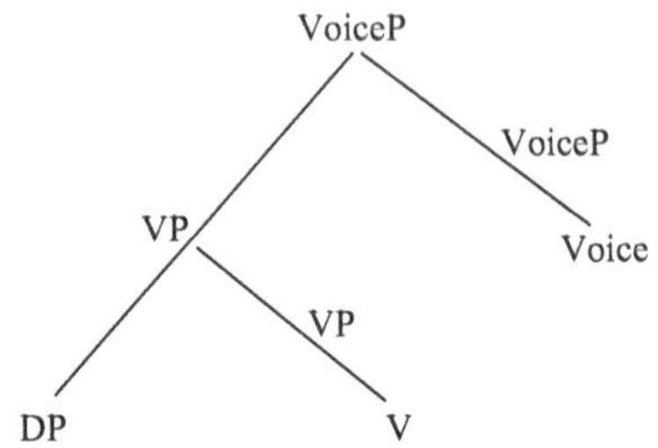

On top of each projection, Verb Phrase (VP), VoiceP, etc. (given for concreteness in X-bar format, with a null complement position [see section 3.3]), an empty agreement projection, such as $Agr_{VP}P$ or $Agr_{Voice}P$, will have to be assumed to host the movement of the respective head. See below for these agreement projections and for the associated projections that contain the corresponding modifier (e.g, "probably" for $Mod_{Epistemic}P$ in the clause). I keep the notions of segment and c-command as given in Kayne (1994) to allow the LCA to derive the desired word orders. For a brief discussion of how this approach could be cast in a bare phrase structure and labeling approach (perhaps not entirely straightforwardly), see the end of section 3.3.

The reason for having nothing below/to the right of a head is the pervasive left-right asymmetry found in every domain: to the left of a head (e.g., N, V, A) the order of complements and modifiers is unique, while to the right of the head more possibilities exist; among others, either the same order as that found to the left of the head or, more frequently, its mirror image (cf. the generalization in (5b), a particularly clear example of which is Greenberg's [1963] Universal 20, which is briefly taken up in section 2.1). For more detailed discussion of this point see Cinque (2009) and Abels (2016a).

In my view this left-right asymmetry can be made sense of if the order of the elements found to the right of a head is a function of how the head raises (with or without pied piping) past them, which are merged in hierarchically higher specifiers (preceding the head if linear order is part of narrow syntax). It is in fact difficult to see how this pattern could be derived otherwise from a *single* universal structure. Under the widespread idea that complements and modifiers to the right of a head are in their external Merge position there, one would have to base-generate the two (or more) orders to the right of the head, as well as the one to the left of the head, independently of the others, even though they are literally the same, or in the case of the mirror order, the same at a more abstract level. If one assumes instead that all complements and modifiers of a head are externally merged higher up (prenominally, preverbally, if linear order is part of narrow syntax), the observed left-right asymmetry necessarily follows from independent properties of movement (movement of the head with or without pied piping). This assumption also has the advantage over a specifier head complement order of dispensing with the necessity of "evacuating" the complements from VP in the derivation of final and certain head-initial orders. The complements start out as already "evacuated."

To go back to the generalizations governing linear order across languages, chapter 2 begins with the first one, (5a).

Significantly, in each of the subdomains that we consider (the subprojections that make up the nominal, verbal, and so on, extended projections), of all the mathematically possible orders of the elements involved, only a subset is invariably attested. This cannot be an accident, especially if we find that the missing orders are missing for the same reason.

In chapter 2 I illustrate the generalization in (5a) with a number of cases drawn from the nominal domain (returning later to what the reason for the missing orders may actually be, which is not as trivial as it might seem).

2 Nominal Subprojections and Their Word Orders

2.1 Orders of Demonstrative, (Cardinal) Numeral, Adjective, and Noun

To illustrate why out of the mathematically possible orders of *n* elements only a subset is ever found, I begin with the more complex case of the attested orders of the four elements Demonstrative, (cardinal) Numeral, Adjective, and Noun (actually DemP, NumP, AP, and Noun), as this is better known from previous work (Greenberg 1963; Cinque 2005; Abels and Neeleman 2009, 2012; and other works since). In Cinque (2005) I claimed that only a subset of the mathematically possible orders of those elements, namely 14 of 24 (factorial 4), are actually attested (those in (1A)), proposing a set of conditions able to derive them without also deriving the 10 unattested ones of (1B).

(1) A.	B.
a. N A Num Dem	a. *Dem A Num N
b. Dem Num A N	b. *Num A Dem N
c. Dem N A Num	c. *A Num Dem N
d. Dem Num N A	d. *Num Dem A N
e. Num N A Dem	e. *A Dem Num N
f. N A Dem Num	f. *A Num N Dem
g. N Num A Dem	g. *A Dem N Num
h. Dem N Num A	h. *Num Dem N A

i. Dem A N Num
l. N Dem Num A
m. Num A N Dem
n. N Dem A Num
o. A N Num Dem
p. A N Dem Num

i. *Num N Dem A
l. *N Num Dem A

There I also stressed the importance of not considering informationally special orders, to the extent that it is possible to recognize them in the relevant sources. I take up that work again because, despite some apparent counterevidence,[1] that claim and that general approach seem to me to be correct and capable of providing the simple principle at the base of the orders that are systematically missing in the subdomains just reviewed (and in all other phrasal domains). There I assumed that the 14 possible orders of Demonstrative, (Cardinal) Numeral, Adjective, and Noun are a function of the way the N(P) heading the nominal extended projection moves, by itself or by pied piping a phrase containing it via the two existing modes of pied piping (the *whose-pictures* type and the *pictures-of-whom* type, modulo NP rather than [$_{XP}$ *wh-*] as the element undergoing movement). As noted in Cinque (2005), to obtain the correct result of ruling in the 14 attested orders while ruling out the 10 unattested ones, no other movement except that of the N(P) (or of phrases containing it) must be allowed. In particular neither AP nor NumP movements by themselves should be allowed to build the canonical order of Determiner phrases. The marked AP movement above demonstratives in languages such as Chinese (Zhang 2015) and Bangla (see Guha 2017), from this point of view, is not directly relevant. Also not relevant are those orders derived by movement to scope positions, as with the movement of English APs to a superlative high position in front of numerals, for example, *The black*(est) two dogs that I've (ever) seen* (Kayne 2008b: fn15, also on Persian; and in this volume, see chapter 4, note 39 on Maltese), and above higher adjectives, reversing the canonical order: *The <hard*(est)>occasional <hard(*est)>worker* . . . (Cinque

2010b: 32). Similarly outside of such a theory is the fronting of APs before the indefinite determiner in English in the presence of a degree word (e.g., *how, too*) pied piper: *<How big> a <*how big> house did John buy*? (Kayne 2007: section 8.3) and in the similar Bavarian constructions discussed in Plank (2003a: section 2.9). On this construction see Zompì (2020).[2]

In Cinque (2005) I had assumed that one order, the order Dem Num A N, involved no movement, being the order of Merge. But that was incorrect because certain nominal heads, like Singular/Dual/Plural (PL), . . . (number), Determiner (Det), and Case (K), interspersed at Merge among the prenominal modifiers,[3] generally follow the noun in head-final languages while modifiers precede it (DemP NumP AP N PL Det Case).[4] So I would now take even that order to be derived by moving the heads of the nominal extended projection (N, PL, Det, Case) with the *pictures-of-whom* pied piping. See the discussion in section 3.3.

The fact that more orders are found to the right of a head than to its left (the left-right generalization mentioned in chapter 1) is a consequence of the way the head of a projection moves. For example, illustrating only the case where all modifiers are on the same side of the noun, the leftward movement of the N(P) by itself to a position above the demonstrative or by the *whose-pictures* pied piping mode (whereby the noun drags along stepwise constituents c-commanded by it) gives rise to two orders to the right of the noun ((2a) and (2b), respectively). The leftward movement of the noun via the *pictures-of-whom* pied piping mode (whereby it drags along stepwise constituents c-commanding it) gives rise instead to the single order attested to the left of the noun ((2c)).

The derivations in (2) are very much simplified. See sections 3.3 and 3.4 for a more detailed discussion of (this part of) the nominal domain. The representation X(P) is meant to underline the undetermined head (X°)/phrasal (XP) status of the core element of the projection (something that projects but also moves to a specifier position) (cf. Chomsky's [1994] bare phrase structure approach, according to which every nonbranching element is automatically both a phrase and a head, and Kayne's [2008a] notion of singleton set).

(2) a. N Dem Num A (derived via movement of the N(P) without pied piping)

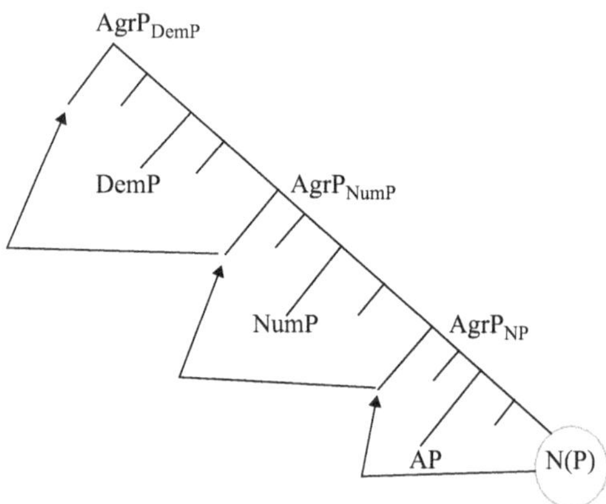

b. N A Num Dem (derived via movement of the N(P) with the *whose-pictures* pied piping, vacuously in the first movement)

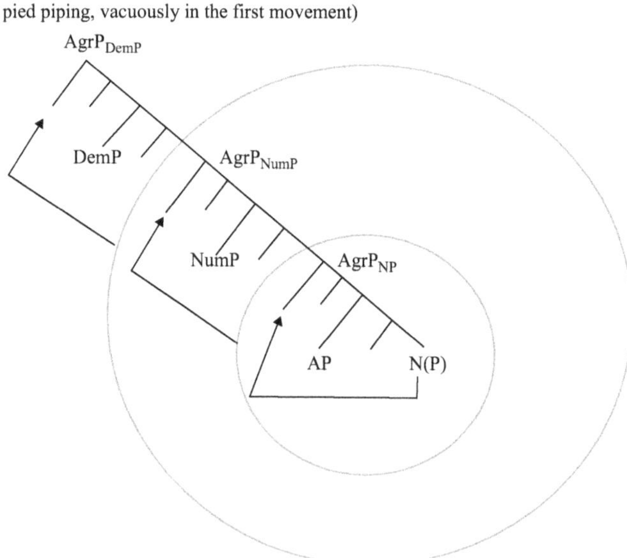

c. Dem Num A N (derived via movement of the N(P) with the *pictures-of-whom* pied piping)

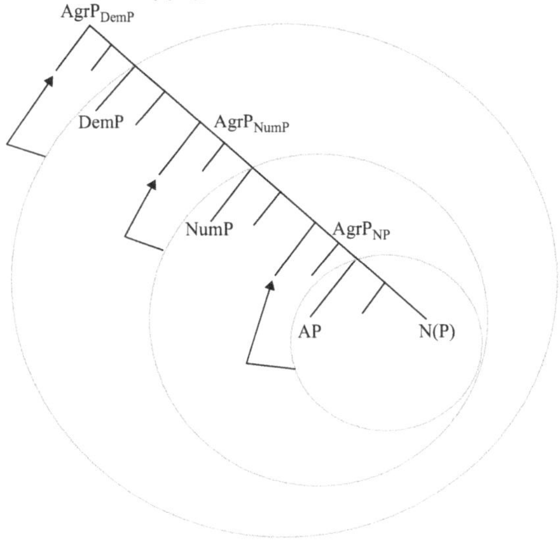

While the movement shown in (2a) could be represented as successive movement from head to head, that in (2b) and (2c) is clearly phrasal, which suggests generalizing phrasal movement to (2a) as well.[5]

An approach allowing the movement of the N(P) in one of the possible derivational options, and only the N(P), appears capable of discriminating between the 14 attested and 10 unattested orders of the 4 elements Dem Num A N (see Cinque 2005, as updated here).

The clausal counterparts of the three derivations in (2) have something in common with the derivations termed "climbing," "inverted order," and "English order" in Koopman and Szabolcsi (2000) (cf. also Koopman 2002); "skipping," "curl/roll-up," and "straight" in Svenonius (2007); and "stranding" and "pied piping" in Jayaseelan (2010). See chapter 4 for the derivations assumed here.

The same situation is found with nominal phrases comprising three elements, such as those discussed in sections 2.2–2.7. Here too the attested orders are a subset of the mathematically possible ones: 4 of 6 (factorial 3).

2.2 Orders of (Cardinal) Numeral, Classifier, and Noun

As Greenberg (1972: 28) observes, of the six potential orders of N(oun), Num(eral), and Classifier (CLF), only four are attested (cf. (3)) (on the relative rarity of the N CLF Num and CLF Num N orders, mainly concentrated in Northeast India and neighboring regions, see Evans, 2022):

(3) a. Num CLF N[6]
b. N CLF Num[7]
c. N Num CLF[8]
d. CLF Num N[9]
e. *CLF N Num
f. *Num N CLF

Greenberg's conclusion has been confirmed by subsequent investigations (Adams and Conklin 1973: 1; Conklin 1981: 4–5; Aikhenvald 2000: 104–105; Hall 2015: chapter 5, 2019; Her 2017a, 2017b; Allassonnière-Tang and Her 2020: section 2; Her and Tsai 2020). The alleged instances of the orders in (3)e. and (3)f. pointed out in the literature have been shown in Hall (2015: chapter 5) and Her (2017a, 2017b) to be apparent only, as is the case of Ejagham (also mentioned in Aikhenvald 2000: 105), and of other Niger-Congo languages (Kießling 2018), where the "classifier" is in fact the true syntactic head of the nominal phrase triggering noun class agreement on the numeral.[10] The same can be said for the apparently exceptional case of cardinal 'one' in certain Tibeto-Burman and Tai-Kadai languages, which is plausibly an "indefinite article" (Her 2017a: section 2.2) (in this connection, Kayne [2017] is relevant).

2.3 Orders of Multiplier, Base, and Noun

A similar pattern is found with the orders of the noun with multiplier and base (in complex cardinals such as 'three hundred'). Interestingly, Greenberg notes that the order between a multiplier and a base tends to "harmonize" with the order between a (cardinal) numeral and a classifier (cf. Greenberg 1989: 111), as well as with the order of (cardinal) numeral and noun (see Greenberg's [1990] Generalization 28). I return to these (partial) correlations later (on the notion of base, also see Kayne [2006a], Comrie [2016], and additional references cited therein).

(4) a. multiplier base N[11]
    b. N base multiplier[12]
    c. N multiplier base[13]
    d. base multiplier N[14]
    e. *base N multiplier
    f. *multiplier N base

2.4 Orders of Cardinal and Ordinal Morphemes (to Form Ordinal Numerals) and Noun

Ordinal numerals, which give the number position of an item in an ordered sequence, are often composed of a cardinal and an ordinal morpheme. When the two morphemes are realized separately and combine with the noun one observes the same pattern of four possible orders out of six. See (5) (a pattern pointed out in Tatsumi [2020]; also see Tatsumi [2021: Chapter 4] for other strategies for expressing ordinals).

The orders in (5) should not be confused with the relative orders of cardinal numerals and ordinal numerals when these co-occur, as in "the first three pages." This is clearly seen in Vietnamese (Vietic) and Lakkja (Kam-Tai), where cardinal numerals precede the noun while ordinal numerals (composed of an ordinal morpheme preceding a cardinal numeral) follow the noun: Num_{card} CLF N A [$_{\text{OrdP}}$ Ord Num_{Card}] (Nguyen 2004: 51; and respectively Fan 2019: sections 4.1.8.1 and 4.4.2).

(5) a. Card Ord N (Maale, Kashmiri,..)[15]
 b. N Ord Card (Uab Meto, Tai Lue,..)[16]
 c. N Card Ord (Kove, Koromfe,..)[17]
 d. Ord Card N (Àhàn,..)[18]
 e. *Ord N Card[19]
 f. *Card N Ord

In certain languages, perhaps universally, ordinals are actually merged in two distinct positions. The higher position is arguably part of the subprojection headed by the cardinal numeral, following "other" and preceding the cardinal ([ʻother' [ordinal [cardinal]]]). The lower position occurs after the cardinal (outside of the subprojection containing the cardinal). The two ordinals can even co-occur (see Cinque's [2015: 24n4, 2022c: section 4] examples from Italian, French, and Russian. See, e.g., the Italian example [*gli* [*ultimi due*] *primi giorni di scuola*] 'the last two first days of school'). If only the Head of a (sub)projection can move, as I suggest later, a comparison of Italian and French provides evidence that it is the cardinal that heads the subprojection containing the higher ordinal and 'other', because in French the cardinal obligatorily crosses over the ordinal and 'other' ([les [deux_i autres premiers t_i] membres] "lit." "the two other first members"), while it does not in Italian, nor in English, [gli [altri primi due] membri] 'the other first two members'. More complex is the case of Hebrew, which has the overall order $\text{Num}_{\text{Cardinal}}$ N Adj $\text{Num}_{\text{Ordinal}}$ Dem (Shlonsky 2004; section 5). If anything, the order that combines the two ordinals in Hebrew is 'two days last first' (Ur Shlonsky, pers. comm., August 5, 2021).

2.5 Orders of Degree Adverb, Adjective, and Noun

Consider also the attested and unattested orders of degree adverb (e.g., intensifier), adjective, and noun, (6). Once again, only four of six orders are apparently attested.

In Greenberg's (1963) sample only languages with the orders degree adverb A N (11 languages), N A degree adverb (8 languages), and N degree adverb A (2 languages) are reported as attested (cf. his table 7 and Universal 21). But the order A degree adverb N is also attested, even if rarely. (See the references in note 23.) Dryer (2008: 62) also reports that the order AdjN&AdjDeg is uncommon (unattested in Tibeto-Burman), while the other three orders (AdjN&DegAdj, NAdj&DegAdj, and NAdj&AdjDeg) are quite common (in Tibeto-Burman too).

(6) a. degree adverb A N (English, Korean[20],..)
    b. N A degree adverb (Ichindali, Daai Chin,..)[21]
    c. N degree adverb A (Italian, Apatani,..)[22]
    d. A degree adverb N (Sakha, Korlai,..)[23]
    e. *A N degree adverb
    f. *degree adverb N A[24]

2.6 Orders of Measure Phrase, Adjective, and Noun

The same pattern is found when a measure phrase, an adjective, and a noun are combined together. See (7):

(7) a. measure phrase A N (English, Bulgarian,..)[25]
    b. N A measure phrase (Italian, Bulgarian,..)[26]
    c. N measure phrase A (Bosnian,..)[27]
    d. A measure phrase N (Chinese,..)[28]
    e. *A N measure phrase
    f. *measure phrase N A

To judge from the possibility of such phrases as *two inches too short a pole* (Peter Svenonius, pers. comm., May 21, 2020), *lipsticks two shades too red* (*for her complexion*), or German *Sie haben einen um einen Meter zu tiefen Graben gegraben* literally, 'they have one of one meter too deep ditch digged' (Roland Hinterhölzl, pers. comm., November 30, 2022) measure phrases (*two inches, two shades, einen Meter*) appear to modify the degree word (*too, zu*) within the degree phrase, which in turn modifies the AP, which modifies the NP.[29]

2.7 Orders of Color, Color Adjective, and Noun

Exactly the same pattern is also found when the noun combines with an adjective of color and the noun for 'color'. In languages like Chinese a particular adjective class can co-occur with the common noun that corresponds to that class; for example, 'white'/'black'/'red'/ . . . with 'color', 'big'/'small'/'medium'/ . . . with 'size', and so on (an instance of the more general co-occurrence of common noun–proper noun, which is known to at least partially correlate with the head-final and head-initial types; see Greenberg's [1963] Universal 23 and Cinque [2011] and references cited there).

It could be objected that, unlike Chinese, English and many other languages do not readily allow for the co-occurrence of a color name with the common noun 'color'. However, there is indirect evidence even in English for a silent, if not overt (for certain speakers), instance of the noun 'color', modified by the proper name of a color. So not only are sentences like *What color car did they buy*? possible for all speakers who are asking for a color name. Even phrases like *a red color car* are acceptable to a number of speakers (see Kayne 2005b: 57, note 20, 2007: section 15; and William Snyder, pers. comm., February 20, 2020), though not to all. In other languages the noun 'color' is optionally pronounced (in addition to Chinese, see the languages mentioned in (9)). This evidence makes it plausible to assume that the name of a color always co-occurs with an overt or silent common noun 'color'.[30] In other words, adjectives (APs) may turn out not to modify the head noun directly but only as part of a nominal projection headed by the corresponding common noun $[_{NP}[_{NP}[AP_{color}]$ color] N], $[_{NP}[_{NP}[AP_{size}]$ size] N], $[_{NP}[_{NP}[AP_{nationality}]$ nationality] N], and so on to the effect that it is this nominal projection that modifies the head noun directly (see Kayne 2005b: 15). This may be true of numerals and demonstratives as well. Although numerals appear to be categorially adjectives in some languages (or in one language for some numbers, see Corver and Tatsumi 2021: section 2), nominal in others (e.g., Galo—Sino-Tibetan; Post 2007: section 8.2.1), and relatives in still others (Ionin and Matushansky 2018: section 3.4), they possibly also modify nouns via a nominal projection (a phrase headed by an overt "amount/number", as obligatorily in Korowai and optionally in Cotabato Manobo and Tawala [see (8)] - or a silent one elsewhere [see Zweig 2006; Kayne 2006a, 2007]). And this may carry over to the internal constituents of complex numerals. Greenberg (1990: 287) observes that "multiplicands are often treated like nouns and multipliers . . . like noun modifiers in general. Hence, it is reasonable to equate the multiplicand with the noun and the multiplier with the adjective."

(8) a. gol wayafül-anop (Korowai—Papuan [de Vries 2012: 186])
pig four(lit. index.finger)-amount
'four pigs'

b. lima kedoo etaw (Cotabato Manobo—Malayo-Polynesian [Kerr 1988: 48])
five number people
'five people'

c. lawa magou-na wohepali (Tawala—Oceanic [Ezard 1984: 91])
person number-its four
'four men'

The same may be true of demonstratives if the head of the demonstrative subprojection is actually a silent PLACE/THING/PERSON modified by a locative reinforcer (e.g., [[this HERE PLACE] square]). See Kayne (2004a) and Leu (2008: section 2.2).

This may turn out to be true of every nominal modifier, and thus render otiose the question whether adjectives, for comparative purposes, should be considered a semantic notion rather than a category given that they sometimes appear to be categorially nouns (*a silver musical box*), sometimes categorially an adverb (*the then prime minister*), sometimes categorially a prepositional phrase (*an off-the-cuff remark*), sometimes categorially a particle (*his ex-girlfriend*), and so on. What seems to count is that each class is plausibly merged in all languages in the specifier of a corresponding overt or silent common noun (e.g., MATERIAL, PLACE, TIME), in the same dedicated position of the nominal extended projection (see, e.g., Scott 2002, and also Dryer 2018: section 4.2), which may suggest, as Ian Roberts observed (pers. comm., June 11, 2021), that some "grammatical categories/modifiers" are really positions rather than features.

To go back to the adjective of color, (9) exemplifies the attested and nonattested orders of the noun 'color' and of a color adjective across languages. Once again, apparently only four of six orders are found.

(9) a. A_{color} 'color' N (Chinese, Bulgarian,..)[31]
  b. N 'color' A_{color} (Niuean, Lao, Vietnamese,..)[32]
  c. N A_{color} 'color' (Mocho', Bulgarian,..)[33]
  d. 'color' A_{color} N (Chinese, Russian,..)[34]
  e. *'color' N A_{color}
  f. *A_{color} N 'color'

In the context of determining which orders are cross-linguistically possible, or impossible, the question of which specific orders are characteristic of head-final or head-initial languages is not directly relevant. The goal is to arrive at a system that specifies all the possible/attestable orders, not just those that are more frequent or that conform to a maximal degree to the head-final/head-initial correlations. The latter appears to be a separate (albeit important) question, to which I return.

In sections 2.2 to 2.7 we have considered triplets of nominal elements that give rise to six potential orders, of which only four have apparently turned out to be attested. Each triplet was composed of the noun and a pair of elements arguably belonging to a separate constituent of the nominal extended projection ([[Num CLF] N], [[Multiplier Base] N], [[Card Ord] N], [[Degree Word A] N], [[Measure Phrase A] N], [[A_{color} 'color'] N]). The constituency [[Num CLF] N] is suggested in Greenberg (1972: 28; 1975[35]), Huang (1982), Lin (1997), Fukui and Takano (2000: section 4), Hsieh (2008: section 2.3.4), Hall (2015), Her (2017b), among others. This constituency is argued for in detail in Brown (2001: 431) for Nias Selatan; in Inglis (2003) for Thai; in Henderson (2006: section 3.2) for Sinhala; in Bale and Coon (2014: section 3) and Bale, Coon, and Arcos López (2019: section 4.1) for Mi'gmaq and Chol; and in Her and Tsai (2020) and Allassonnière-Tang et al.(2021) for Chinese.[36] On the constituent [multiplier base] see Kayne (2005b: section 9), He (2015), and Her (2017a, 2017b). The constituent structure assumed here for the remaining cases ([[Card Ord] N], [[degree word A] N], [[measure phrase A] N], and [[A_{color} 'color'] N]) needs no particular argumentation.

The missing orders (those where N comes between the two elements of the pair) could thus be unproblematically seen as a consequence of the overall hierarchical composition. The N (NP) can be linearized to the right or to the left of the constituent modifying it but not inside it. This apparently simple conclusion, carrying over to the order inside the constituent modifying the noun, that the head of the constituent can be linearized to the right or to the left of its modifier, though essentially correct, is nonetheless insufficiently general. While the simple left or right linearization might seem to work when there are just two elements, it fails when more elements are involved, as in the case of the order of demonstrative, numeral, adjective, and noun that we have discussed in this chapter or in the case to be discussed in section 3.6. What is needed is some principle that may account for the simple and the more complex cases at the same time. One will be suggested in chapter 3.

Notice that if the correct constituencies were different from the ones assumed here, like those proposed for the sequence [numeral classifier noun] by Cheng and Sybesma (1999), Borer (2005: chapter 6), Watanabe (2006), Huang et al. (2009), and Li (2013) (i.e., [Num [CLF [N]]], or for the sequence [multiplier base noun] by Ionin and Matushansky (2006, 2018: chapter 3) (i.e., [Multiplier [Base [N]]]), things would not be as straightforward. More orders than the attested ones would be expected to exist (e.g., *[Num [N] [CLF]], [[CLF N] Num], *[Multiplier [N] [Base]], *[[Base N] Multiplier]). The principle to be suggested in chapter 3 that only the head of a subprojection can move provides an additional argument for the constituencies assumed here, and, in a sense, a novel type of diagnostic for constituency.[37]

3 Toward a Restrictive Theory of Linear Order

3.1 The Role of the Head in Each (Sub)projection

The considerations discussed in chapter 2 prompt me to advance the general hypothesis in (1) as the basis of a more restrictive theory of word order variation discriminating possible from impossible canonical orders.

(1) The Head, and only the Head, of each (sub)projection (N(P), A(P), V(P), . . .) can move within its projection.[1]

The theory proves rather simple once we recognize the complex articulation of the sentence and of the phrases that compose it; that is (again limiting ourselves for the moment to the nominal extended projection) once we recognize that this projection is not a unique downward/rightward spine, as in (2b), but a more highly articulated constituent, similar, to a simplified first approximation, to that in (2c), for the dialectal English phrase in (2a) (the Agreement phrases [AgrPs] on top of each subprojection that are needed to host the movement of its Head are not indicated here—see (5), (14), (15), and (16) below, for more detailed derivations). The overall projection is made up of a number of hierarchically arranged subprojections, within which the constituent heading the subprojection, and only this, can move in one of only three ways: (i) by itself or by pied piping some larger phrase containing it in the

(ii) *whose-pictures* or (iii) *pictures-of-whom* mode. (I address these derivations, and the elements that determine the way in which the Head moves, in sections. 3.2, 3.3, and 3.4)

(2) a. these here two hundred two shades too red lipsticks

b.

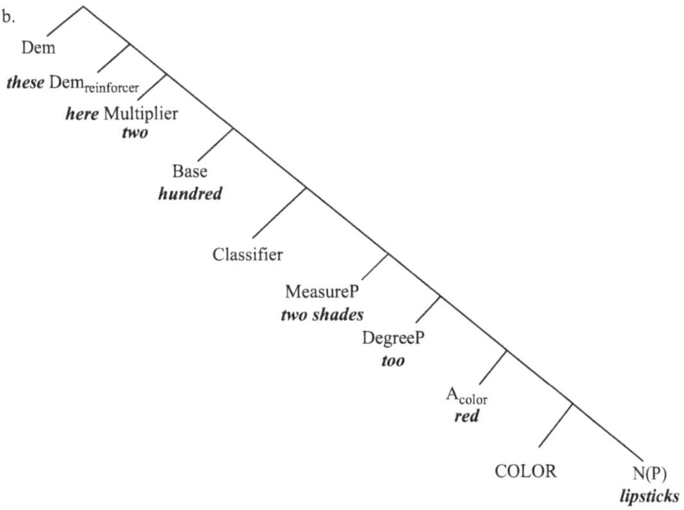

c.

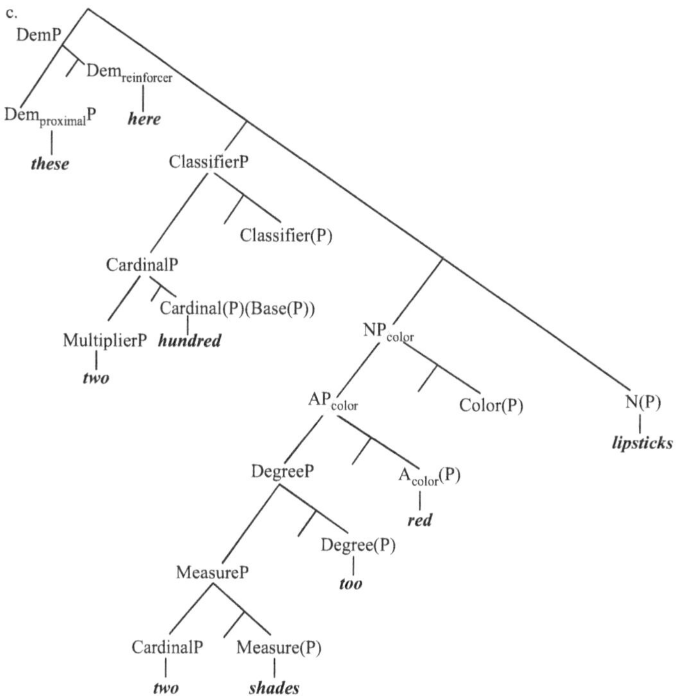
DemP
Dem$_{reinforcer}$
Dem$_{proximal}$P
here
these
ClassifierP
Classifier(P)
CardinalP
Cardinal(P)(Base(P))
MultiplierP
hundred
two
NP$_{color}$
AP$_{color}$
Color(P)
N(P)
lipsticks
DegreeP
A$_{color}$(P)
red
Degree(P)
MeasureP
too
CardinalP
Measure(P)
two
shades

If the internal articulation of the nominal projection is essentially as in (2c) rather than as in (2b), and if, given (1), only the Head of each subprojection can move within its subprojection (to the Specifier of the, here missing, associated AgrP), the two unattested orders of each of (3)–(7) and (9) of chapter 2 cannot be derived (as the Head would have to move into another subprojection). I return to the other missing labels in (2c).

The factorial numbers stemming from the combinations of n elements (which when $n = 8$, already amount to 40,320 possible orders if no restrictions are introduced) are thus drastically reduced if the combinations are limited to each subprojection and if only the Head of that subprojection can move within it and determine the order inside it.

Consider the addition of a fifth element, the numeral classifier, to the four elements Demonstrative, (cardinal) Numeral, Adjective, and Noun, assuming the latter to have just 14 possible orders, as claimed in chapter 2. As already mentioned, there is evidence that cardinal numerals form a constituent with the classifier (where the classifier is the Head). See note 35 of chapter 2. This means that within the subprojection ClassifierP only the Head, the classifier, will be able to "change place" with respect to the (cardinal) numeral. Factorial 5 (demonstrative, [cardinal] numeral, numeral classifier, adjective, and noun) is 120. But if we assume that only 14 orders of demonstrative, (cardinal) numeral, adjective, and noun are possible, due to the fact that only the Head N(P) can move (in one of the permitted ways), and we multiply this number by 2, due to the possibility for each of the 14 orders to vary according to whether the classifier moves coming to precede or follow the (cardinal) numeral, we get not 120 but just 28 possible orders. This seems correct. See (3), where only 2 of the 28 expected orders are not (yet) documented, no other order being found distinct from those in (3), as far as can be ascertained:[2]

(3) a. Dem Num CLF A N (Mandarin, Cantonese [Hall 2019: 29fn28])
a′. Dem CLF Num A N (Upper Necaxa Totonac, Eastern Tamang)[3]

b. Dem Num CLF N A (Yao[4], Trukese[5])
b′. Dem CLF Num N A (Nêlêmwa, Zuanga)[6]

c. Dem N Num CLF A (Lahu, Shiwilu)[7]
c′. Dem N CLF Num A (Hakha Chin—Sino-Tibetan)[8]

d. N Dem Num CLF A (Stiêng—Austroasiatic)[9]
d′. N Dem CLF Num A (Kiriwina—Oceanic)[10]

e. A N Dem Num CLF (Yunnan Bai, Puxi Qiang—Sino-Tibetan)[11]
e′. A N Dem CLF Num (?)

f. N A Dem Num CLF (Kayan Lahta, Yao`an Lolo—Sino-Tibetan)[12]
f′. N A Dem CLF Num (Awara, West Makian—Papuan)[13]

g. Dem A N Num CLF (Newari, Dulong—Sino-Tibetan [Hall 2019: 29fn28])
g′. Dem A N CLF Num (Mising, Nyishi—Sino-Tibetan)[14]

h. Dem N A Num CLF (Burmese, Maru—Sino-Tibetan [Hall 2019: 29fn28])[15]
h′. Dem N A CLF Num (Kokborok, Apatani - Sino-Tibetan - Hall 2019: 29fn.28)

i. N Dem A Num CLF (Nias Selatan - Malayo-Polynesian - Brown 2001: §4.10 and §8.5.2))
i′. N Dem A CLF Num (Tongan[16], Diola-Fogny[17])

l. Num CLF A N Dem (Coast Tsimshian, Tojolabal)[18]
l′. CLF Num A N Dem (Kavalan, Q'anjob'al)[19]

m. Num CLF N A Dem (Chrau, Vietnamese - Austroasiatic)[20]

m′. CLF Num N A Dem (Rongga—Malayo-Polynesian)[21]

n. N Num CLF A Dem (Kele, Lele - Oceanic)[22]
n′. N CLF Num A Dem (Buglere, Teribe - Chibchan)[23]

o. A N Num CLF Dem (?)
o′. A N CLF Num Dem (Galo, Mising—Sino-Tibetan)[24]

p. N A Num CLF Dem (Thai, Lao—Tai-Kadai [Nguyen 2004: 143])
p′. N A CLF Num Dem (Abun, Sudest)[25]

Adding another element by taking Num to be a complex cardinal numeral, composed of a multiplier and a base (see (4) of chapter 2), would yield 720 possible combinations (factorial 6). Yet, if the multiplier and base form a constituent (cf. Kayne 2005b: section 9; He 2015; Her 2017a, 2017b; and Tatsumi 2018, 2021: chapter 2; pace Ionin and Matushansky 2018: chapter 3), and if only the base can move because it is the Head of that constituent, at most 56 (rather than 720) orders are expected to be available (the 28 possibilities of (3) multiplied by the 2 possible orders between base and multiplier in each of the 28 orders).[26]

It is possible that even "simple" numerals are actually "complex," having either a silent multiplier (typically '1': compare Italian *cento*, without *un(o)* 'one', with *duecento, trecento* 'two hundred, three hundred', etc.; similarly French [Kayne 2020b: section 6] versus English *one hundred, two hundred, three hundred,* etc.; possibly Italian *dieci,* English *ten* when compared with 'ten' in the Papuan languages Adang [Haan 2001: 324] and Savosavo [Wegener 2012: 75] ('ten one' = 10, 'ten two' =20, etc.), or in the Austronesian language Mokilese [Harrison 1976: 98] ('one-ten' = 10), or in Chajul Ixil (Mayan) *va'l dies* 'ten' (lit. one ten) (cf. also *va'l nueeve* 'nine', lit. one nine) [Adell 2019: 403])[27], or a silent base (see Greenberg's [1990] Generalization 36 "The only numeral expressions deleted are those for 1 and for bases of the system," and Greenberg [1975, note 2], and Hurford's [2003:

section 4.2.3] rule of 1-Deletion). Bases like 'hundred' in (American) English ("*three sixty-five* for *three hundred sixty-five*" [Stampe 1976: 595]) or *cento* 'one hundred' and *mille* 'one thousand' in (certain) dates in Italian (*nel mille e due* 'Lit. in.the thousand and two' = in 1,200; *nel cinquecento* lit. 'in.the five hundred' = in 1,500) can also be silent, leading to ambiguity (cf. Comrie 1997: section 4 for other such cases). This may not be completely general if there are languages whose numerical system does not involve multiplication (Greenberg 1990: 277; Epps et al. 2012: section 3.4; Allassonnière-Tang and Her 2020: section 3.1). If one were to add additive numerals to the complex numeral containing multiplicatives, then one would have to add additional dimensions of variation, as additives are found to follow multiplicatives in some languages, ('(((thousand one) nine hundred) and five and fifty)' = 1,955 in Kinubi [Arabic-based Creole]),[28] but to precede them in others ('(two (ten three))' = 32 in Yemba [Harro and Haynes 1991: 31]), and within the additive subprojection higher numbers precede smaller ones in some languages (e.g., English: *twenty one*) while the opposite is true in other languages (e.g., in the Papuan language Ekari: '((one and ten) and sixty)' = 71 [Comrie 2016: section 2; cf. Doble 1987: section 7]; and in German (below 'hundred'): *ein und zwanzig* 'one and twenty'. Teen numerals (12–19) tend to be "ten-with-unit" in head-initial languages and "unit-ten" in head-final ones (see Polinsky and Magyar 2020: 14) (but see Lehmann 1978a: section 1.3 for an opposing view, exemplified with Sinhala and Irish). Again the number of the possible orders can be kept severely limited if we understand what the overall constituent structure is and which is the Head of each subprojection, the only element that can change place. Ionin and Matushansky (2018: section 5.2) analyze complex additive numerals as coordinations of NPs with backward deletion; for example, *twenty six books* would derive from (*twenty ~~books~~*) (*and*) (*six books*). While this analysis may be correct for certain languages and/or constructions

(Russian: *Ja delayu dvacat' odin šag* lit. 'I make twenty one step (sing.)'; German: *dreihundertundein Haus/*Häuser* 'three hundred and one house/houses'; Italian: *le mille e una notte* lit. 'the(pl.) thousand and one night (sing.)'), it is not for other languages and/or constructions (English: *three hundred and one students/*student*; Italian: *Cento e un modi* lit. 'hundred and one way (pl.)'), where the complex cardinal makes up a constituent that does not involve coordination and backward deletion, as shown by plural rather than singular agreement after 'one'. See Meinunger (2015) and Tatsumi (2019, 2021: chapter 3) for detailed discussion and arguments that both analyses are needed.[29] For further discussion, also see Hurford (2003: section 4.1), where the following constituent structure is given for 230,567: [[[[two **hundred**] and **thirty**] **thousand**] [[five **hundred**] and [**sixty** [**seven**]]]] (the possible Heads of each subprojection are indicated in boldface), and He (2015: 200) for the complex phrase structure of 5,000,601 in Chinese. On an arguably even more complex structure underlying cardinal numerals, see Wągiel and Caha (2020).[30]

If we were then to add to Demonstrative, Multiplier, Base, CLF, Adjective, and Noun three more elements (a single additive numeral, the DegreeP of (6) of chapter 2, and the common noun corresponding to a certain class of adjectives, say 'color' for adjectives of color, (9) of chapter 2), we would obtain in the absence of any restrictions 362,880 possible combinations of the 9 elements (factorial 9). The adoption of the restriction in (1), on the other hand, yields, once we consider the right constituencies, only 448 possible orders (56×2×2×2). I have left aside additional multiplier-base constituents, which may linearize differently from the first one, as in the Kinubi example ('thousand one nine hundred' = 1,900), ordinal numerals ((5) of chapter 2), and measure phrases ((7) of chapter 2) (all of them composed of a Head and a modifier). If added, they would further increase these numbers to several millions were we to ignore the right constituencies and the restriction in (1).

The nominal subprojections considered in this discussion are actually only a subset of those characterizing the nominal extended projection. I have not considered, among others, universal quantifiers, which are of (at least) two types, collective/distributive (*all*) or just distributive (*every*), which are apparently merged in two distinct positions—one above and the other below the definite determiners;[31] indefinite quantifiers (*some/any*), which can even co-occur with universal distributive quantifiers (see Italian *una volta ogni qualche mese* and its English counterpart *once every some months*); multal and paucal modifiers (*many/ few*);[32] prenumeral adjectives (e.g., 'same', 'next', 'usual', 'occasional'); nominal classifiers;[33] nor relative clauses.[34]

If we were to consider these additional elements we would have further combinatorial possibilities. What remains to be done is to calculate how many more possible, and impossible, orders the system explored here, if correct, leads one to expect once we reach a precise understanding of the right constituencies. Recognizing the subprojections that make up the maximal extended projection thus drastically reduces the number of combinations, due to the way the Head moves within each subprojection.

Some of the possible orders are very rare, such as some of those involving different types of movement at different layers of embedding. (I return to this question in section 5.3, after the cross-linguistic tendencies underlying the head-initial and head-final types in the nominal extended projection and in the clause are introduced.)

3.2 Head-Initial and Head-Final Correlations in the Nominal Extended Projection

So far I have not addressed the question of which orders correlate with the head-initial or head-final character of the language; I have just observed that this is, strictly speaking, an orthogonal issue.[35] Two of the four orders attested (out of six) of each of the orders in (3)–(7) and (9) of chapter 2 do correlate to some extent with the head-initial and head-final type. So, for example, the World Atlas of Language Structures online gives the correlations in (4) for the order of Degree word and Adjective with object verb (OV) and verb object (VO) languages. Degree words precede the adjective more often in head-final languages than in head-initial ones and conversely the order adjective > degree word is more frequent in head-initial languages than in head-final ones, "cross-category harmony" being here rather weak as the other two correlations are also attested in significant numbers.[36]

(4) a. OV and degree word-adjective: 114 languages
 b. VO and adjective-degree word: 102 languages
 c. VO and degree word-adjective: 81 languages
 d. OV and adjective-degree word: 63 languages

A similar picture appears to hold of the other orders. The order adjective of color > noun 'color' > Noun is characteristic of head-final languages, while the order N > noun 'color' > adjective of color is characteristic of head-initial languages and is actually a special case of the order proper noun–common noun found in head-final and head-initial languages (see Greenberg's (1963) Universal 23; Cinque 2011, and references cited therein).

Num CLF N is the order more typically found in head-final nominal phrases, and N CLF Num is found in several head-initial ones, though, as Greenberg (1975: 29) notes, N Num CLF is more frequent than N CLF Num even in head-initial nominal phrases. As mentioned at the beginning of section 2.3, the order of multiplier and base tends to "harmonize" with the order of numeral and noun and with the order of numeral and classifier (noun, classifier, and base being the Heads of the respective subprojections).[37] See the cases of (in this regard, "head-final") Chinese $[_{NP}$ $[_{CLFP}$ Num CLF] N], in (3a) of chapter 2, and $[_{NP}$ $[_{CardP}$ multiplier base] N] in (4a) of chapter 2, that is, $[_{NP}$ $[_{CLFP}$ $[_{CardP}$ multiplier base] CLF] N], and the cases of head-initial Adang (Papuan), Helong, and Uab Meto (Malayo-Polynesian) [$_{NP}$ N [$_{CLFP}$ CLF Num]], in (3b) of chapter 2, and [$_{NP}$ N [$_{CardP}$ base multiplier]], in (4b) of Chapter 2, that is, [$_{NP}$ N [$_{CLFP}$ CLF [$_{CardP}$ base multiplier]]].[38]

In other words the Head of ClassifierP (the classifier), that of CardinalP (the base), and that of NP (the noun), tend to behave in the same way, that is, by moving via the same pied piping mode. See (5a), which shows the ideal case involving movement of all the Heads with the (vacuous) *whose-pictures* pied piping mode (which affects the order of the Heads and the modifiers), and (5b), involving movement of all the Heads with the *pictures-of-whom* pied piping mode (which does not affect the order of the Heads and modifiers).[39] I give the structures in X-bar format, recalling however what said in note 1 of this chapter, that the X-bar heads are actually (minimal) phrases (in (5a) they raise by themselves to Specifier [Spec] positions). Each functional subprojection is dominated by an associated projection, which is there to host the movement of the subprojection Head. I call it for convenience Agr(eement)P. The structure is compatible with Antisymmetry if the subprojections $Agr_{CardinalP}$, selected by Classifier(P), and $Agr_{ClassifierP}$ selected by N(P), are merged in specifier position with the complement merged empty and if the Agr Heads are also null. This way the specifiers are in an asymmetric c-command relation with the rest and thus linearize to its left. The Agr Heads are instead irrelevant for linearization because they are null. For simplicity I omitted some of the subprojections of (2c), also ignoring antilocality (Abels 2003: chapter 2; Kayne 2005b: section 5.6). These structures are still simplified (omitting intermediate X-bar projections). See section 3.3 for more detailed representations.

(5) a.

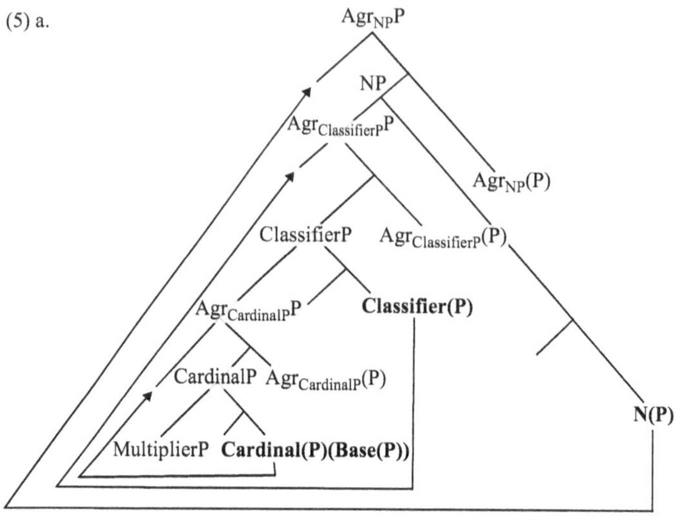

Agr$_{NP}$P
NP
Agr$_{ClassifierP}$P
Agr$_{NP}$(P)
ClassifierP
Agr$_{ClassifierP}$(P)
Agr$_{CardinalP}$P
Classifier(P)
CardinalP
Agr$_{CardinalP}$(P)
N(P)
MultiplierP
Cardinal(P)(Base(P))

(5) b.

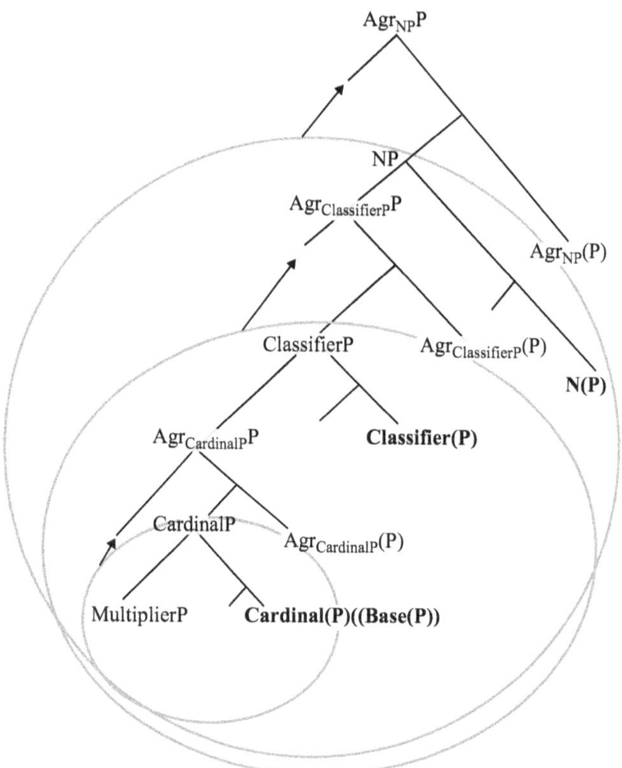

Agr$_{NP}$P
NP
Agr$_{ClassifierP}$P
Agr$_{NP}$(P)
ClassifierP
Agr$_{ClassifierP}$(P)
N(P)
Agr$_{CardinalP}$P
Classifier(P)
CardinalP
Agr$_{CardinalP}$(P)
MultiplierP
Cardinal(P)((Base(P))

The structure in (5a), is ultimately linearized under the LCA as N Classifier Base Multiplier and (5b) as Multiplier Base Classifier N. It is thus clear that the *whose-pictures* pied piping leads to head-initial orders and the *pictures-of-whom* pied piping to head-final ones.

In the *whose-pictures* pied piping mode of (5a) the Head drags along to its Spec,Agr constituents c-commanded by it (here vacuously), while in the *pictures-of-whom* pied piping mode of (5b) what the Head drags along to its Spec,Agr are constituents that c-command it.

Strictly speaking (5a) could also involve movement of the Heads without pied piping, but given that in consistent head-initial languages when the Head and more than one modifier are present we observe a roll-up derivation involving the *whose-pictures* pied piping mode, it seems plausible to generalize this to all cases.

Harmony in the collocation of Demonstrative, Numeral, and Adjective within the nominal extended projection is also fairly strongly obeyed. In the larger sample on which Cinque (in preparation) is based (as of June 2022) cases (6a) and (6b), derived via the consistent application of the same type of movement at all levels, involve many more genera, and languages (with some skewing for the order derived with the *whose-pictures* pied piping, (6a)), than the disharmonic ones involving different, nonuniform, types of movement (those in (6c–p)):

(6) a. N A Num Dem: 606 languages; 137 genera
 b. Dem Num A N: 425 languages; 110 genera
 c. Dem N A Num: 207 languages; 79 genera
 d. Dem Num N A: 182 languages; 67 genera
 e. Num N A Dem: 226 languages; 47 genera
 f. N Num A Dem: 67 languages; 35 genera
 g. N A Dem Num: 101 languages; 34 genera
 h. Dem N Num A: 47 languages; 29 genera

i. Dem A N Num: 46 languages; 24 genera
l. N Dem Num A: 81 languages; 22 genera
m. Num A N Dem: 51 languages; 22 genera
n. N Dem A Num: 30 languages; 18 genera
o. A N Num Dem: 31 languages; 13 genera
p. A N Dem Num: 20 languages; 8 genera
Total: 2,120 languages

The consistent application of the same pied piping mode to subprojections embedded one inside the other is at the base of the mirror image found between (more rigid) head-final and (more rigid) head-initial languages in many other nominal orders. For example, in the case of family name, given name, occupational title, and honorific title (Lehmann 1978a: section 1.3), this is the order found in Japanese (7a), while Italian shows the exact mirror-image order (7b):[40]

(7) a. Kuroda Shige-Yuki kyooju san
family name given name occupational title (professor) honorific title (Mr.)

b. il signor[41] professore Gianfranco Folena
the honorific title (Mr.) occupational title (professor) given name family name

There is thus evidence for a rather articulated structure (see (8)a), where the constituents heading their subprojection, the honorific title and the given name, are raising to $\text{SpecAgr}_{\text{HonorTitleP}}\text{P}$ and to $\text{SpecAgr}_{\text{GivenNameP}}\text{P}$, respectively, in one or the other pied piping mode, in concert with the N(P) heading the projection (some intermediate X-bar projections are not labeled):[42]

(8) a.

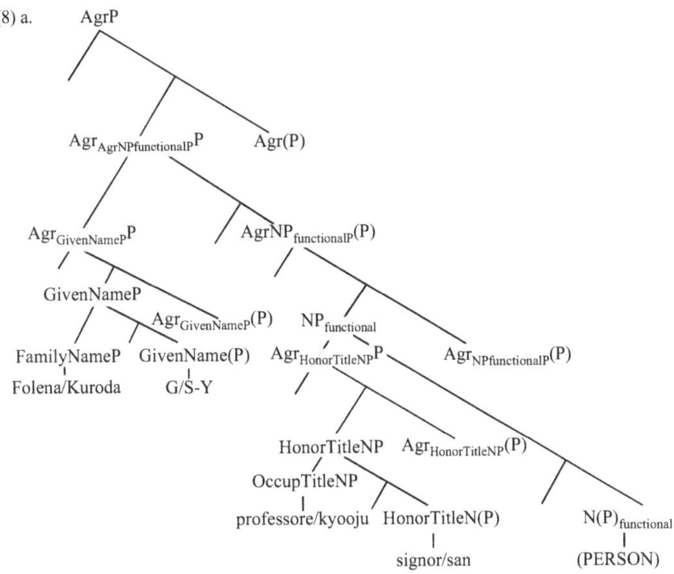
AgrP
Agr_AgrNPfunctionalP P
Agr(P)
Agr_GivenNameP P
AgrNP_functionalP(P)
GivenNameP
Agr_GivenNameP(P)
NP_functional
FamilyNameP
GivenName(P)
Agr_HonorTitleNP P
Agr_NPfunctionalP(P)
Folena/Kuroda
G/S-Y
HonorTitleNP
Agr_HonorTitleNP(P)
OccupTitleNP
professore/kyooju
HonorTitleN(P)
N(P)_functional
signor/san
(PERSON)

(8) b.

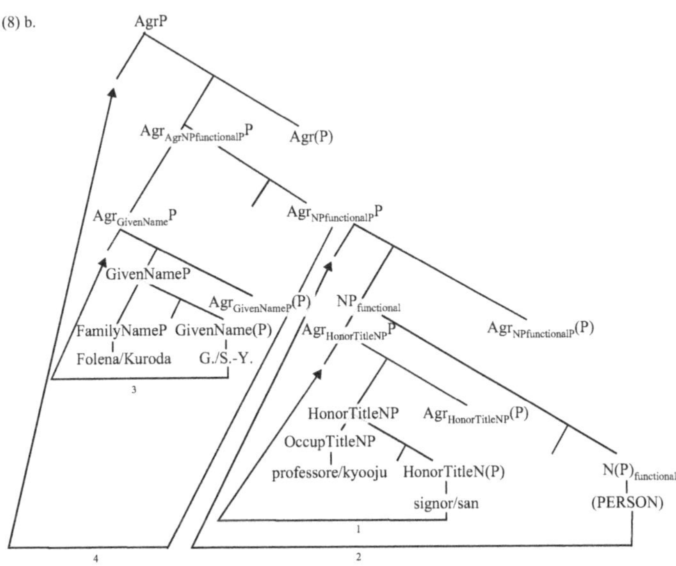
AgrP
Agr_AgrNPfunctionalP P
Agr(P)
Agr_GivenName P
Agr_NPfunctionalP P
GivenNameP
Agr_GivenNameP(P)
NP_functional
FamilyNameP
GivenName(P)
Agr_HonorTitleNP P
Agr_NPfunctionalP(P)
Folena/Kuroda
G./S.-Y.
3
HonorTitleNP
Agr_HonorTitleNP(P)
OccupTitleNP
professore/kyooju
HonorTitleN(P)
N(P)_functional
signor/san
(PERSON)
1
4
2

The Italian order in (7b) is obtained via movement of HonorTitleN(P) to the Spec of $Agr_{HonorTitelNP}P$, movement of $N(P)_{functional}$ to the Spec of $Agr_{NPfunctional}P$, movement of GivenName(P) to Spec of $Agr_{GivenNameP}P$, followed by movement of $Agr_{NPfunctional}P$ to the Spec of AgrP, as shown in (8b). All movements are of the *whose-pictures* pied piping type, with the effect of reversing the order of Merge of the constituents completely (if order is part of narrow syntax).

The head-final order (7a) is instead obtained via movements of the Heads in the *pictures-of-whom* pied piping mode (not indicated here), which retains the order of Merge (if order is part of narrow syntax).[43]

The N(P) heading the main projection line in (8a) and (8b) may be taken to host the generic noun that accompanies a specific noun, overtly in certain languages and, arguably, covertly in others (see Kayne 2007: section 15). As Hackstein (2010: 8) puts it: "The ordering of the generic and the specific noun is not random. There is a tendency for head-final languages to postpose the generic noun (wallaby—animal), and for head-initial languages to prepose the generic noun (animal—wallaby)."[44] See the case of head-final languages in (9) and that of the head-initial/medial languages in (10) (once again the *pictures-of-whom* pied piping is more typical of head-final languages and the *whose-pictures* pied piping of head-initial/medial ones):[45]

(9) a. lalaŋ abmal (Kunjen—Pama-Nyungan, SOV [Sommer 1970: 138])
uncle person
'the uncle'

b. hel-tːi k'ʷel=ra zunra admi=ra (Sanzhi Dargwa—Northeast Caucasian SOV [Forker 2020: 406])
that-PL two=add neighbor person=add
'and those two neighbors'

c. c'c'um hinč' (Avar—Northeast Caucasian, SOV [Hackstein 2010: 16])
eagle.Nom bird.Nom
'an eagle'

d. arrano hegazti-a (Basque—language isolate, SOV [Hackstein 2010: 16])
eagle.NOM bird.NOM-DET
'the eagle'

(10) a. nŏk čítam (Chuj—Mayan, VOS [Hopkins 1967: 147–148]).
animal pig
'a pig'

b. benhe bila ka (San Bartolomé Zoogocho Zapotec—Zapotecan,VSO [Sonneschein 2005: section 7.4.4])
person sister PL
'sisters'

c. baːr naʔ caw ʔuːr (Ko'ho Sre—Mon-Khmer, SVO [Olsen 2014: 62])
two CLF person woman
'two women'

d. ø-an ø-aare a-arɔ (Eegimaa—Kwa, SVO [Bassene 2012: 22])
CM-person woman SR-pretty
'a pretty woman'

This suggests that it is the (overt or silent) generic noun that heads the extended nominal projection.

Less frequent orders are apparently those that combine the two pied pipings modes, yielding cases that are less harmonic; for example, when the base moves with the (vacuous) *whose-pictures* pied piping, the classifier moves with the (vacuous) *whose-pictures* pied piping but the N moves with the *pictures-of-whom* pied piping, giving rise to the order (Heads in boldface) [[**CLF** [**Base** multiplier]] **N**] of Rongga (see (3d) and (4d) of chapter 2). Also mixed are the cases of Stiêng with movement of the base and the classifier with the *pictures-of-whom* pied piping and movement of the N with the *whose-pictures* pied piping (see (3c) and (4c) of chapter 2), yielding the order [**N** [[multiplier **Base**] **CLF**]]], and Jingpo with the base moving with the *pictures-of-whom* pied piping and the classifier and the N with the *whose-pictures* pied piping (see (4c) and (3b) of chapter 2), yielding the order [**N** [**CLF** [multiplier **Base**]]]. I return to the rarest combination among these disharmonic cases in section 5.3.

3.3 The Heads of the Maximal Nominal Extended Projection

In the preceding sections I let it be understood that the entire nominal projection is headed just by N(P) (possibly the generic N just discussed taking the lexical N(P) as its first merged specifier), but this is not completely accurate. In many languages in addition to N(P), Case (K(P)), Determiner (D(P)), and singular, dual, . . . , plural Number (PL(P)),[46] *overtly* head a specific subprojection of the overall nominal projection, to the effect that they also move in one of the two pied piping modes ending up to the left of the Noun in rigid head-initial languages (where argument and modifier phrases end up instead to its right) and to the right of the Noun in rigid head-final ones (where arguments and modifier phrases end up to its left). See (11), which is partially illustrated in (12) for head-initial languages and in (13) for head-final ones. On this segregation of Heads and arguments and modifier "phrases" also see Cinque (2017: section 2). Here I present a more accurate picture of the derivations that result in such a segregation.[47]

(11) a. K(P) D(P) PL(P) N(P) AP NumP DemP QP_{univ} (typical of rigid head-initial languages)
b. QP_{univ} DemP NumP AP N(P) PL(P) D(P) K(P) (typical of rigid head-final languages)

(12) a. 'a e ngaahi fale (Tongan—Polynesian, VSO /VOS [Ball 2009: 116])[48]

Case_{ABS} DET PL house

'the houses'

b. e te kau tagata (East Uvean—Polynesian, VOS/VSO [Livingston 2016: 106])[49]

Case_{ERG} DET PL man

'the men'

(13) a. ham oxorza-lepe-şi (Laz—South Caucasian, SOV [Kutscher 2001: 36])

Dem woman-PL-GEN

'of these women'

b. ʔo lam-ɨti–n (Argobba—Ethio-Semitic, SOV [Getahun 2018: 133])[50]

that cow-DEF-ACC

'that cow'

In other languages these Heads may be silent, as are those that head additional nominal projections, such as ClassifierP, ColorP, and others.

Let me sketch the derivation of (consistent) head-initial languages (14) and (consistent) head-final ones (15) for the nominal domain. Section 4.1 will present the parallel derivations for the verbal domain.

I am assuming that each substantive functional projection (abstracting away from AgrPs) is constituted by a Head that selects its complement in specifier position.[51] This assumption, which is compatible with antisymmetry, rejects the idea that anything is merged below the Head (to its right, if linear order is part of narrow syntax). The reason for that is the already mentioned left-right asymmetry of natural languages (whereby more orders are found to the right of a Head than to its left). The asymmetry can be derived as a consequence of the way in which the Head moves in relation to its dependents, merged above it in the order in which they compose with the Head.

Above each substantive functional projection a correponding agreement projection is merged to host in its specifier the movement of the Head of the substantive functional projection (which raises by itself or via one of the two pied piping modes). On top of the agreement projection a modifier projection associated with the substantive functional projection is merged (NumeralP containing CardinalP for PL(P); DeicticP containing DemonstrativeP for D(P), much like what happens in the verbal domain, where on top of the AgrP associated with (irrealis) Modal(P) there is an adverbial projection containing the associated modal adverb (*This possibly may qualify as one.*). See section 4.1.

Consider (14) and (15). On top of the N(P) and its agreement projection one, or more, associated modifier projections are merged, represented here by the projection of $[_{NP}$ 'color'], which selects in its specifier the corresponding AP ($[_{AP}$ $A_{color}]$) (should $[_{NP}$ 'color'] be spelled out an extra layer would be needed). This will be followed by the merger of the next nominal Head, PL(P), and the subsequent merger above it of an AgreementP to host the movement of the PL(P) Head. The derivation proceeds with the merger of a Numeral(P), the modifier projection associated with PL(P), which selects a CardinalP in its specifier, which has a corresponding AgreementP (I omit here the more articulated substructure seen in (2c) containing a ClassifierP and, inside the CardinalP, a MultiplierP); then D(P), the next nominal Head is merged with its AgreementP and selects a DemonstrativeP in its specifier, and the associated modifier projection, DeicticP, which comes with its AgreementP. Finally the highest nominal Head, K(P), is merged with its AgreementP. To ensure compatibility with Antisymmetry either the complement (as in the nominal Head projections, NP, PLP, DP, KP) or the Head (as in the AgreementPs, and in the associated modifers projections) will be null and thus uninfluential for linearization under the LCA. The derivation in (14), which involves movement of the nominal Heads N(P), PL(P), D(P), and K(P) with the *whose-pictures* pied piping mode, will give rise under the LCA to the order K D PL N AP

NumP DemP (typical of VOS/VSO languages), and that in (15), which involves movement of the same Heads with the *pictures-of-whom* pied piping mode, to the order DemP NumP AP N PL D K (typical of rigid SOV languages).

(14)

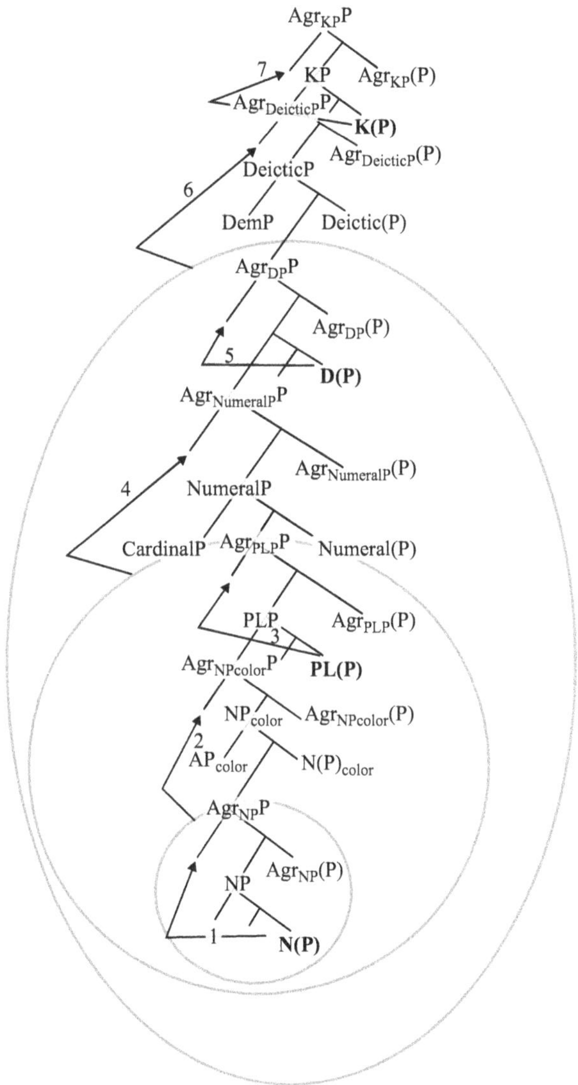

(15)

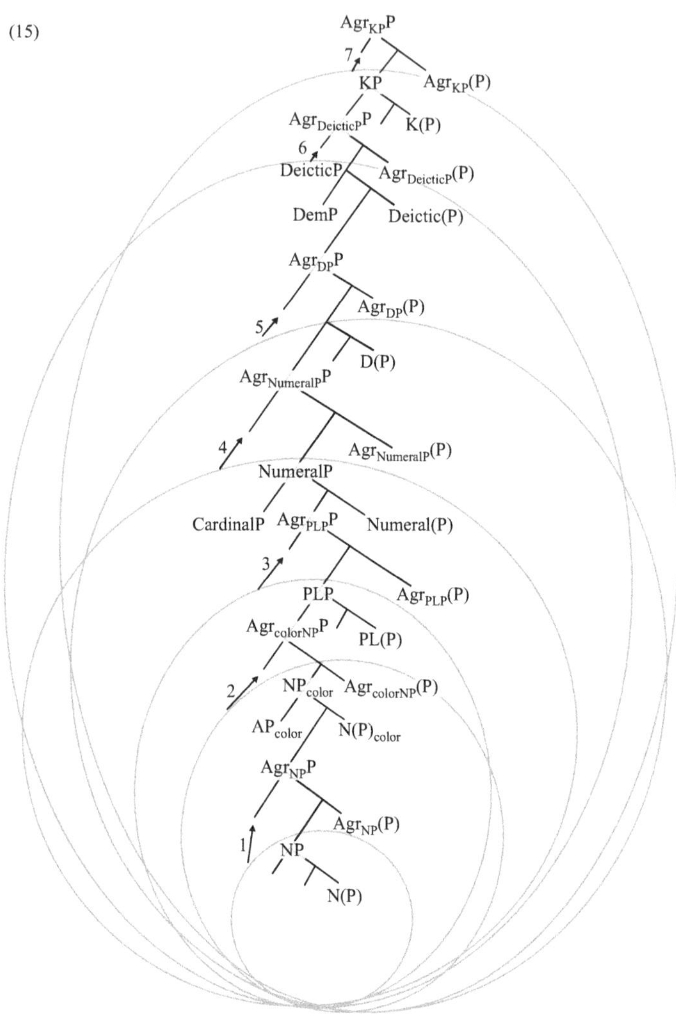

The preceding derivations of head-initial and head-final structures are couched within traditional X-bar theory, with overt selected complements and modifiers merged in specifier position when the Heads are overt and in complement position when the

Heads are null (to comply with antisymmetry). Perhaps these derivations, with movements of the Heads with pied piping, or without pied piping, "to yield the proper hierarchies" (Chomsky 2004: 110) for the LCA could also be obtained in a Bare Phrase Structure system with a labeling algorithm of the type developed in Chomsky (2013, 2015) and Rizzi (2016). For the LCA to apply properly, which requires asymmetric c-command to yield a linearization, the first-merged ("structural complement") XP of an overt nominal (verbal, etc.) Head is merged empty, so that the Head can label the resulting XP with its categorial feature, and its Lex (lexical) feature in Rizzi's (2016: section 4) sense. The next step will then involve the merger of this XP with another XP: DP, AP, CardinalP, DemP, to limit attention to the nominal extended projection. If, as noted in section 2.7, the latter are themselves all modifiers of an N(P) (AP_{color} of [$_{NP}$ color], AP_{size} of [$_{NP}$ size], CardinalP of [$_{NP}$ Classifier] (itself possibly a modifier of [$_{NP}$ amount/number], DemP of [$_{NP}$ ..PLACE], and so on), the phrases merged together are two XPs that are "identical in a relevant respect, providing the same label" (Chomsky 2013: 43), say both +N, thus arguably labeling the resulting XP as a +N phrase (also see Rizzi's [2016: 107–109] labeling convention when the two phrases being merged agree in their categorial feature). What remains to be seen is how best to ensure asymmetric c-command by one of the two merged categorially identical XPs and how to reconcile the successive cyclic movement of the N(P) discussed in the next section with Rizzi's (2016: 116) Maximality principle, which in theory could provide a rationale for the privileged status of pied piping over lack of pied piping. Problems remain, such as the labeling of the projection created by +V XP and a non-+V one such as AdvP, unless AdvP is also +V (which may be the case if each adverb is paired with a distinct verbal functional Head, as argued in Cinque [1999]). On the possible reconciliation of the LCA with bare phrase structure see Kayne (2008a: section 3), and on a labeling approach to head-initial and head-final orders, see Moro and Roberts (2021) and their work in progress.

3.4 Movement of the N(P) Spanning Over the Entire Nominal Projection

One case that could be interpreted as showing that the N(P) has after all a special status among the nominal Heads is the fact that it can move (at least in some languages) all the way up the entire nominal projection on top of the demonstrative. This is Greenberg's (1963: 52) "less popular" N Dem Num A order found in several Bantu languages and in some Nilo-Saharan, Cushitic, and Chadic languages (with very few languages outside of the African continent).

It is nonetheless possible to retain the uniform articulated structure in (14) and (15) if we consider the possibility that (a silent token of) the Head of each of the subprojections N(P), PL(P), D(P), K(P) raises to its own AgrP (solid lines in (16)) as part of the derivation for head-initial languages, with N(P) (the Head of the extended nominal projection) incorporating successive cyclically PL(P), D(P), and K(P), up to the highest Spec of the entire nominal projection (dashed line in (16)) (alternatively, checking their features in its successive cyclic movement through the various Specs containing the silent Heads moved there):

(16)

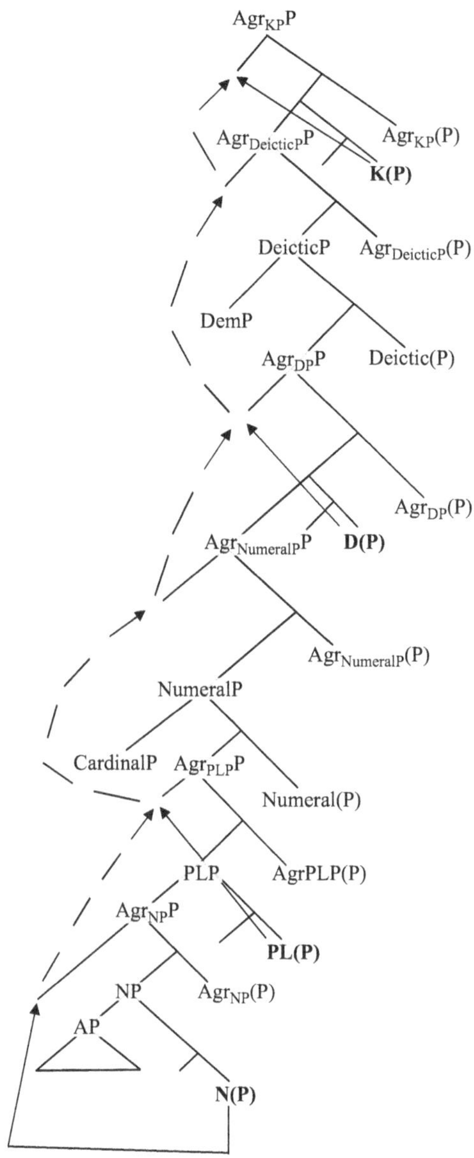
AgrKPP
AgrDeicticPP
AgrKP(P)
K(P)
DeicticP
AgrDeicticP(P)
DemP
AgrDPP
Deictic(P)
AgrDP(P)
AgrNumeralPP
D(P)
AgrNumeralP(P)
NumeralP
CardinalP
AgrPLPP
Numeral(P)
PLP
AgrPLP(P)
AgrNPP
PL(P)
NP
AgrNP(P)
AP
N(P)

This is rendered plausible by the fact that languages with the order N Dem Num A, unlike those with the order N A Num Dem, apparently never show separate K(P), D(P), and PL(P) Heads before the noun (as when each of these moves up with the *whose-pictures* pied piping mode illustrated in (14)). Rather, they display PL, D, and K suffixes on the noun, in this order, if any. As just mentioned, these can either be thought of as being picked up during the raising of the N(P), or as being part of the morphological make-up of the N(P), checked as the N(P) raises successive cyclically through the relevant Specs to which the silent Heads have raised. See, for example, the case of the Eastern Cushitic language Gawwada (Ale) in (17a), with an example of its N Dem Num A order in (17b):[52]

(17) a. t'rak-o-si [[e] lala-ɗe-si-si ɓitam-n-a] (Mekonnen 2010: 49)
man-m-DEF cloth-PL-DEF-ACC buy-FUT-Impf .3SGmasc
'the man who will buy clothes'
b. orħami-sa kora salaħ sikapoma (Prisecaru 2015: 17)
spears those four long
'those four long spears'

Similar is the case of Nilo-Saharan languages. In Majang (Surmic) the noun has the structure stem-(optional number and Case suffixes)=enclitics (Joswig 2019: 146) (see (18a)), and in Gaahmg (Eastern Sudanic) the structure stem-number (followed by definiteness/Case clitics) (see (18b)). The same holds in the Nilotic languages Kipsigis (Kouneli 2019: chapter 5) (see (18c)) and Lopit (Moodie 2019: section 4.8) (see (18d)):

(18) a. ʤóop sigoj ʤiit-ík ʤéedɗúwatu-ŋɔŋk koʤutú-ŋɔŋk. (Majang [Getachew 2014: 198])
people those three-GEN long-DEF black-DEF
'those three tall black men'

b. t̪ɔ́-gg nìì ásámán d̪ùìgg=ə̀ ə́ ənəgg=ə̀ (Gaahmg [Stirtz 2012: 303])
cow-PL these five black=DEF 1sPoss.PL=COP
'These five black cows are mine.'

c. làag-óo-chù sómòk chù kárâarán (Kipsigis [Kouneli 2019: 136])[53]
girl-PL-PROX three PROX beautiful
'these three beautiful girls'

d. xìsʊ́ŋ xʊ́ná ùnìk l-ò-bwór (Lopit [Moodie 2019: 100])
cows.ABS this.F.PL three Subord-3-be.white
'these three white cows'

Nor is in Bantu languages with the order N Dem Num A the noun preceded by separate number, definiteness, or Case Heads. It is rather preceded by just a class prefix. See, for example, (19):[54]

(19) a. mí-rí éső mi-raarú dhí-nddímúwa (Cuwabo [Guérois 2015: 154])
4-tree 4.dem 4-three 4-old
'these three old trees'

b. e-itu a-ya ma-kwa a-tatu a-seo (Kikamba [Mbuvi 2005: 68])
C2-girls 2AGR-those 2AGR-mine 2AGR-three 2AGR-good
'those three good girls of mine'

Among the few languages outside of the African continent displaying the order N Dem Num A, the noun of the Papuan (Torricelli) language Abu Arapesh (Nekitel 1985: section 3.4.1.1) is only followed by singular/plural suffixes, as in (20a), and the Oceanic language Namakir (Sperlich 1991: section 5.2.1.4.1) has a determiner prefixed to the noun (20b):

(20) a. aleman ana atena ubahineri (cf. Nekitel 1985: 95)
man this one big
'this big man'

b. na-bokah iŋa laru aŋino ?(ara) ahoh (Sperlich 1991: 189)
ART-pig this eight my (REL) good
'these eight beautiful pigs of mine'

In this class of languages the N(P) moves above demonstratives successive cyclically (by itself) rather than in one of the two pied piping modes.

On the determinants of the pied piping or no pied piping mode see section 4.5.

Interim Summary

So far we have seen evidence that the extended nominal projection is made up of a number of subprojections, headed the N(P), PL(P), D(P), K(P), a fragment of which was given in (14) and (15). On top of each such subprojection there is an agreement projection in whose specifier the subprojection Head moves, either by itself or via one of the two pied piping modes (recall the possibility that these Heads are actually minimal phrases comprising just an X°). Above the Head's agreement projection there is a specific modifier projection that is paired with the Head: for example, NumeralP with PL(P), DemonstrativeP with D(P) (and in the case of the clause, say, an $\text{Adverb}_{\text{modal}}$P with ModalP). The variety of orders obtainable are a function of the way each Head raises, yielding a head-initial language if every Head moves with a consistent *whose-pictures* pied piping and a head-final one if it moves in a consistent *pictures-of-whom* pied piping, otherwise yielding a mixed word order language.

3.5 A Movement/Internal Merge Account versus a (Partially) Symmetric External Merge Account

Though appealing in its apparent simplicity, a symmetrical Merge of the phrasal modifiers DemP, NumP, and AP, either to the left or to the right of the NP, to derive the 8 "symmetrical" orders of the 14 attested orders (Abels and Neeleman, 2009, 2012) (see (21)), may not be the best option, quite apart from its abandonment of the LCA and Antisymmetry.

(21)

'direct' order	[lgs]	[genera]	'mirror-image order	[lgs]	[genera]
a. Dem Num A N	425	110	a'. N A Num Dem	606	137
b. Dem Num N A	182	67	b'. A N Num Dem	31	13
c. Num A N Dem	51	22	c'. Dem N A Num	207	79
d. Dem A N Num	46	24	d'. Num N A Dem	226	47

First, one would think that the mirror-image order (21a′) would be represented by approximately the same number of languages and genera as the direct order (21a), given that both involve no marked principle in the (partially) symmetric external Merge account of Abels and Neeleman (2009: section 4.2, 2012: section 3). However, as is apparent from the numbers of languages and genera in Dryer's (2018) 576-language sample and in the enlarged, over 2,000-language sample mentioned earlier (with N A Num Dem totalling 606 languages and 137 genera vs. Dem Num A N totalling 425 languages and 110 genera, as reported in (21)), it is clear that they are far from being approximately equal.[55] Under an internal Merge account involving movement of the *whose-pictures* pied piping for the order N A Num Dem and of the *pictures-of-whom* pied piping for the order Dem Num A N the difference in frequency can arguably be attributed to the more marked status of the latter type of pied piping (see sections 5.2 and 5.3 for discussion).

Second, the symmetrical Merge account has to be supplemented with some instances of internal Merge to derive the remaining 6 attested orders (see (22)), which cannot be merged by symmetrical Merge without violating the no-tangling condition[56] or the underlying hierarchical order (Abels 2016a: 185):

(22) a. N Dem Num A
b. Dem N Num A
c. N Num A Dem

d. N Dem A Num
e. A N Dem Num
f. N A Dem Num

But once internal Merge is allowed to derive the "nonsymmetrical" orders of (22) it is also available to derive the "symmetrical" ones of (21), thus exposing the redundancy inherent in any account that can derive certain orders both by symmetric external Merge and by internal Merge.[57]

Third, if ellipsis is dependent on movement (Johnson 2001; Ntelitheos 2004; Kayne 2006b, 2012) and if nominal subdeletion is governed by the same principles that derive Greenberg's Universal 20 (see Cinque 2012, 2021; 2022a: sections 3 and 4), then there is further evidence that movement is crucial in accounting for all the 14 attested orders of demonstrative, numeral, adjective, and noun.

3.6 Reason, Manner, Directional PPs in Dutch and Italian

Another consideration that seems to favor a generalized movement approach over a direct symmetric one for the derivation of the possible/attested orders of *n* elements may come from the unmarked order of reason, manner, and directional Prepositional Phrases (PPs) in head-final Dutch and head-initial/-medial Italian.[58]

In Dutch the unmarked preverbal order of these PPs is Reason > Manner > Directional (23a), an order that is retained when the verb moves to second position (23b) (cf. Koster 1974: 612).[59]

(23) a. Hij is [$_{PP3}$ door 'n stuurfout] [$_{PP2}$ met een knal] [$_{PP1}$ op het hek] [$_{VP}$ gestrand]
he has [$_{PP3}$ by a steering error] [$_{PP2}$ with a bang] [$_{PP1}$ on the fence] [$_{VP}$ got stranded]
b. Hij strandde [$_{PP3}$ door 'n stuurfout] [$_{PP2}$ met een knal] [$_{PP1}$ op het hek]

he got stranded [$_{PP3}$ by a steering error] [$_{PP2}$ with a bang] [$_{PP1}$ on the fence]
'He got stranded on the fence with a bang by a steering error'

In Italian the unmarked (postverbal) order of the same PPs is the mirror image of Dutch (VP > Directional > Manner > Reason) with both participial and finite verbs. See (24):[60]

(24) a. Lui si è incastrato [$_{PP1}$ nella recinzione] [$_{PP2}$ con un botto] [$_{PP3}$ per un errore di manovra]
he has got stranded [$_{PP1}$ on the fence] [$_{PP2}$ with a bang] [$_{PP3}$ by a steering error]
b. Lui si incastrò [$_{PP1}$ nella recinzione] [$_{PP2}$ con un botto] [$_{PP3}$ per un errore di manovra]
he got stranded [$_{PP1}$ on the fence] [$_{PP2}$ with a bang] [$_{PP3}$ by a steering error]
'He got stranded on the fence with a bang by a steering error'

In Dutch the participial V(P) can also raise above all the PPs in the middlefield, in which case the only order possible is the mirror image of the preverbal order. See (25) (Barbiers 1995: 103):

(25) a. Hij is [$_{VP}$ gestrand] [$_{PP1}$ op het hek] [$_{PP2}$ met een knal] [$_{PP3}$ door een stuurfout]
he has got stranded [$_{PP1}$ on the fence] [$_{PP2}$ with a bang] [$_{PP3}$ through to a steering error]
b. *Hij is [$_{VP}$ gestrand] [$_{PP3}$ door 'n stuurfout] [$_{PP2}$ met een knal] [$_{PP1}$ op het hek]
he has got stranded [$_{PP3}$ through a steering error] [$_{PP2}$ with a bang] [$_{PP1}$ on the fence]
'He got stranded on the fence with a bang due to a steering error'

This seems to suggest, given the basically head-final nature of Dutch (cf. note 58), that the head-initial/-medial order, VP>

$PP_{Directional} > PP_{Manner} > PP_{Reason}$, with participial verbs raised to the middlefield (cf. (25a)), is a function of the movement of the VP with pied piping of the *whose-pictures* type from the final position, much like the main clause order V2 > $PP_{Reason} > PP_{Manner} > PP_{Directional}$ (23b) is a function of the successive cyclic movement (or movement in one fell swoop) of the VP from a final position to CP without pied piping. The head-final order, $PP_{Reason} > PP_{Manner} > PP_{Directional}$ > VP of (23a) is instead a function of the movement of the VP with the *pictures-of-whom* pied piping. That means, if this is correct, that in the (partially) symmetric external Merge account the mirror-image order of (25a) in Dutch would plausibly involve the roll-up movement of the participle with the *whose-pictures* pied piping mode, while that of Italian (24) (where there is no alternation with the order $PP_{Reason} > PP_{Manner} > PP_{Directional}$ > VP) would involve a direct (scope-complying) merger of the phrases to the right of the participial verb. In such an account, then, the order VP > $PP_{Directional} > PP_{Manner} > PP_{Reason}$ would arise in two different ways, either via internal Merge or via external Merge, again exposing a redundancy. By contrast no such redundancy is present in the antisymmetric internal Merge account assumed here, which generalizes the role of movement.

It may be interesting to consider the entire paradigm of possible and impossible orders given by Barbiers (1995: 103). In addition to the just discussed grammatical alternatives of (23a) and (25a), repeated here as (26a) and (26b), Barbiers provides additional grammatical orders in (27) and ungrammatical ones in (28) and (29):

(26) a. Hij is [$_{PP3}$ door 'n stuurfout] [$_{PP2}$ met een knal] [$_{PP1}$ op het hek] [$_{VP}$ gestrand]
he has [$_{PP3}$ through a steering error] [$_{PP2}$ with a bang] [$_{PP1}$ on the fence] [$_{VP}$ got stranded]

b. Hij is [$_{VP}$ gestrand] [$_{PP1}$ op het hek] [$_{PP2}$ met een knal] [$_{PP3}$ door een stuurfout]

he has got stranded [$_{PP1}$ on the fence] [$_{PP2}$ with a bang] [$_{PP3}$ through a steering error]
'He got stranded on the fence with a bang due to a steering error'

(27) a. Hij is [$_{PP3}$ door 'n stuurfout] [$_{PP2}$ met een knal] [$_{VP}$ gestrand] [$_{PP1}$ op het hek]
b. Hij is [$_{PP3}$ door 'n stuurfout] [$_{VP}$ gestrand] [$_{PP1}$ op het hek] [$_{PP2}$ met een knal]
c. Hij is [$_{PP3}$ door 'n stuurfout] [$_{PP1}$ op het hek] [$_{VP}$ gestrand] [$_{PP2}$ met een knal]
d. Hij is [$_{PP1}$ op het hek] [$_{VP}$ gestrand] [$_{PP2}$ met een knal] [$_{PP3}$ door een stuurfout]
e. Hij is [$_{PP2}$ met een knal] [$_{PP1}$ op het hek] [$_{VP}$ gestrand] [$_{PP3}$ door een stuurfout]
f. Hij is [$_{PP2}$ met een knal] [$_{VP}$ gestrand] [$_{PP1}$ op het hek] [$_{PP3}$ door een stuurfout]

(28) a. *Hij is [$_{VP}$ gestrand] [$_{PP3}$ door 'n stuurfout] [$_{PP2}$ met een knal] [$_{PP1}$ op het hek]
b. *Hij is [$_{PP3}$ door 'n stuurfout] [$_{VP}$ gestrand] [$_{PP2}$ met een knal] [$_{PP1}$ op het hek]
c. *Hij is [$_{PP2}$ met een knal] [$_{VP}$ gestrand] [$_{PP3}$ door 'n stuurfout] [$_{PP1}$ op het hek]
d. *Hij is [$_{PP1}$ op het hek] [$_{VP}$ gestrand] [$_{PP3}$ door 'n stuurfout] [$_{PP2}$ met een knal]
e. *Hij is [$_{PP1}$ op het hek] [$_{PP3}$ door 'n stuurfout] [$_{VP}$ gestrand] [$_{PP2}$ met een knal]
f. *Hij is [$_{PP1}$ op het hek] [$_{PP2}$ met een knal] [$_{VP}$ gestrand] [$_{PP3}$ door 'n stuurfout]
g. *Hij is [$_{PP2}$ met een knal] [$_{PP3}$ door 'n stuurfout] [$_{VP}$ gestrand] [$_{PP1}$ op het hek]
h. *Hij is [$_{VP}$ gestrand] [$_{PP3}$ door 'n stuurfout] [$_{PP1}$ op het hek] [$_{PP2}$ met een knal]

i. *Hij is [$_{VP}$ gestrand] [$_{PP2}$ met een knal] [$_{PP3}$ door 'n stuurfout] [$_{PP1}$ op het hek]
l. *Hij is [$_{VP}$ gestrand] [$_{PP2}$ met een knal] [$_{PP1}$ op het hek] [$_{PP3}$ door 'n stuurfout]
m *Hij is [$_{VP}$ gestrand] [$_{PP1}$ op het hek] [$_{PP3}$ door 'n stuurfout] [$_{PP2}$ met een knal]

(29) a. *Hij is [$_{PP3}$ door een stuurfout] [$_{PP1}$ op het hek] [$_{PP2}$ met een knal] [$_{VP}$ gestrand]
b. *Hij is [$_{PP2}$ met een knal] [$_{PP3}$ door een stuurfout] [$_{PP1}$ op het hek] [$_{VP}$ gestrand]
c. *Hij is [$_{PP2}$ met een knal] [$_{PP1}$ op het hek] [$_{PP3}$ door een stuurfout] [$_{VP}$ gestrand]
d. *Hij is [$_{PP1}$ op het hek] [$_{PP3}$ door een stuurfout] [$_{PP2}$ met een knal] [$_{VP}$ gestrand]
e. *Hij is [$_{PP1}$ op het hek] [$_{PP2}$ met een knal] [$_{PP3}$ door een stuurfout] [$_{VP}$ gestrand]

In the present framework, where word order is a function of movement, the Dutch patterns of grammatical orders ((26) and (27)), and of ungrammatical ones ((28) and (29)) seem to follow from a subset of the set of conditions assumed here, which comprise the axioms and theorems of Antisymmetry (Kayne 1994) and the condition that movement can only involve the Head of the construction (here the VP). Specifically, the (successive cyclic) movement of the participial VP without pied piping above the PPs is disallowed (see (28a) and (28b)).[61]

The grammatical (27a) would involve movement of the VP above the Directional PP, arguably with vacuous *whose-pictures* pied piping, as one can gather from the grammaticality of (27b), where the prenominal order of the Manner and Directional PPs is reversed, due to the roll-up movement induced by the *whose-pictures* pied piping, and the ungrammaticality of (28d), which instead appear to have been derived by movement of the VP (within a larger phrase containing it) without any *whose-pictures* pied piping.

Example (27c) would involve movement of the larger constituent [[$_{PP1}$ op het hek] [$_{VP}$ gestrand]], containing the VP, above the next higher PP [$_{PP2}$ met een knal]. Example (27d) would involve movement of the larger constituent [[[$_{PP1}$ op het hek] [$_{VP}$ gestrand]] [$_{PP2}$ met een knal]], previously obtained as in (27c), above the higher PP$_{Reason}$. Example (27e) would instead involve movement of the larger constituent [[$_{PP2}$ met een knal] [$_{PP1}$ op het hek] [$_{VP}$ gestrand]] above the PP$_{Reason}$, and finally (27f) would involve the larger constituent [[$_{PP2}$ met een knal] [$_{VP}$ gestrand] [$_{PP1}$ op het hek]], partly obtained as in (27a), again above the higher PP$_{Reason}$. As noted, the movement of all these constituents involve the *whose-pictures* pied piping mode, whether vacuously or not, because movement of the same constituents by themselves, successive cyclically or in one fell swoop without the *whose-pictures* pied piping, invariably appears to yield an ungrammatical result. I already mentioned the ungrammaticality of (28a, b, and d). Example (28c) cannot be derived. After raising above the PP$_{Directional}$ (PP$_1$) the VP would have had to raise past the PP$_{Reason}$ (PP$_3$) dragging along the PP$_{Manner}$ (PP$_2$), stranding the PP$_{Directional}$ (a nonconstituent). Examples (28e–g) have the wrong order/hierarchy of PPs preverbally (an order/hierarchy that is retained under the *pictures-of-whom* pied piping). Examples (28h, i, l, and m) are ungrammatical as the PPs are in the wrong order/hierarchy of Merge whether the VP has raised with the *whose-pictures* pied piping or by itself without pied piping. The examples in (29) are similarly ill-formed as the PPs are in the wrong order/hierarchy of Merge preverbally. When I said previously that the data in (26)–(29) in Dutch follow from a subset, rather than the full set, of the conditions assumed here, I meant that the movement of the participial VP in Dutch can only proceed with the *whose-pictures* pied piping (like that of Italian), or the more complex pied piping involving simultaneously the *whose-pictures* and the *pictures-of-whom* pied piping modes found in the nominal extended projection to derive, for example, A N Num Dem, and in relative *wh*-movement (*Aylan, pictures of whose body* . . . [cf. note 5 of chapter 1]). Crucially, however, it cannot proceed exploiting the no pied piping possibility open to the finite verb in V2 contexts.[62]

4 Extending the Analysis to the Clause

4.1 Verbal Subprojections and Their Word Orders

As already apparent from the discussion in chapter 3 of Dutch reason, manner, and directional PPs, the same general picture is found with the elements that compose the verbal extended projection, the clause, though a detailed calculation of their possible and impossible orders is out of the question here, because the clause hierarchical structure is richer than that of nominals and our knowledge of the structure's precise constituency is even poorer. What I present here is only an extremely simplified picture of this articulation and of the derivations that lead to different orders, just to illustrate the logic of the matter. Here too, as in previous chapters, I take the different orders to derive from a unique hierarchy(/order) via the different ways the Heads of the clausal subprojections, and just these, move. Section 4.5 briefly considers the possible lexical determinants of the different types of movement.

Like the nominal extended projection, the verbal extended projection is also made up of a number of subprojections headed by verbal, aspectual, modal, tense, and so on, Heads (Cinque 1999), a very tiny fragment of which is given in (1). The Head of each subprojection targets the specifier of an associated AgrP, which is there to host its movement. This in turn is paired with a corresponding adverbial modifier projection (see (1)). Languages vary as to whether they overtly realize the Head or the corresponding associated AdvP or both (as is the case with English alethic modality in (1)).

(1) a. (this) <may> possibly <may> create problems.

b.

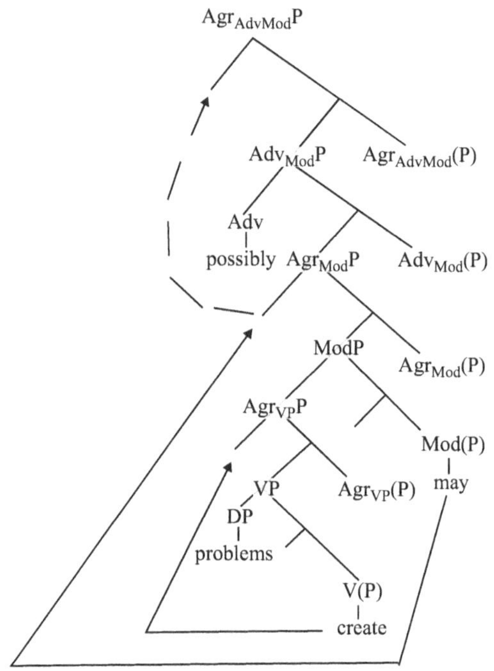

The modal in English moves without pied piping. The first movement to the specifier of its AgrP is obligatory. The second, above the associated adverb, is optional. English active finite or participial V(P)s pied pipe the direct object obligatorily above the lowest adverbs (*well, early* (*on*), . . .) (see (2)) and optionally above the next higher one (*completely*) (see (3)).[1]

(2) a. *She (has) well/early on understood the problem.
b. She (has) understood the problem well/early on.
c. *She (has) understood well/early on the problem.

(3) a. She (has) completely understood the problem.
    b. She (has) understood the problem completely.
    c. *She (has) understood completely the problem.[2]

When passive they raise to a lower head, Voice, obligatorily crossing over *early (on)* in (4) but not necessarily over the higher *well* and *completely* in (5).

(4) The problem had been <*early on> understood <early on>.

(5) The problem had been <understood> completely/very well <understood>.

Some subprojections of the clause are given in (6). As already stated, this is only a very tiny fragment of the overall clausal projection, which can be taken as neutral between a purely hierarchical and a hierarchical/linear representation:[3]

(6)

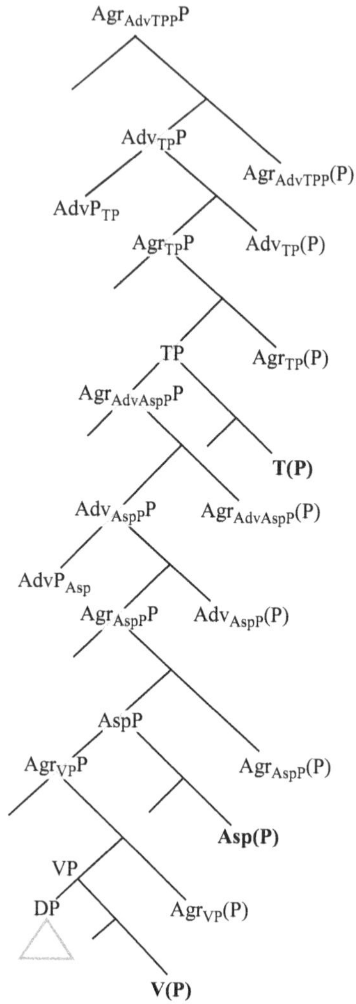

For clarity we may start from the characteristic word orders of the more rigid head-initial and the more rigid head-final languages (cf. Cinque [2017: section 2], in particular concerning the segregation of the Heads on one side of the V(P) and of the arguments and modifiers on the other side). The terms (rigid)

head-initial and head-final should not be taken to suggest that VOS or SOV languages (or, for that matter, VSO and SVO) constitute uniform "types" of languages. See Cinque (2013b: 50fn8), Chung (2017), Clemens and Polinsky (2017) and references cited there on head-initial languages, and Cinque (2017) and references cited there on head-final ones. Be that as it may, one should not be disturbed by the possibility that each language is different from every other language of its own type (in addition to being different from those belonging to other types). The hope of deriving the orders of all languages from the same hierarchical organization of the clause via the same basic principles is not lost if the differences are a consequence of slightly different combinations of the few movement options admitted by Universal Grammar (UG). See section 4.3 for a brief illustration of other possible derivations of VOS/VSO, SVO, and SOV languages.

The templates in (7) and (8) are simplified representations of the order of the main Heads and argument/modifier phrases that characterize the more rigid head-initial and head-final languages, respectively, with three illustrative examples each:

(7) C(P) T(P) Asp(P) V(P) DP PP AdvP[4]

a. Chol (Mayan, VOS [Coon 2010: 241])
Tyi k-sub-u [che' mi i-bajb-eñ ts'i' aj-Wãn]
PRFV ERG1-say-TV [COMP IMPF ERG3-hit-NMLZ dog CLF-Juan]
'I said that Juan hits the dog.'

b. Sakun (Sukur) (Chadic, VOS [Thomas 2014: 88])
a ɗá-r kərá=j nə dʒíf Lawu
PRFVhit-EXT dog=REL with stick Lawu
'Lawu hit the dog with the stick.'

c. Seediq (Austronesian, Formosan, VOS [Lin 2005: 116])
ye uxe dheya wada gmeeguy di
Yes/No Neg. 3PL Aux_{Past} steal Part
'Have/Had they stolen (the basket of pears)?'

(8) AdvP PP DP V(P) Asp(P) T(P) C(P)

a. Japanese (SOV [Endo Yoshio, pers.comm., July 15, 2015])
Watasi-wa [kare-ga osoraku sore-o zyoozuni okona-e-ru to] it-ta
I-TOP [he-NOM probably it-ACC well do-Mod-PRESCOMP] say-PST
'I said that probably he can do it well'

b. Tangsa (Tibeto-Burman, SOV [Boro 2017: 326])
ibə́ kʰiʔhî dà meʔ nɤʔ cʰí t-aʔ[5]
that deer leg ABL tread DUR PST-3
'(They) trod with deer legs (to leave deer foot marks on the ground).'

c. Maranungku (Australian, Daly, SOV [Tryon 1970: 46])
yer ngeti tyapat me tu
tomorrow I sit.swim PROG FUT
'Tomorrow I shall be swimming'

Asp(P), T(P), and C(P) heading their projections (as minimal phrases) are, as noted, an abbreviation for more numerous aspectual, tense, and complementizer categories (see Cinque 1999; Rizzi 1997; Rizzi and Bocci 2017), as are the AdvP PP DP arguments/modifiers indicated, but this will do to illustrate the derivations responsible for the ultimate order of (7) (see, for example, (9), with English glosses), and (8) (see, for example, (10), again with English glosses):

(9)

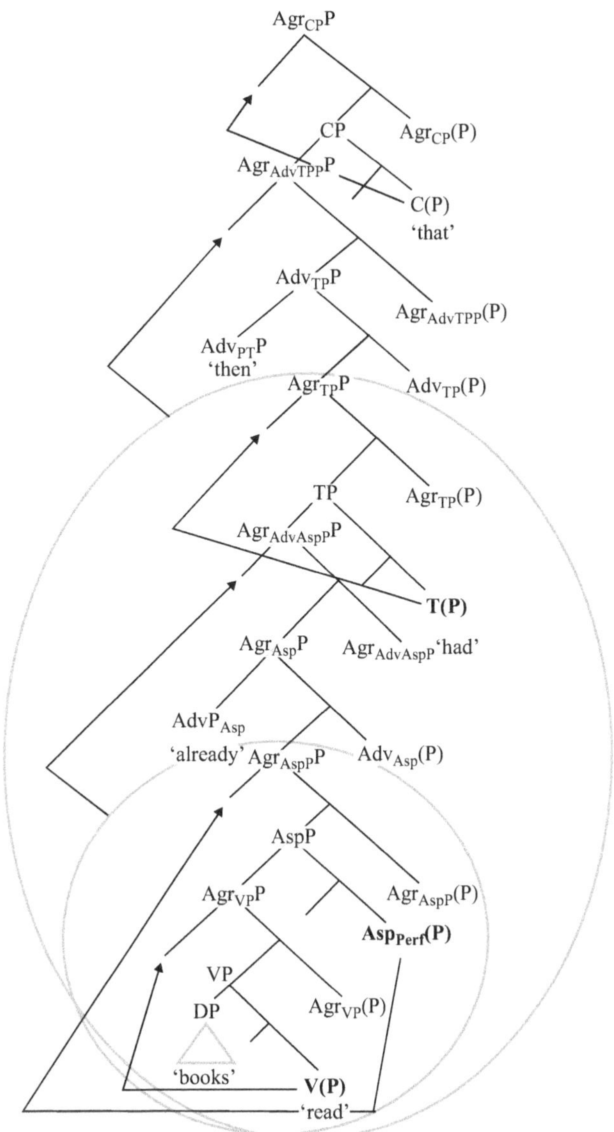

Agr_CP P
CP
Agr_CP(P)
Agr_AdvTPP P
C(P)
'that'
Adv_TP P
Agr_AdvTPP(P)
Adv_PT P
'then'
Agr_TP P
Adv_TP(P)
TP
Agr_TP(P)
Agr_AdvAspP P
T(P)
Agr_Asp P
Agr_AdvAspP 'had'
AdvP_Asp
'already'
Agr_AspP P
Adv_Asp(P)
AspP
Agr_VP P
Agr_AspP(P)
Asp_Perf(P)
VP
DP
Agr_VP(P)
'books'
V(P)
'read'

The derivation in (9) yields under the LCA the order 'that' 'had' 'read' 'books' 'already' 'then'.

(10)

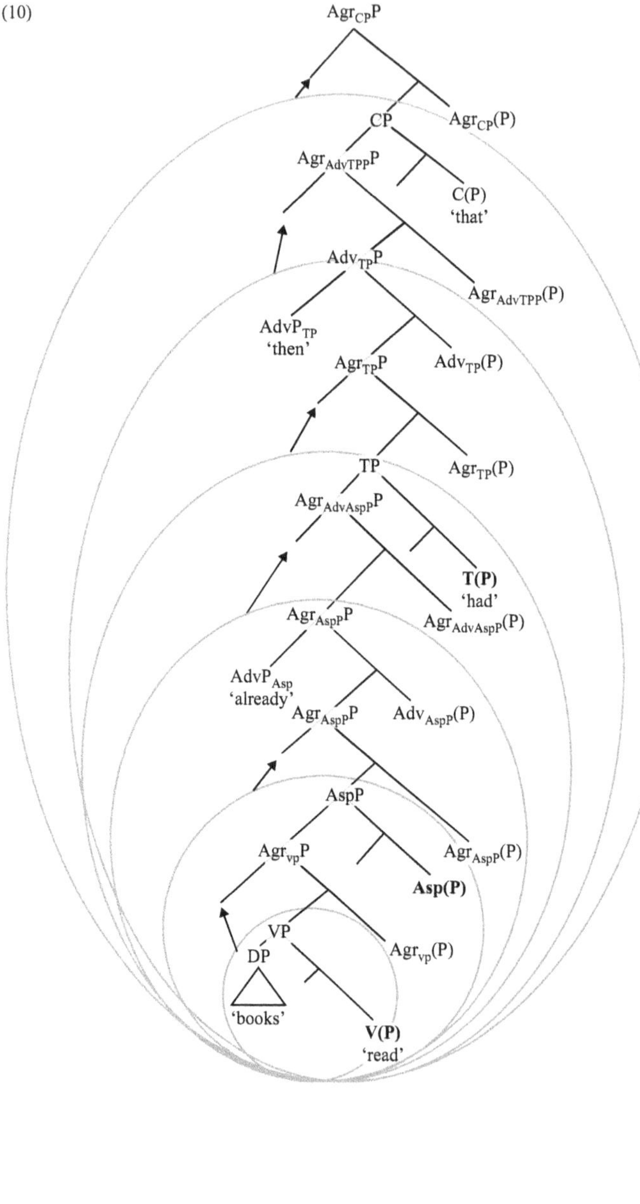

The derivation in (10) yields under the LCA the order 'then' 'already' 'books' 'read' 'had' 'that'. The cases of head-final Tangsa in (8b) and Maranungku in (8c) are cases in which the clausal Heads of Tense and Aspect are independent morphemes following the V, but in other head-final languages the corresponding Aspect and Tense Heads are morphemes bound to the verb, as in the Japanese example (8a). In such cases one should determine whether they are inflectional suffixes arguably making up a lexical word with the verb or retain a relatively independent status, making up a "syntactic word" (for lack of a better term) with the verb. Particularly relevant in this respect is Jaklin Kornfilt's work (1996; 2012) on Turkish, which apparently displays both types of suffixes. As Kornfilt shows, the two types of suffixes can be told apart by their ability/inability to participate in "suspended affixation" (whereby only the last conjunct in a coordination bears a certain word-final suffix that distributes over all conjuncts). While the reportive past suffix *-mIş* can be suspended, the homophonous perfect participle suffix *-mIş* cannot. See the contrast between (11a) and (11b) (from Kornfilt 2012: 189fn7):

(11) a. Ali her gün [[havyar ye-r-], [şampanya iç-er-]]-miş
Ali every day [[caviar eat-AOR]- [champagne drink-AOR]- REP.PST
'Ali reportedly eats/used to eat caviar (and) (reportedly) drinks/used to drink champagne every day.'

b. *[[kok-] ve [çürü-]]-müş balık
smell- and rot-PART fish
'smelly and rotted fish'

Kornfilt shows however that the suspendable suffixes are really nonsuspendable at all. They are suffixed to a silent auxiliary (which in certain cases can be overt) (Kornfilt 1996). This suggests that they are after all the same type of affix. This is not very different (modulo the head-final linearization of the coordinated structure in Turkish to the left of the suspended (auxiliary)-suffix) from the "suspended" auxiliary+suffix in such Italian cases as (12), where the coordinated structure is to the right of the suspended auxiliary-suffix (with the auxiliary necessarily spelled out):[6]

(12) Loro ha-nno [[mangia-to] e [bevu-to]]
they have-3PL eat-PST.PART and drink-PST.PART
'They have eaten and drunk.'

In other terms, "all suffixes that can be successfully 'suspended' are *syntactically* merged projection heads" (Kornfilt 2012: 190). This carries over to many head-final languages with agglutinative morphology, such as Korean and Japanese (see Yoon 1994; Takano 2004; Koopman 2005; Kornfilt 2012; Fenger 2020).[7]

The consistent application in each of the subprojections belonging to a certain extended projection of the *whose-pictures* pied piping mode and of the *pictures-of-whom* pied piping mode yields the more rigid head-initial VOS languages and the more rigid head-final SOV languages, respectively.

As noted in Cinque (2013b: 51fn11; 2017: section 4) even the most rigid head-initial languages (including Malagasy) and the most rigid head-final languages (including Japanese) display some inconsistencies, and, more strikingly, they appear to be a minority of the languages of the world. These are two puzzles that remain to be understood.[8]

Most languages display nonfully consistent derivations (i.e., they are not harmonic across their different phrases). Section 3.2 briefly discussed some of the nonharmonic orders found in the nominal extended projection, and section 4.3 will address the same question with respect to the clause (the verbal extended projection). Nonetheless there appear to be some clear word order correlations uncovered in the typological literature since Greenberg (1963) that have to be taken into account and will be discussed in the next section. Section 4.4 will instead address the particular challenge for the present movement account of word order represented by the Germanic verb clusters.

4.2 The (Partial) Correlations of Head-Initial and Head-Final Languages

The word order variation found in the languages of the world clearly involves different departures from the simple derivations seen so far.

Within the present perspective, one type of departure from such uniform derivations resides in the presence of opposite values in the mode of pied piping for the verbal and the nominal extended projections. For example the Trans-New Guinea language Bargam (like several other Papuan languages) is head-final in the verbal extended projection (quite strictly so [Hepner 2006: chapter 5]) and in the PP (which is rigidly postpositional), but head-initial in the nominal extended projection (Hepner 2006: section 4.1):[9]

(13) Bargam (Papuan [Trans-New Guinea] SOV)
   a. AdvP Subj PP Obj V (head-final)
   b. N AP NumP DemP (head-initial)

Many Mayan languages, like Tzutujil in (14), show the reverse situation, being head-initial in the verbal extended projection and head-final in the nominal one (Dayley 1981: sections 8.2.3 and 8.1.1):

(14) Tzutujil (Mayan [Qichean] VOS)
   a. V Obj Subj AdvP PP (head-initial)
   b. DemP NumP AP N (head-final)

Yet, clear tendencies of different strength are observable. Harmony of heads within the same extended projection is rather strongly obeyed. As apparent from Dryer (1992) (also see Biberauer et al. 2014: section 3), modal verbs, auxiliaries and subordinating conjunctions are predominantly verb patterners. They predominantly follow the lexical verb in OV languages and predominantly precede the lexical verb in VO languages. See (15) (with modal= 'want'), (16), and (17), all from Dryer (1992: 94, 100, 103):

(15) a. OV and V modal: 29 genera
b. VO and modal V: 42 genera
c. OV and modal V: 10 genera
d. VO and V modal: 4 genera

(16) a. OV and VAux: 36 genera
b. VO and AuxV: 28 genera
c. OV and AuxV: 3 genera
d. VO and VAux: 4 genera

(17) a. OV and IP Subordinator: 38 genera
b. VO and Subordinator IP: 59 genera
c. OV and Subordinator IP: 17 genera
d. VO and IP Subordinator: 1 genus

Harmony of modifiers within the same extended projection is also fairly strongly obeyed.

To judge from Dryer (1992: 123) (see (18)), the position of AdvP and PP modifiers with respect to the verb in the clause also tends to be harmonic:

(18) a. PPV and AdvV: 42 genera
b. VPP and VAdv: 36 genera
c. PPV and VAdv: 1 genus
d. VPP and AdvP: 6 genera

Harmony across different extended projections seems to be more strongly obeyed by heads with respect to their complements than by heads with respect to their modifiers.

For example, if one composes the features "order of object and verb" and "order of adposition and NP" or those of "order of object and verb" and "order of genitive and noun" in the interactive tool of the World Atlas of Language Structures (WALS Online), the cross-categorial harmony between the extended projections of VP and PP and VP and NP with respect to heads and their complements (to the extent that N GEN includes genitive complements of the noun in addition to genitive subjects) appears to be fairly robust. See the figures in (19) and (20):

(19) a. OV and OP: 427 languages
 b. VO and PO: 417 languages
 c. VO and OP: 38 languages
 d. OV and PO: 10 languages

(20) a. OV and GEN N: 434 languages
 b. VO and N GEN: 352 languages
 c. VO and GEN N: 113 languages
 d. OV and N GEN: 30 languages

And even if no comparable composition of the feature "order of object and verb" with "order of adjective and complement" is available from WALS, it seems not too far-fetched to hypothesize that a similar harmony obtains (at least to judge from a number of OV languages, which have PP/DP A as their canonical order, and, conversely, from a number of VO languages, which have A PP/DP as their canonical order).

Harmony across different extended projections is instead much weaker (if present at all) when heads and their modifiers are considered. Compare the order of P and its complement and the order of the N and its genitive object just reviewed (which align fairly well with the order of the verb and its complements), with the figures in WALS Online for the composition of the features "order of object and verb" and "order of adjective and noun" (see (21)) or "order of numeral and noun" (see (22)) (as well as the cases of Bargam and Tzutujil in (13) and (14)):

(21) a. OV and AN: 201 languages
b. VO and NA: 404 languages
c. OV and NA: 287 language
d. VO and AN: 100 languages

(22) a. OV and Num N: 180 languages
b. VO and N Num: 246 languages
c. OV and N Num: 230 language
d. VO and Num N: 208 languages

Note that it would not do to assume that nominal modifiers are adjuncts, rather than specifiers, and as such are outside the purview of the headedness parameters; this is because within the nominal extended projections they largely follow the relevant headedness parameter, as shown by the fact that (6a) of chapter 3 is the predominant order of more rigid head-initial languages and (6b) is the predominant order of more rigid head-final ones.

Similarly for adjectives (in predicate position), whose order with respect to their PP complements appears to show more cross-category harmony than their order with respect to modifiers. For example, the combination of OV and VO with the order of degree word and adjective shows only rather weak cross-category harmony. See (4) of chapter 3, repeated here as (23):

(23) a. OV and degree word-adjective: 114 languages
b. VO and adjective-degree word: 102 languages
c. VO and degree word-adjective: 81 languages
d. OV and adjective-degree word: 63 languages

4.3 'Nonharmonic' Derivations in the Clause

As noted, VOS and SOV, or for that matter VSO and SVO, languages do not constitute uniform types. For each, many subtypes appear to exist (possibly one for each language).[10] For example in the more rigid VOS language Malagasy DPs/PPs and AdvPs appear to precede the subject in the inverse order (V > direct object DP [DP_{DO}] > indirect object DP [DP_{IO}] > manner AdverbP > frequency AdverbP > subject DP).[11] This suggests that in Malagasy the VP moves around the complement DPs and AdverbPs, merged above it, via the *whose-pictures* pied piping mode, with the ultimate effect of reversing their order entirely (see (25) and (i) of note 12).[12] Other Austronesian VOS languages, like Toba Batak (Keenan 1978; Cole and Hermon 2008), and, marginally, Seediq (Holmer 2005: section 3.1), display an order in which PPs and AdverbPs follow the subject (VOSX). Also those VOS languages where VOS alternates with VSO differ as to whether adverbials and PPs precede the subject or follow it. All of these differences may suggest that the VP raises above different chunks of the clause (above just a low indefinite NP object, or also above a higher DP object, or even above a higher PP or adverbial, or Topic XP) pied piping them above the subject (as a function of attracting features located at different heights).[13] Also see Clemens and Polinsky (2017: section 3.2.1). Other languages that alternate VOS with VSO (like Maori and Tongan) differ from VSO-only languages (like Irish and Arabic) concerning the order of topic and focus constituents (Polinsky 1997). Needless to say, each language should be looked at individually to sort out the types of derivations that yield its canonical orders (hopefully via different combinations of the very same options allowed by UG, including attraction of different projections dominating the V(P)).

Many languages display orders that mix the two types of pied piping, or movement with pied piping (in one of the two modes) and movement without pied piping. This is typical of head-medial (SVO) languages, but also of many SOV languages. For example Hindi and other Indo-Aryan languages, as already noted, have initial complementizers (C AdvP DP/PP V Asp T), thus applying the *pictures-of-whom* pied piping mode in the most deeply embedded subprojections and the *whose-pictures* pied piping one in the highest CP subprojection. For the very rare opposite case see section 5.3.

Some SVO languages, like Italian, appear to have movement of V(P) + object over the lower adverbs without pied piping (thus not reversing their order, which then corresponds to the preverbal order of the same adverbs in OV languages). This contrasts with rigid head-initial VO languages like Malagasy, where the order of the same lower adverbs is the mirror image of that of Italian. See (24) and (25), and Rackowski (1998), Cinque (1999), Pearson (2000), and Sabel (2011) for discussion.[14]

(24) Rakoto non lava i vestiti più sempre bene (cf. Cinque 1999: section 1.1)
R Neg washes the clothes anymore always well
'Rakoto does not wash clothes anymore always well.'

(25) Tsy manasa lamba tsara foana intsony Rakoto (cf. Rackowski 1998: section 4.3)
Neg wash clothes well always anymore R.
'Rakoto does not wash clothes anymore always well.'

Pearson (2000) calls the Italian order (in (24)) *direct* and that of Malagasy (in (25)) *inverse*. The direct order is reminiscent of the N Dem Num A order of the nominal extended projection of certain languages, where the N(P) alone raises above the demonstrative successive cyclically (hence not reversing the order of the modifiers). It is also reminiscent of the order of PPs in the German Verb Second main clauses when it is the finite lexical V(P) that raises to CP without pied piping ($[_{CP}$ C PP_1 PP_2 PP_3 V$] \rightarrow [_{CP}$ V_i PP_1 PP_2 PP_3 $t_i]$ [see Schweikert 2005: chapter 6, and Hinterhölzl 2020 for recent discussion]).

4.4 A Note on Germanic Verb Clusters

German and other Germanic languages pose a particular puzzle for any approach to linearization. Quite apart from their V2 character, they have verb clusters in embedded clauses that display virtually the same pattern as Greenberg's Universal 20, as pointed out in Abels (2011, 2013, 2016a).[15] See especially Abels's (2016a) insightful discussion, showing that the Universal 20 pattern is displayed by a subset of restructuring (clause-mate) predicates (auxiliaries, modals, causative 'let') that are merged together with the main verb (or a verbal particle, if one is present), which behaves as the Head of the entire verbal cluster (in the digit representation 1-2-3-4 the highest number, 4, represents the main verb/verbal particle, corresponding to the noun in Greenberg's Universal 20). What is puzzling is that the adverbial modifiers, the DPs and PPs, are in the direct head-final order irrespective of the different orders within the verb cluster (as if the main verb, or verbal particle, the modals, and the auxiliaries moved in an independent plane, ultimately raising as one complex Head in the *pictures-of-whom* pied piping, which preserves the Merge order of their AdverbP, DP, and PP dependents).[16]

The syntax of Germanic verb clusters thus raises a challenge to the movement approach developed so far, much as it does to nonmovement approaches, as these do not contemplate separate planes of derivation. Here I sketch a possible solution that involves a minimal departure from the set of assumptions adopted here, pending a more principled analysis.

To keep things manageable I will consider the possible orders in clusters composed of three (rather than four) elements: (i) an auxiliary, (ii) a modal, and (iii) a main verb (perhaps the most researched triplet). On the basis of a vast documentation of Germanic varieties Wurmbrand (2004, 2017: section 2.2), and Barbiers (2005: 238) for Dutch varieties, show that of the six possible orders of the three elements only five are attested, which Abels (2011: section 3.1, 2016a: section 3) claims are those instantiating the Universal 20 pattern.[17] As just noted, the modal > auxiliary > main verb order (2-1-3) "is completely absent as a neutral order" (Abels 2016a: 197), just as the order A > Dem > N order

(2-1-3) is absent as a neutral order in the subset of the Universal 20 elements represented by demonstratives, adjectives, and the noun (see Cinque 2005). Compare the case of the theoretically possible Germanic clusters in (26a)—(26f) with the case of the theoretically possible Dem A N orders within the extended nominal projection in (26a′)—(26f′).

(26)							
a.	V	Mod	Aux	a′.	N	A	Num
	3	2	1		3	2	1
b.	Aux	Mod	V	b′.	Num	A	N
	1	2	3		1	2	3
c.	Aux	V	Mod	c′.	Num	N	A
	1	3	2		1	3	2
d.	Mod	V	Aux	d′.	A	N	Num
	2	3	1		2	3	1
e.	V	Aux	Mod	e′.	N	Num	A
	3	1	2		3	1	2
f.	*Mod	Aux	V	f′.	*A	Num	N
	2	1	3		2	1	3

Here, unlike the Universal 20 DemonstrativeP, (cardinal) NumeralP, and AdjectiveP, which are modifiers, the elements involved are all Heads of a subprojection of the clause, with the main verb Head of the entire extended projection and cluster. Being a Head each can move, either by itself or by pied piping some larger constituent containing it in one of the two possible modes of pied piping. Interestingly the resulting pattern turns out to be the same as that of Universal 20.[18]

The generalization hinted at (earlier in this section) that the adverbial modifiers, the DPs, and the PPs are in the direct head-final order (e.g.'he' > 'probably' > ('to us') > 'the letter' > 'carefully' > [verb cluster]) irrespective of the five different orders attested for the verbal elements in the Germanic cluster suggests that the cluster eventually moves as a single Head with the *pictures-of-whom* pied piping mode, which does not alter the direct order of the arguments and modifiers of the clause.

The problem in the present account is how to derive the different orders of the elements of the cluster while keeping the order of the dependents, or "satellites," constant.

The possibility that I tentatively explore here is a particular implementation of Abels' (2016a) idea that the derivation of the order of the verbal Heads in a cluster takes place separately, essentially subject to the same conditions on movement that derive the Universal 20 pattern (albeit, I assume, without multidimensional representations, in line with Chomsky 2019: 267–268; 2021: 20).[19]

In the spirit, if not the details, of Barbiers's (2005) derivation of verb clusters, I assume that in the workspace Aux(P), Mod(P), and the V(P) are assembled in a hierarchy that respects their relative scope (see (27)), with an agreement phrase on top of each such projection to host the movement of the Head. Each Head moves in one of the available ways (with *whose-pictures* pied piping, *pictures-of-whom* pied piping, or without pied piping) to form the five possible clusters (out of six) (see (28)) before building up the clause containing their respective dependents (see (29)).[20] If Kayne (2016) is right every overt Head may be selected by a (necessarily silent) X-bar head, which is not indicated in (27). Unlike him, but still in compliance with Antisymmetry, I also assumed that what is selected by a Head is merged in its specifier, with the Head moving across it in the *whose-pictures* pied piping mode in head-initial languages. As in section 2.1 and section 3.1n1, the (bare) phrasal nature of the Heads of (27) is suggested by the fact that they target in their movement a specifier position.[21]

(27)

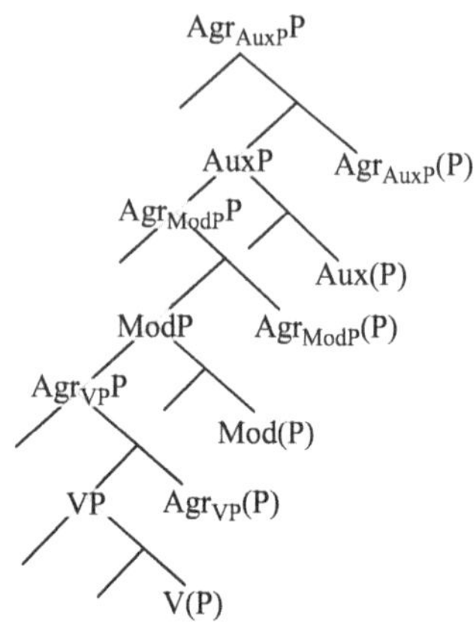

Let's consider how the five attested orders of the cluster composed of V(P) Mod(P) and Aux(P) (see (26a)–(26e)) are derived by movement (see (28)–(32)), and how the sixth order (i.e., (26f)) fails to be derived.

I take each Head to obligatorily move to the specifier of its AgrP. If each moves there with the *pictures-of-whom* pied piping (see (28)), the order under the LCA will be V(P) Mod(P) Aux(P) (3-2-1), as $Agr_{VP}P$ comes to asymmetrically c-command Mod(P), so that everything dominated by it precedes Mod(P), and $Agr_{ModP}P$ asymmetrically c-commands Aux(P), so that everything dominated by it (including V(P) > Mod(P)) precedes Aux(P).[22]

(28)

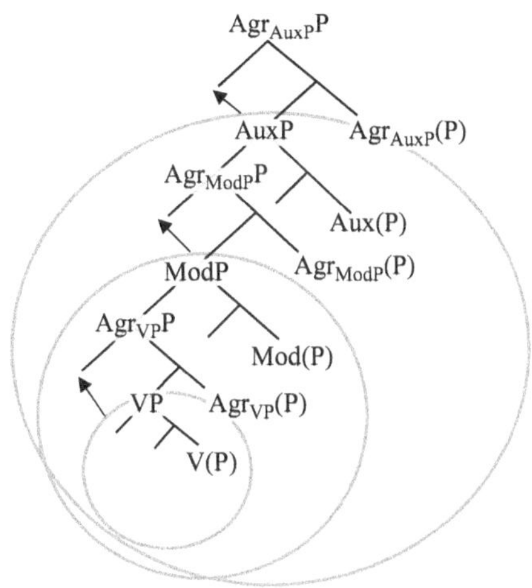

On the other hand if each Head moves with (vacuous) *whose-pictures* pied piping to the specifier of its AgrP (see (29)), the order under the LCA will be Aux(P) Mod(P) V(P) (1-2-3). This is because Mod(P) comes to asymmetrically c-command Agr$_{VP}$P and Aux(P) comes to asymmetrically c-command Agr$_{ModP}$P.

(29)

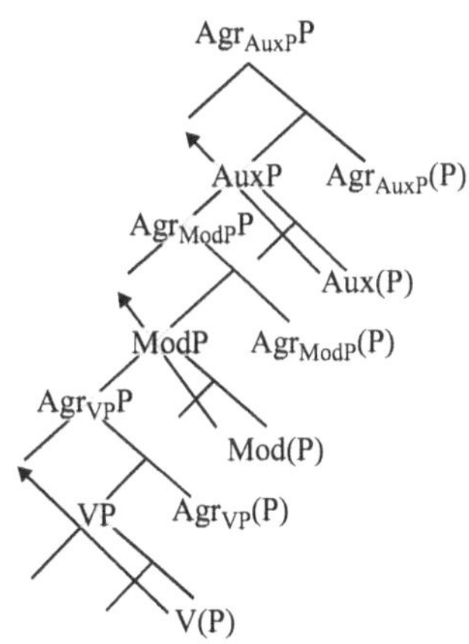

The order Aux(P) V(P) Mod(P) (1-3-2) is instead obtained if V(P) and Mod(P) move to the specifier of their AgrP via the *pictures-of-whom* pied piping while Aux(P) moves to the specifier of its AgrP via the (vacuous) *whose-pictures* pied piping. See (30):

(30)

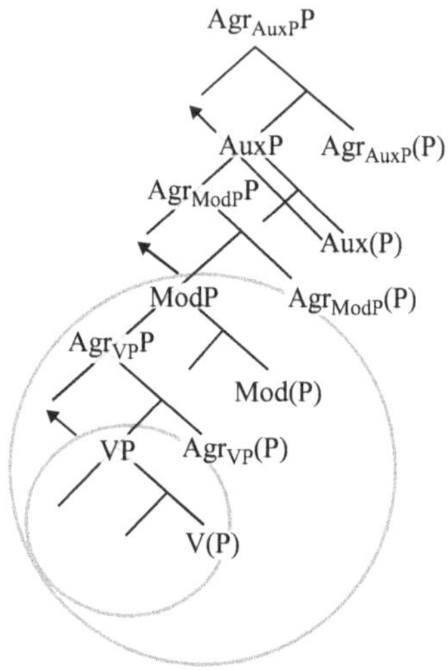

The order Mod(P) V(P) Aux(P) (2-3-1) is obtained if V(P) and Mod(P) move via the (vacuous) *whose-pictures* pied piping mode to the specifier of their respective AgrP and Aux(P) moves to the specifier of its AgrP via the *pictures-of-whom* pied piping, as shown in (31). This is because Mod(P) will asymmetrically c-command $Agr_{VP}P$, giving rise in $Agr_{ModP}P$ to the partial order Mod(P) V(P), which will precede Aux(P) as $Agr_{ModP}P$ asymmetrically c-commands Aux(P). Its relative rarity compared with the other attested orders (Svenonius 2007; Abels 2013) is tentatively attributed in section 5.3 to its involving a change in its derivation from the less marked *whose-pictures* pied piping mode to the more marked *pictures-of-whom* pied piping mode, a general determinant of the rarest word orders.

(31)

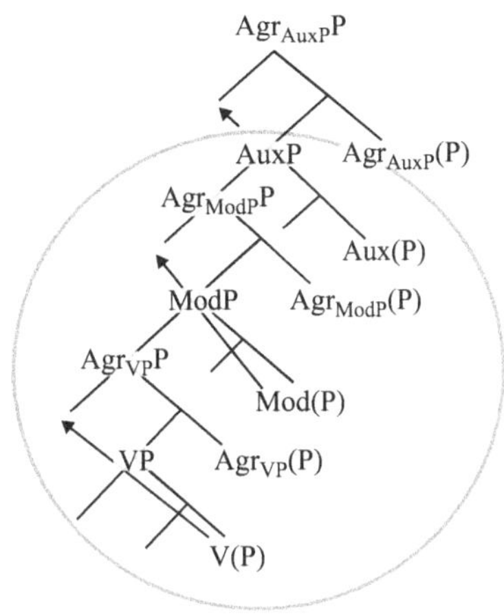

The final attested order of the cluster is V(P) Aux(P) Mod(P) (3-1-2).[23] This order is reminiscent of the order N Num A of (26e′) (and the full N Dem Num A order of Greenberg's Universal 20). Recall from section 3.4 how this order was obtained within a configuration that contains the other Heads of the nominal extended projection (PL(P), D(P), and K(P)), with the Head of the entire projection, N(P), incorporating them in its raising to the top of the extended projection (see in particular the derivation in (16) of chapter 3).

What I would then like to propose is the essentially parallel derivation in (32), in which the Head of the entire extended verbal projection, V(P), raises to the top of its extended projection (except that here V(P) does not incorporate [a silent copy of] them in its raising to the top).

(32)

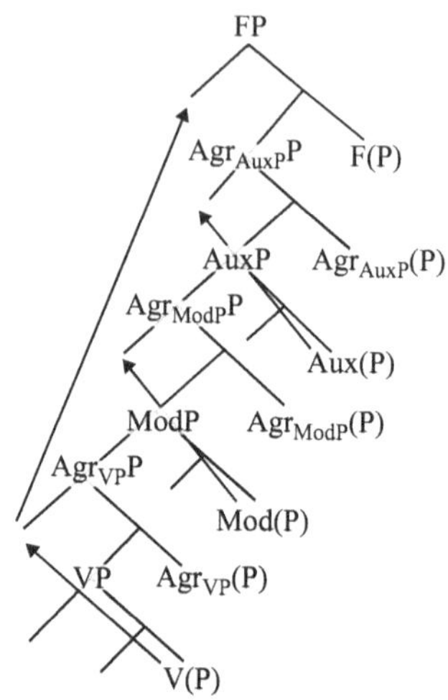

The order Mod(P) Aux(P) V(P) (2-1-3) (see (26f)) is instead underivable. If Mod(P) raised to the specifier of $Agr_{ModP}P$, coming to asymmetrically c-command $Agr_{VP}P$ and Aux(P) (thus ultimately preceding both), there would still be no way for Aux(P) to come to asymmetrically c-command V(P) so as to intervene between Mod(P) and V(P).

Extending to dependents other than DPs (e.g., PPs and AdvPs) Neeleman and Weerman's (1993: section 4) idea that the selectees of a verb cluster are derived from the selectees of its parts I will tentatively assume that given that the V(P) is the most deeply embedded category (under reconstruction), it will be the first to license its dependents, followed by the Modal(P) and the Aux(P). Raising of the verb cluster to Spec,FP via the *pictures-of-whom* pied piping, as shown in (33), will preserve the hierarchy/order of the dependents.

(33)

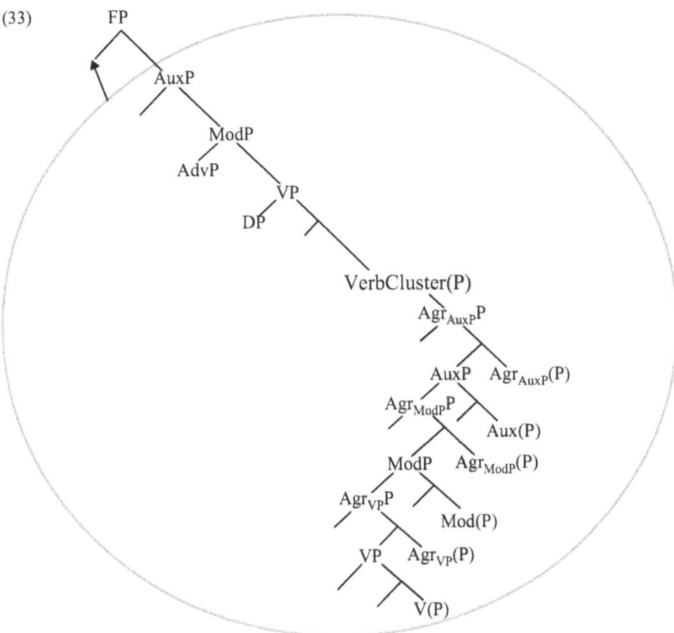

In V2 constructions only the finite verb will raise to Spec,CP in main clauses.

I believe that once verb clusters are set aside (treated separately, perhaps as in the preceding text, from run-of the-mill verbs embedding IP/CP complements) AdverbPs, PPs, DPs, and V(P)s can still be taken to be merged together in fixed positions within a single hierarchy.[24]

The evidence discussed in Bobaljik (1999), Svenonius (2002), Nilsen (2003), Zwart (2007b), and Abels (2016a: 191) that DPs, PPs, AdverbPs, and verbs belong to separate tiers, ultimately conflated like different decks of cards shuffled together, is, I think, not warranted, quite apart from its conceptual unattractiveness.

The first apparent paradox discussed by Bobaljik (1999) concerns the rigidity of adverb order (say, in Italian, *mica* 'presuppositional NEG' > *più* 'any longer') and the rigidity of the order of finite auxiliaries and participles (say, in Italian, *ha* 'has' > *telefonato* 'called'). Now, the fact that the auxiliary and the participle can both follow or precede one or both of the two adverbs, as apparent from (34), would seem to lead to a violation of the Head-Movement Constraint, because one verb would appear to be crossing over the trace of the other.[25]

(34) a. Mica più gli ha_i $telefonato_k$ (da allora)
b. Mica gli ha_i più t_i $telefonato_k$ (da allora)
c. Mica gli ha_i $telefonato_k$ più t_i t_k (da allora)
d. Non gli ha_i mica t_i $telefonato_k$ più t_i t_k (da allora)
e. Non gli ha_i $telefonato_k$ mica t_i t_k più t_i t_k (da allora)
'(S)he has no longer called him (since then).'

The second paradox discussed by Bobaljik concerns the rigid order of adverbs and the equally rigid order of DPs, once we abstract away from topicalization and focalization: namely, $DP_{Subject} > DP_{BareIndirectObject} > DP_{directObject}$. Given that the DPs can be found interspersed among the adverbs while retaining their relative order, it would seem difficult to accommodate adverbs and DPs in unique merge positions within a single hierarchy. Bobaljik adds that this could even be taken to suggest that it is the DPs that occupy fixed positions while adverbs achieve their relative freedom via movement, rather than vice versa, concluding that "it is clearly impossible to maintain that the internal ordering of adverbs, that of heads and arguments, and the ordering of the groups with respect to each other, all follow directly from a single phrase-structure representation. Any such account must be supplemented minimally by displacements that may violate strict locality constraints (i.e., crossing paths must be tolerated), in tandem with an independent stipulation to preserve the original word order" (6). But this is precisely what Relativized Minimality enforces if one adopts Chomsky's insight that links of a chain do not count as interveners (see Krapova and Cinque 2008: section VII; Chomsky 2013: 44fn33; Rizzi 2017: 255–256, 2018: 354;

Shlonsky and Rizzi 2018: 50).[26] Under this assumption (34e) involves the derivation in (35), which incurs in no locality violation, as each movement crosses only one link of a chain, not a full chain, ensuring at the same time preservation of the original order:[27]

(35) Non gli ha$_i$ telefonato$_k$ mica t_i t_k più t_i t_k (da allora)

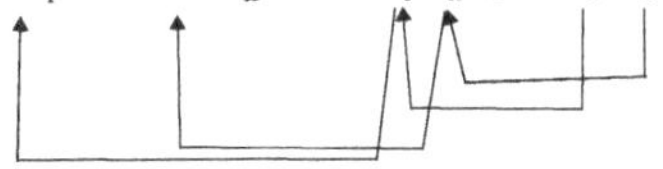

If we take into consideration the proneness to displacement of V(P)s and DPs and, after Pollock (1989), the essential immobility of AdvPs (except for limited and recognizable cases of movement to CP or NegP positions [Rizzi 2004; Garzonio and Poletto 2012; Cuonzo 2019]), the fact that the same order of DPs ($DP_{Subject}$ > $DP_{BareIndirectObject}$ > $DP_{directObject}$) is found before or after a certain adverb is simply due to the possibility of moving the DPs in compliance with the just mentioned version of Relativized Minimality.

There is thus no reason to abandon the idea that the maximal extended projection of the V(P), the clause, is one *single* hierarchy of DPs, PPs, AdverbPs, and verbal functional heads merged in fixed positions; in fact, there is every reason to adopt it and to reject "a multi-dimensional theory of phrase-structure in which the principles ordering adverbs occupy a different plane than those ordering verbal elements and arguments" (Bobaljik 1999: 6).[28] After their merger within the maximal extended projection of the V(P), DPs, PPs, and verbal heads may raise to different positions interspersed among the AdverbPs (with possible semantic effects).[29]

And the same holds of the clause's major phrases.

4.5 Determinants of the Pied Piping and No Pied Piping Modes[30]

In the derivational approach I've sketched movement of the Heads with consistent *whose-pictures* pied piping gives rise to the (ideal) head-initial type and movement of the Heads with consistent *pictures-of-whom* pied piping to the (ideal) head-final one, even if the most consistent ("rigid") head-initial and head-final languages are, as noted, a tiny minority (and possibly never totally consistent). The majority of languages appear to mix the three modes of movement (no pied piping, *whose-pictures* pied piping, and *pictures-of-whom* pied piping), both across different phrasal extended projections and (less frequently) even within a single one, as noted in sections 4.2 and 4.3 (also see section 5.3). What determines the type of pied piping with which each Head moves seems quite generally to be the modifiers of the Head's projection, with different degrees of generality (suggesting the appropriateness of a micro-parametric approach to word order [Cinque 2017]). Fewer times it is the Head itself of the projection that determines the type of pied piping that it undergoes (except perhaps for verbs). Pending a more principled account, here I utilize for clarity the terms [*whose-pictures* pied piping] feature, [*pictures-of-whom* pied piping] feature, and [-pied piping] feature.

4.5.1 Cases of Movement Determined by the Modifier

These cases will be arranged along a scale of successively larger generalizations.[31]

4.5.1.1 Single lexical item[32]

In English the adjectival degree modifier *enough*, which has to follow the adjectives that it modifies (e.g., *good enough*) (Maling 1983: section 1.4; Webelhuth 1992: 23–24f; Kayne 2005b: section 3.6; and references cited in these works),[33] may be taken to be endowed with a [*whose-pictures* pied-piping] feature that forces the A(P), the Head of the projection, to move above it.[34] The other elements belonging to the same class of adjectival modifiers (e.g., *very, quite, so, too*), which have to precede the adjectives that they modify (e.g., *very good, quite good, so good*), may instead be taken to be endowed with a [*pictures-of-whom* pied-piping] feature that forces the A(P) to drag the modifier along in its raising without inverting their relative order.

The same appears to be true of certain direct modification adjectives in Italian.[35] *Vecchio* 'old' in the sense of 'long-standing' is only prenominal (hence, in the present context, endowed with a [*pictures-of-whom* pied-piping] feature that does not cause the N(P) to raise above it; see (36a)). *Medio* 'average' is instead only postnominal (hence endowed with a [*whose-pictures* pied-piping] feature that causes the N(P) to raise above it; see (36b):

(36) a. *un vecchio amico* (**un amico vecchio*)
'a friend of long-standing'
b. *l'italiano medio* (**il medio italiano*)
'the average Italian'

4.5.1.2 Single adjectival subclass

Cypriot Maronite Arabic color adjectives of Arabic origin necessarily follow the NP while those of Greek origin may either follow or precede the N(P). See (37), from Panayidou (2013: 179–180):

(37) a. (tin-i) varka χabra (with *whose-pictures* pied-piping) (**tin-i χabra varka*)
(give-me) paper.DEF.F red.DEF
'(Give me) the red book/paper.'
b. (tin-i) li-prasini varka (with *pictures-of-whom* pied-piping) (but also *varka li-prasini*)
(give-me) the-green.f paper.DEF.F
'(Give me) the green book/paper'

Istro-Romanian (Zegrean 2012: 93) presents a minimal pair of the same general type. The provenance adjective *taljanski* (of Slavic origin) has to precede the noun (thus imposing a [*pictures-of-whom* pied-piping] movement of the N(P)), while the adjective *taljan* (of Romance origin) has to follow the noun (thus imposing a [*whose-pictures* pied-piping] movement of the N(P)).[36]

(38) a. ur taljanski fečor (*ur fečor taljanski)
     b. ur fečor taljan (*ur taljan fečor)
     'an Italian boy'

Another case is provided by Italian provenance adjectives, which are only postnominal (see (39a)), in contrast with size adjectives, which can either be pre- or postnominal. See (39b)):[37]

(39) a. l'invasione romana della Tracia (*la romana invasione della Tracia)
     'the Roman invasion of Thrace'
     b. l'enorme cupola di S.Pietro/la cupola enorme di S.Pietro
     'the enormous cupola of S.P.'s'

4.5.1.3 Single category within an extended projection[38]

Farsi adjectives are all postnominal (except those in the superlative form [cf. Kayne 2008b, note 15]). This can be achieved, in the spirit of Webelhuth (1992: section 1.6), if all lexical items that contain the [+Adj] categorial feature are marked as imposing a [*whose-pictures* pied piping] movement of the N(P) (the prenominal position of superlative adjectives being instead a function of the movement of the adjective to a high position within the extended nominal phrase [cf. Cinque 2010b: 124n13]).[39]

All modifiers within a particular extended projection[40]

In the Niger-Congo (Defoid) Bantu language Yorùbá, adjectives, numerals, and demonstratives are all post-nominal in "the mirror image of English modifier sequences" (Ajíbóyè 2005: 18). See (40):

(40) a. àwọn ajá dúdú dúdú méje wòn-yí (263)
     PL dog black black(=black.PL) seven Dem-PL
     'these seven black dogs'

b. ẹṣin funfun n'lá dáradára méjọ (cf. 18)
horse white big nice eight
'eight nice big white horses'

In the present context, this means that all lexical items of any of the nominal modifier classes force a [*whose-pictures* pied piping] movement of the N(P). Bulgarian or German adjectives, numerals, and demonstratives, which are all necessarily prenominal, instead force the N(P) to move with the *pictures-of-whom* pied piping mode.

4.5.1.4 All categories within all extended projections[41]

All modifiers (whatever their categorial label) of Japanese would instead be marked as imposing a [*pictures-of-whom* pied piping] movement on their Head (thus yielding virtual "cross-category" harmony, with the exception of numerals that can also be postnominal, possibly with a discourse-related difference with respect to prenominal ones [see Kim 1995]).

So far, we have observed cases in which the [*pictures-of-whom* pied piping] or the [*whose-pictures* pied piping] feature appears to be imposed by the modifier.

As mentioned earlier, there are reasons to endow also the modified category with the same type of features, in those cases where it is the modified category that apparently determines the kind of movement. This implies that the features of the modifier and those of the modified category must match for the derivation not to crash.[42]

4.5.2 Cases of Pied Piping Mode Determined by the Head (the Modified Category)

In Swedish, adjectives taking a DP complement fall into three classes (Platzack 2014: section 4): (i) those that can only follow their DP complement, such as *bekant* 'known to', *kär* 'dear', *värdig* 'worthy of', *likgiltig* 'indifferent to', and so on (see (41)); (ii) those that can only precede their DP complement, such as *kvitt* 'be rid of' *lik* 'like' *värd* 'worth', and so on (see (42)); and (iii) those that can either precede or follow their DP complement, such as *trogen* 'true to', *underlägsen* 'inferior to', *överlägsen* 'superior to', and so on (see (43)):

(41) a. Hon var honom likgiltig.
She was him indifferent
b. Hon var likgiltig *(för) honom.
She was indifferent to him
'She was indifferent to him'

(42) a. Han är kvitt sina plågor.
He is rid-of his.REFL pains
b. *Han är sina plågor kvitt.
He is his.REFL pains rid-of
'He is rid of his pains'

(43) a. Hunden är sin husse trogen
The dog is his master faithful
b. Hunden är trogen sin husse
The dog is faithful his master
'The dog is faithful to his master'

Assuming, as we have done throughout, that nothing is merged below/to the right of a lexical category (with the consequence that any complement will be merged in the Spec of a projection above the lexical X(P)),[43] in (41), the adjective must be endowed with a [*pictures-of-whom* pied piping] feature; in (42) with a [-pied piping] feature;[44] and in (43) with either a [*pictures-of-whom* pied piping] or a [-pied piping] feature.

In certain languages Nouns also appear to determine the mode of pied piping. Especially in SVO languages, where variation is substantive, single common nouns appear to determine their order with respect to their modifying proper noun. So, for example, in English the common noun *cape* typically precedes the proper name of the cape (e.g., *Cape Cod, Cape Canaveral, Cape Horn*), while the common noun *road* typically follows the proper name of the road (e.g., *Abingdon road, Portobello road, Kensington road*).[45] Thus *cape* must be marked with a [*whose-pictures* pied-piping] feature, and the common noun *road* with a [*pictures-of-whom* pied piping] feature. Some (like *river*) appear to avail themselves of both possibilities: *the Mississippi river/the river Mississippi.*[46]

In Yugambeh-Bundjalung (Bandjalang) (Pama-Nyungan, Australia) adjectives "follow nouns denoting humans, but precede those denoting trees and neuters" (N_{+hum} AP and AP N_{-hum} [Sharpe 2005: 98]).[47] This would seem to suggest that also in this case it is a feature of the N(P) that determines the mode of pied piping (whether it is of the *whose-pictures* or of the *pictures-of-whom* type, yielding N_{+hum} AP or AP N_{-hum}). As I've noted previously, the AP must have a feature matching the feature of the N(P).

Similarly, in Tuyuca (Tucanoan, South America) "numerals precede inanimate nouns and follow animate nouns" (Barnes 2000: 446; my translation), suggesting once again that it is the noun that dictates the type of pied piping involved:

(44) a. sika-'ga 'dii-ga
one-CLF ball-CLF
'one ball'

b. ĩbĩ-'ã iti'a-rã
man-PL three-PL
'three men'

A comparable situation is found with adpositions, which in certain languages also appear to determine, depending on the particular adposition, the mode of movement.[48] See, for example, the case of Michif (Mixed [French-Cree] language [Bakker 1997: 112]), where *d* 'of' is a preposition (i.e., endowed with a [*whose-pictures* pied piping] feature, or a [-pied piping] feature (see (45a)) and *pour* a postposition (i.e., endowed with a [*pictures-of-whom* pied piping] feature (see (45b)):

(45) a. d sa:b
of sand
b. bi:bi: pour
baby for
'for the baby'

In other languages the DP complement can, indifferently, precede or follow certain adpositions, which we consequently take to be endowed with either a [*whose-pictures*] or a [*pictures-of-whom*] pied piping feature. See, for example, the case of German, (46) (Haider 2015: section 2):[49]

(46) a. nach meiner Meinung
b. meiner Meinung nach
'in my opinion'

Also modals, auxiliaries, and complementizers in the extended projection of the VP appear to be able to determine the type of pied piping involved.

In Vietnamese the deontic modal precedes the lexical verb while the ability modal follows:

(47) a. Cô ấy sẽ không phải gặp em. (Duffield 1999: 97)
PRN DEM FUT NEG must meet PRN
'She will not have to meet with you.'
b. Cô ấy sẽ không gặp em đuọc. (ibid.)
PRN DEM FUT NEG meet PRN can
'She will not be able to meet with me.'

In Persian Farsi, "the perfect auxiliary *budan* ('to be') must appear after the main verb. On the other hand, the future tense auxiliary, used in formal contexts, is expressed by adding the auxiliary verb *xastan* ('to want'), inflected for person and number immediately before the verb stem" (Goldberg 2002: section 6.1). See (48a) and (48b):[50]

(48) a. (man) rafte budan
(I) go.PART be-PAST.PERF.1.sg
'I had gone'
b. (man) xâham raft
(I) FUT-1.sg go
'I will go.'

As for complementizers, within the same language, Bangla, one complementizer (of nominal origin), *je* (which we take to be endowed with a [*whose-pictures* pied piping] feature), precedes its complement clause (cf. (49a)), and another (of verbal origin), *bole* (which we take to be endowed with a [*pictures-of-whom* pied piping] feature), follows it (cf. (49b)):

(49) a. Chele-Ta Sune-che [je [or baba aS-be]] (Bayer 1996: 255)
boy-CLF hear-PST3 COMP his father come-will
'The boy heard that his father will come'
b. Chele-Ta [[or baba aS-be] bole] Sune-che (ibid.)
boy-CLF his father come-will COMP hear-PST3
'The boy heard that his father will come'

All of this seems to suggest that modifiers as well as nouns, adjectives, prepositions, auxiliaries, modals, and complementizers (hence, by inheritance, their maximal projections) must be endowed with either a [*pictures-of-whom* pied piping] feature or a [*whose-pictures* pied piping] feature (or a [-pied piping] feature), because it is them in some cases that determine the type of movement. This suggests generalizing the endowment of such features to either the modifier or the modified category, whose movement features then will have to match.

Differently from such categories, it would seem that single verbs cannot be endowed with a special pied piping feature, for, as Webelhuth (1992: 49) observes, all of them take their complements on the same side. In other words no verb can apparently differ from any other verb in the direction in which it takes a complement.[51] This, however, remains to be ascertained at a cross-linguistic level because all other categories, as seen, seem to be able to be endowed lexically with one such pied piping feature.

5 The Generalizations That Characterize Linear Order and What They Follow From

5.1 The Absence of Certain Orders and the Left-Right Asymmetry

As noted at the outset, the widespread idea "that the physics of speech [leaves] just two options: the head either precedes or follows its complements" (Eguren et al. 2016: 12) seems far from being sufficient. Among others it falls short of accounting for the first two generalizations cited in (5) of chapter 1: the systematic absence of certain orders (among the mathematically possible ones), and the fact that there are more ordering possibilities to the right of a lexical Head than to its left (the pervasive left-right asymmetry discussed in Cinque [2009] and briefly taken up in chapter 1, section 1).[1] The first generalization was argued to follow from the articulation of the subprojections of an extended projection and the restriction that only the Head can move within each subprojection, thus excluding orders obtainable if the Head moved out of its subprojection (into another subprojection except for the Head of the extended projections (N(P), V(P), and so on)). The second generalization can instead be seen to follow from the way the Heads, N(P), V(P), and so on raise, either with the *pictures-of-whom* pied piping, which does not alter the hierarchical Merge order of modifiers, or with the *whose-picture* type of pied piping, which reverses it, or without pied piping, which relocates the N(P), V(P), and so on above (hence before) the modifiers without altering their order. This is at the basis of the fact that, when all modifiers are on the same side, only one order is possible to the left of a Head (the one derived by a single type of movement: the *pictures-of-whom* pied piping), while to its right two are possible, as a consequence of the fact that two types of movement are available (movement of the Head with a *whose-pictures* pied piping, or movement of the Head without pied piping).

5.2 The Final-over-Final Condition (FOFC)

The idea that linearization reduces to whether a Head precedes or follows its complements is also unable to account for the empirical asymmetry in the domain of word order uncovered in Holmberg (2000), Biberauer et al. (2009, 2014), and Sheehan et al.'s (2017) FOFC,[2] whether this is an absolute universal or a robust cross-linguistic tendency that accounts for the extreme rarity of certain configurations (as suggested in Philip 2010, 2012; Abels 2013: section 4.2; and Clem 2018, 2020).

While Sheehan et al. (2017) manage to explain away a number of apparent exceptions to the FOFC by restricting α and β to heads of the same extended projection and α to inflecting auxiliaries rather than to invariant particles (see in particular Holmberg 2017 and Biberauer 2017, respectively), there may still be some residual exceptions, which nonetheless do not detract from its importance as an extremely strong cross-linguistic tendency. I will argue that its relevance extends (possibly in weaker form) across the main extended projection and its subprojections (just as Roberts [2017] generalizes it in weaker form across different extended projections). Bona fide exceptions to FOFC may be the final complementizers of the SVO Tibeto-Burman language Hkongso ("The sole instance in my database of a VO language with final complementizer is Hkongso, a Tibeto-Burman language of Burma" [Dryer 2012: 76fn8]), of the SVO Khoisan language East !Xóõ (Güldemann [2004: 7] reports a sentence from Traill [1994: 17] that exemplifies the order V O C, confirming in personal communication (January 16, 2010) that "the language indeed is an exception to the supposed universal SVO → initial complementizer" see Cinque [2013a: 245n31]), or the final subordinators of the VOS Austronesian language Seediq (Holmer 1996: 60, 2005: section 2). Also exceptional may be the [[V DP/PP] inflecting auxiliary] order of the Sese and Northern varieties of Gumuz (Nilo-Saharan). See (1):

(1) a. kà gìž ànjinééla ná ma-dok'ʷ mec'a ḿʔiirà (Sese Gumuz [Uzar 1989: 379])
next year time.this in INF-build house1:FUT:AUX
'Next year at this time I will build a house'
b. nágó-m↓-dók' máts'á d-ée-ot-ára (Northern Gumuz [Ahland 2012: 379])
PROG-NMLZ-build house AFF-FUT-EXT-1SG.INTR
'I will be building a house.'

Equally exceptional may be the Tupí-Guaraní language Ka'apor ("Although the SOV is the more general word order in narratives and spontaneous speech, we also find other linear order possibilities, such as VSO-Aux and SVO-Aux" [Duarte 2019: 812]). See, for example, (2):

(2) ihẽ a-py'a-katu ne r-ɛhɛ a-ʃɔ
I 1-think-INTNS you about 1-be
'I am thinking about you a lot.'

Kokama-Kokamilla, another Tupí-Guaraní language, also has SVOAux orders (Vallejos 2010: section 7.3.3.1) with auxiliaries inflected for tense (though not for person agreement).

Within the present approach to linear order, based on the LCA applying (in narrow syntax or PF) to hierarchical structures built by movement of a Head (by itself or through pied piping of one of the two available types), there may be a derivational account of the FOFC. It was noted in section 3.5 that pied piping of the *pictures-of-whom* type is more marked than pied piping of the *whose-pictures* type. This is shown, for example, by the following contrasts in English *wh*-interrogative contexts:[3]

(3) a. Whose pictures do you keep in your wallet?
 b. ?Pictures of whom do you keep in your wallet?

(4) a. I wonder whose pictures they published yesterday.
 b. *I wonder pictures of whom they published yesterday.

Given the more marked character of the *pictures-of-whom* pied piping and the less marked one of the *whose-pictures* pied piping, it is not unreasonable to think that changing mode from the more marked type to the less marked one bottom up within the same extended projection may be less severely sanctioned than changing mode from the less marked to the more marked one.[4] In the illustrative derivations in (14) of chapter 3 and (9) of chapter 4 for the more rigid head-initial languages and in (15) of chapter 3 and (10) of chapter 4 for the more rigid head-final ones, the Heads of each extended projections (N(P) PL(P) D(P) K(P) and V(P) Asp(P) T(P) C(P)) move in unison, with the same pied piping mode at every level, from the most deeply embedded domain to the highest one (with the *whose-pictures* type for head-initial languages and the *pictures-of-whom* type for the head-final ones, yielding in the case of the clause the fragments $[_{TP}$ Aux $[_{VP}$ V O]] and $[_{TP}$ $[_{VP}$ O V] Aux], respectively). The question is what happens when a change of pied piping obtains. $[_{TP}$ Aux $[_{VP}$ O V]] involves pied piping of *pictures-of-whom* type in the most deeply embedded domain, VP, and (vacuous) pied piping of the *whose-pictures* type at the next higher level, and is attested, even if less widely than the harmonic derivations $[_{TP}$ Aux $[_{VP}$ V O]] and $[_{TP}$ $[_{VP}$ O V] Aux]. The FOFC-violating structure,[5] involves instead the less marked *whose-pictures* pied piping in the most deeply embedded domain, VP, followed by the more marked *pictures-of-whom* pied piping type at the next higher level. Though apparently attested in at least some cases, this is an extremely rare case, where the rarity can be imputed to the change from a less marked to a more marked option.[6]

From the present perspective, one might think that languages involving the more marked *pictures-of-whom* pied piping mode (SOV/OSV/OVS) should be fewer than those involving the putatively less marked *whose-pictures* pied piping mode (VOS/VSO/SVO). Yet the two groups are more or less equally represented (see the counts, and references, reported in Cinque [2013b: 70 and reproduced here in n7]).[7]

5.3 The Rarity of Certain Orders

The rarity of 2-3-1 orders in verb clusters (Svenonius 2007: section 4; Abels 2013) also appears to be amenable to a FOFC-violating derivation. Recall the fact that to obtain that specific order the V(P) and Mod(P) move via the (vacuous) *whose-pictures* pied piping mode, and Aux(P) moves via the *pictures-of-whom* pied piping mode (as illustrated in (31) of chapter 4). This implies a change from the less marked *whose-pictures* pied piping occurring in the more deeply embedded layers to the more marked *pictures-of-whom* pied piping in the top one. None of the other orders have one such transition from a less marked to a more marked derivational option.

I am also tempted to interpret the contrast between (5a) and (5b), noted in Hinterhölzl (2006b: section 6.3), and the generalization that he draws ("The formation of right-branching verb clusters is also subject to the following condition. Once a right-branching structure is introduced at one level . . . the structure has to be right-branching also at the next level" [175]), as a consequence of the sanctioned status of a change from the *whose-pictures* pied piping mode, which creates right-branching structures, to the *pictures-of-whom* pied piping, which gives rise to left-branching ones.

(5) a. weil er den Text [wird [müssen [lesen können]]]
since he the text will must read can
'since he will have to be able to read the text'

b. ??/*weil er den Text [[müssen [lesen können]] wird]
since he the text must read can will

If we turn to the Heads of the subprojections of the nominal extended projection seen in chapter 2 (e.g., A of AP, 'color' of NP_{color}, classifier of ClassifierP, base of CardinalP), we find a similar situation. One order out of the possible ones, that involving a change from the less marked (*whose-pictures*) to the more marked (*pictures-of-whom*) pied-piping mode, is the rarest order.

Recall from section 2.5 Dryer's (2008: 62) observation that the order adjective-degree word N is uncommon (unattested in Tibeto-Burman), while the other three orders, degree word-adjective N, N degree word-adjective, and N adjective-degree word, are quite common (an observation corroborated by the WALS correlations with OV/VO reported in (4) of chapter 3 if OV commonly correlates with N final and VO with N initial). Example (4d) is the least represented, the reason for that being that the order $[_{NP}[_{AP}$ adjective degree word] N] involves movement of the adjective across its degree word specifier via pied piping of the *whose-pictures* type in the most deeply embedded domain AP, while N in the immediately higher domain NP moves with the *pictures-of-whom* pied piping mode, without crossing over the AP (thus changing from a less marked option to a more marked one).

A similar case is represented by the extremely rare order [[base multiplier] N], which, as observed in note 14 of chapter 2, Greenberg (1989: 106) and Hurford (2003: 596) reported as being absent from their samples (as opposed to [[multiplier base] N], [N [base multiplier]], and [N [multiplier base]]). It is however found at least in Rongga. Once again the extreme rarity of this order may be related to the fact that the Head of the complex numeral, the base, moves with (vacuous) *whose-pictures* pied piping across the multiplier while the noun moves in the higher domain with the *pictures-of-whom* pied piping, involving a change of pied piping from a less marked option to a more marked option (which seems to invariably yield the worst result).[8]

Another case is that of [[CLF Num] N] (cf. (3d) of chapter 2), which Greenberg (1972: 28–30, 1975: 29) says is less common (together with [N [CLF Num]]) than [[Num CLF] N] and [N [Num CLF]], with movement of the Head of the embedded domain, CLF, via the *whose-pictures* pied piping and movement of the Head of a higher domain, the N, via the *pictures-of-whom* pied piping.

In the case of the order between an ordinal morpheme and the cardinal (to yield an ordinal numeral) and N ((5) of chapter 2), Tatsumi (2020) lists several languages for the harmonic orders [[Card Ord] N] and [N [Ord Card]], with N and Ord as the Heads of their respective projections, somewhat fewer languages for the nonharmonic order [N [Card Ord]], and just one language for the order [[Ord Card] N] (Àhàn, though few others can be added—see chapter 2, n18). It thus appears that the rarest orders ([[A_i degree word t_i] N], [[$base_i$ multiplier t_i] N], [[CLF_i Num t_i] N], [[Ord_i Card t_i] N]) are the ones reminiscent of a FOFC-violating pattern.

Concerning the order between the measure word, the adjective, and the N ((7) of chapter 2), and that between the adjective of color, the noun 'color', and the lexical N ((9) of chapter 2), I am not aware of any systematic counts, but there are some suggestive cues that the FOFC-reminiscent orders [[A_i measure phrase t_i] N] (see (7d)), and [['color'$_i$ A_{color} t_i] N] (see (9d)) are quite marked (they are found in Chinese and Russian, but only under some kind of emphasis, or in nonordinary styles [see notes 28 and 34 of chapter 2]).

The increasing rarity of the nonharmonic orders of Demonstrative Numeral Adjective and Noun (see (6c)—(6p) of chapter 3) needs to be looked into to determine whether it is due to more and more marked derivational choices.

5.4 Meaningless Movement

To capture the generalizations in (5) of chapter 1, meaningless movement in narrow syntax appears to be crucially involved "to yield the proper hierarchies" (Chomsky 2004: 110) that may provide the correct linear orders under the LCA. As already noted, meaningless movement is often rejected because movement in narrow syntax, it is assumed, should have both PF and LF consequences; whence the idea that linear order is not in the purview of narrow syntax but is a matter of some externalization mechanism (to be specified). This question however remains open because there appear to be numerous cases where meaningless movement is actually needed in the derivation of the neutral order of sentences and phrases. To the various cases discussed by Kayne (2018: sections 3 and 10, 2020a: sections 2 and 11), one can add the case of Punjabi (Indo-Aryan, SOV), where "adverbials are generally placed at the preverbal position following a direct object" (Bhatia 1993: 93), as shown in (6):

(6) ó pañjaabii sadaa can,gii boldii ai.
she Punjabi always good.F.SG speak.PRES.F.SG is
'She always speaks Punjabi well.'

Here, movement of the object is involved to obtain the canonical order from a position close to the verb to a position above certain adverbs, without any incidence on the meaning of the structure.

Another clear case is the obligatory movement of the DP complement of an adjective across a degree modifier of the adjective. See the Swedish case discussed in notes 43 and 44 of chapter 4, and the analogous case found in German:[9]

(7) a. Ein mir$_i$ völlig t$_i$ ungeläufiges Wort (cf. Riemsdijk 1983: 229)
A to.me completely unfamiliar word
b. *Ein völlig mir ungeläufiges Wort
A completely to.me unfamiliar word
'A completely unfamiliar word to me'

Once again, this type of movement to build the canonical order has no semantic import.

If Internal Merge is the unmarked form of Merge,[10] it comes in a sense for free (subject to whatever governs the forms Internal Merge can take, with pied piping of the two types or no pied piping), and might well be available for functions other than the discourse-/information-related ones. Suppose that the head of each (sub)projection has to internally merge to the top of its (sub)projection (perhaps something that might be seen as even having some "categorial/semantic" function). This would open up the possibility for Internal Merge "to yield the proper hierarchies" that permit the LCA to apply (whether in narrow syntax or at S-M).

In this perspective the bewildering variation in word order among languages might not be an imperfection, It could be just a side-effect of the central displacement property of UG.

5.5 Language Change and Language Acquisition

Concerning syntactic change, if it is indeed the case that the documented changes from one order to another have in essence occurred unidirectionally, from SOV to SVO to VSO/VOS (the rare cases of change from SVO to SOV being possibly due to language contact) (Gell-Mann and Ruhlen 2011 and references cited there), then the more marked character of the *pictures-of-whom* pied piping mode, involved in the derivation of SOV languages, might provide some rationale for it.[11] Change from a more marked derivational option (SOV) to a less marked one (SVO, involving the *whose-pictures* pied piping mode at least partially) is favored over the reverse change. Biberauer et al. (2017: section 2.6) and Roberts (2019: section 2.3.5) consider word order change from an FOFC perspective, saying that the rare changes from head-initial to head-final "must go 'bottom up,' starting at VP, then affecting TP, and then affecting CP" (21). If the change proceeded "top down," reversing first C from initial to final, there would be an FOFC violation (and indeed they cite one case of putative change from head-initial to head-final that complies with the expectation [22]). The opposite holds with changes from head-final to head-initial, which starts with CP, then TP, and finally VP (they cite the history of English and the development of the Romance languages from Latin as bearing out these expectations). From the present perspective there are identical expectations. If every derivation starts with the Head of the extended projection (VP), only changes from the more marked *pictures-of-whom* to the less marked *whose-pictures* pied piping will be favored. Hence in changes from a head-final to a head-initial word order the change cannot start from the VP (→ VO), because one would then go, in the next layer up, from a less marked option (*whose-picture* pied piping) to a more marked one (*pictures-of-whom* pied piping). So they should affect first the highest layer and proceed downward. In the rarer changes from a head-initial to a head-final word order the change must instead affect first the VP (→ OV), because then moving up the change would be from a more marked option (*pictures-of-whom* pied piping) to a less marked one (*whose-pictures* pied piping).

As to language acquisition, if the Heads of the extended projections and subprojections (and their hierarchy and selectional properties) are part of the lexicon of UG, if movement of the Heads, by themselves or via the two pied piping modes, is part of UG (together with the features triggering one or the other type of movement), and if Kayne's LCA is also part of UG, then the task of the children is substantially facilitated. What they have to figure out is just the specific movements and the features determining them that lead under the LCA to the linear order of the language they are exposed to. So, for example, the Malagasy order of the adverbs in (25) of chapter 4, where the rightmost corresponds to the highest, the penultimate to the next highest down, and so on, indicates under the LCA that the VP has raised consistently above them with the *whose-pictures* pied piping mode. The Italian order in (24) of chapter 4 indicates instead that the VP has raised above them without pied piping (thus not reversing their order under the LCA). Similarly the order of VSO Peñoles Mixtec in (i) of note 14 of chapter 4 indicates that the VP has raised above the manner adverb with (vacuous) *whose-pictures* pied piping and that the higher PAST Head has also raised via the same pied piping mode above the epistemic adverb and the pronominal subject. The corresponding English sentence *He probably plowed well* indicates instead that the VP has raised without pied piping just above the low manner adverb, remaining lower than the higher epistemic adverb and the subject. In Cinque (2017: section 4.4) I submitted that acquisition may be guided by a default assumption that once the lexical category is attracted in one of the three modes (*whose-pictures* pied piping, *pictures-of-whom* pied piping or without pied piping), the default expectation is that it (or any other category of the same verbal or nominal type) will continue to move in the same mode, up to disconfirmation.[12] This may even lead (in few cases, as seen) to almost perfect cross-category harmony if the default expectation of a uniform attribution of the pied piping feature is not contradicted by the primary linguistic data.

6 Conclusion

In the preceding chapters, after presenting the possible word orders of a number of nominal subprojections, and one crucial restriction on the Head of a projection in building a restrictive theory of linearization for the nominal and the verbal extended projections, I have discussed four generalizations that any theory of linearization should try to account for that the physics of speech does not help us understand: (i) the systematic absence of certain orders, (ii) the left-right asymmetry found in every domain, (iii) the word order asymmetry falling under the FOFC, and (iv) the increasing rarity of certain attested orders. While it is not be excluded that a linearization algorithm distinct from the LCA may perhaps be conceived that can account for these generalizations, I suggested that the LCA may provide a unified answer to all of them once we admit the existence of meaningless movement and the restriction that just the Head of each (sub)projection can move (with pied piping of the two available types, *whose-pictures* and *pictures-of-whom*, or without pied piping).

Needless to say, the above-mentioned considerations have only scratched the surface of the complex system underlying word order variation, trying to impose additional restrictions on how hierarchical structures are built before they map to linear order. For this program to make progress, more needs to be learned about the fine structure of the subprojections of the clause and of its phrases and about the word orders characterizing each language, which ideally involve just different options among the movement possibilities made available by UG.

Notes

Chapter 1

1. Also see Chomsky (2020: 16): "linear order and other aspects of externalization don't strictly speaking belong to the I-language."

2. As Hall [Partee] (1964: 407) put it: "Šaumjan's theory seems to rest in part on the assumption that word order is independent of syntactic structure in all languages." Later proponents of an unordered underlying structure include Staal (1967: chapter 1), Sanders (1970, 1975), Bartsch and Vennemann (1972: 38–39), and Hudson (1972). For the abbreviations in (1) and (2) see the list of Abbreviations and Symbols in the front matter.

3. This is the Final-over-Final Condition of Sheehan et al. (2017) and related work by the same authors. See section 5.2 for further discussion.

4. That movement is the basis of word order variation is argued for persuasively, to my mind, in Kayne (1994, 2018).

5. There are also more complex cases where the target moves within a larger constituent containing both higher and lower nontarget material, as in *Aylan, [pictures of [**whose** body]] [__] have stirred great global sympathy*, . . . (with analogues in the movements possible within nominal and verbal projections of N(P) and V(P)).

6. Larson's (1988: 346fn11) generation of a direct object in the specifier of a VP shell in the presence of other postverbal complements and/or adjuncts ([$_{\text{IP}}$ *I* [$_{\text{VP}}$ *wrote*$_{\text{i}}$ [$_{\text{VP}}$ *a letter* t$_{\text{i}}$ [$_{\text{VP}}$ [$_{\text{PP}}$ *to Mary* t$_{\text{i}}$ [$_{\text{PP}}$ *in the morning*]]]]]]) is a precursor of this idea, even though it is problematic in other respects. For one thing it violates Baker's (1988) Uniformity of

Theta Role Assignment, because a direct object would be merged as a complement when no Prepositional Phrase (PP) is present and as a specifier when one or more PPs are present. Another problem, pointed out by Cecilia Poletto (pers. comm., 04.08.2021), is that a temporal adjunct and the indirect object would be composed with the V before its closest argument, the direct object. Another problem still is that languages with the order V PP_{manner} PP_{place} PP_{time} would be taken to differ from languages with the order V PP_{time} PP_{place} PP_{manner} (Boisson 1981, 1993; Lu n.d.; Hinterhölzl 2001, 2002, 2009: 243–44) in hierarchical structure and scope relations, which is an unwelcome result as it misses the possibility of assigning one and the same structure and scope to the PPs merged preverbally and ending up in different orders postverbally owing to the different way the V(P) raises around them (with the *whose-pictures* pied piping and without pied piping, respectively).

Chapter 2

1. Dryer (2018) claims that some of the orders that Cinque's (2005) account of Greenberg's Universal 20 ruled out are actually attested in at least few languages. In Cinque (in preparation) I argue, on the basis of the same sources utilized by Dryer and of additional ones, that none of the putative counterexamples is real. In every one of those languages the unexpected order is not the only possible order of demonstrative, numeral, adjective, and noun. Other orders coexist in those languages that conform one or more of the 14 orders admitted by Cinque's (2005) account. Hence, none of them is a convincing counterexample, as we know that some alternative orders are derived by special focus-driven movements, which are distinct from the movements responsible for the canonical orders of the language. In some languages (e.g., Lebanese Arabic, studied in detail in Ouwayda and Shlonsky [2015, 2017], Shupamem, studied in Nchare [2012] and Korean, studied in An [2014, section 7]) numerous alternative orders are reported to be possible, some of which at any rate belong to the 14 orders admitted in Cinque (2005) and here. In a larger sample of over 2,000 languages I have found no evidence that if one of the 10 orders excluded in Cinque (2005) is available, it is the **only** order possible. This suggests to me that only 14 orders are genuinely possible. (I refer to Cinque [in preparation] for more detailed discussion.)

2. Possessive adjectives and relative clauses deserve a separate treatment because they can also move independently; possessives to determiner

position in some languages (his/Bill's many interesting books), or to informationally different positions in others (Italian: *quei<suoi> molti <suoi> altri <suoi> importanti <(?)suoi> contributi <suoi> al dibattito <suoi>* lit. 'those <his> many <his> other <his> important <his> contributions <his> to the debate <his>' as well as Hungarian - Szabolsci 1994 and Dékány 2021: chapter 4). Also see Dryer (2019) on the unexpected word order behavior of possessives across languages. On relative clauses see Cinque (2020).

3. For example, singular, dual, plural, . . . number, as argued for on semantic grounds in Bartsch and Vennemann (1972: 134) and Heycock and Zamparelli (2005: section 4.1) and as is apparent from the word order of some Oceanic, Mayan, Mon-Khmer, Tai-Kadai, and Papuan languages (where it is presumably expressed as a modifier), is merged between cardinal numerals (+classifiers) and adjectives. As for determiners, at least one type is merged between demonstratives and cardinal numerals; and Case is the outermost functional Head (the interface between the nominal domain and the clause): [**Case** [DemP [**DET** [NumP [**PL** [AP [N]]]]]]]. To avoid confusion with the Amount/NumberP dominating (ClassifierP and) CardinalP I indicate singular, plural, dual, . . . number as PL(P).

4. On the segregation of the nominal and verbal Heads and the nominal and verbal modifiers on the opposite side of N and V see sections 3.3 and 4.1, respectively.

5. I ignore here "complements" of the noun, which I take, following Kayne (2002, 2004b), to be later attracted to the front of the nominal projection, eventually appearing in head-initial languages to the right of the noun due to the further fronting of the remnant. See Cinque (2005: fn34), and note 51 of chapter 3.

6. This order is found in many languages, including Chinese (Sinitic [Zhang 2013]), White Tai (Tai-Kadai [Conklin 1981: 47]), Hmong (Hmong-Mien [Niederer 2011: 1295]), Uzbek (Turkic [Beckwith 1998: section 4.2]).

7. This order is found, among others, in the Papuan languages Abun (Berry and Berry 1999: chapter 5), Adang (Haan 2001: chapter 9), and Tobelo (Holton 2003: section 2.1.3); in the Austronesian languages Nga'da (Conklin 1981: 272), Tetun Dili (Williams-van Klinken et al. 2002: 24), Helong (Balle and Cameron 2014: 45–47), and Uab Meto (Metboki and Bellamy 2014: section 1); in the Sino-Tibetan languages Daai Chin (So-Hartmann 2009: section 5.4.3.4) and Jingpo (Cheung

2003: section 4.3.2); and in the Chibchan languages Cuna (Quesada 1999: 232) and Teribe (Quesada 2000: 127).

8. This order is found, among others, in the Sino-Tibetan languages Burmese and Lahu (Goral 1978: 30), in the Mon-Khmer language Stiêng (Bon 2014: section 2.5), and in the Tai-Kadai language Tai Lue (Hanna 1995: section 2).

9. This order is found, among others, in the Totonacan languages Huehuetla Tepehua (Lhiimaqalhqama') (Kung 2007a: section 7.3, 2007b: section 2) and Upper Necaxa Totonac (Beck 2004: section 2.2; García-Vega 2018: section 1), in the Sino-Tibetan language (Eastern) Tamang (Lee 2011: section 5.2), and in the Austronesian languages Rongga (Arka 2008: section 2) and Luangiua (Salmond 1974: 142) (alongside the order in (3)b). Also see Kayne (2020b: 340fn10).

10. See, for example, (i):

(i) ndòó ú-ꜜkwá ɛ́-pɛ́á (Denya; Kießling 2018: 47)
10.CLF:bunch Ass.10- 8-plantain 10-two
'two bunches of plantains'

11. This is the order found in English (*five hundred books*), among other languages.

12. This order is found in the Papuan language Adang (Haan 2001: section 10.3), in the Austronesian languages Uab Meto (Metboki and Bellamy 2014: section 4.1) and Helong (Balle and Cameron 2014: 45–46), in the Sino-Tibetan language Mising (Doley and Post 2012: section 2), and in the Grassfields Bantu language Yemba, exemplified in section 3.1 (Harro and Haynes 1991: 31).

13. Stiêng has the order N multiplier base (Miller 1976: 32), and so does Jingpo (cf. Cheung 2003: section 3.4 for the order N Num and Numeral Systems of the World's Languages [https://lingweb.eva.mpg.de/channumerals/Jingpho.htm] for the order multiplier base: mǎ^{31} li^{33} ʃi^{33} Lit. four ten = 'forty'). Tetun Dili (Central Malayo-Polynesian) has the order N multiplier base for tens and N base multiplier for hundreds and thousands. See (i):

(i) rihun rua atus tolu rua-nulu (Williams-van Klinken et al. 2002: 22)
thousand two hundred three two-tens (= 2,320)

14. While Greenberg (1989: 106) and Hurford (2003: 596) state that no example of [base multiplier] N is found in their samples, this order is attested in the Austronesian language Rongga with multipliers bigger

than 1. See Arka (2008: section 2 and 13–14). As I suggest in section 5.3, the rarity of such an order may bear some relation to Sheehan et al.'s (2017) Final-over-Final Condition (FOFC), or what FOFC follows from.

15. For the Omotic language Maale see (i) and for Kashmiri (and other languages) see Tatsumi (2020: section 2.1).

(i) táɓɓó lamʔ-ása kéll-éll-ó (Amha 2001: 136)
ten two-ORD day-F-ABS
'the twelfth day'

16. See (ia) for the Austronesian language Uab Meto, and (ib) for the Tai-Kadai language Tai Lue (Lɨɨ):

(i) a. uab no n-tenu (Metboki and Bellamy 2014: 65)
talk ORD 3SG-three
'the third talk, third subject matter'
b. maa[1] too[1] thoon[3] soong[1] (Conklin 1981: 107)
dog CLF ORD two
'the second dog'

The same order is found with numbers higher than 6 in the Niger-Congo Atlantic language Mankanya (Gaved 2020: 95).

17. For the Oceanic language Kove see Sato (2013: section 6.1.6.2) and for Koromfe (Niger-Congo, Gur) and other languages displaying this order see Tatsumi (2020).

18. Tatsumi (2020: 2) says that while he found several languages displaying the orders (5a–c), he found only one language displaying the order (5d), Àhàn (Niger-Congo, Atlantic). Also cited as displaying this order per Tatsumi (2021: 2,101.104) are Mandarin Chinese, Maltese and the Oceanic language Belep.

Though rarer than the previous orders, possibly for the same reason mentioned in note 14 for the order base multiplier N, two additional languages displaying the order Ord Card N appear to be Kokota (Oceanic) ((ia)) and White Tai ((ib))

(i) a. fa palu mane (Palmer 2009: 87)
ORD two man
'the second person'
b. ʔan1 chɨɨ saam1 haang6 (Conklin 1981: 47)
CLF Ord three floor
'third floor'

19. Tatsumi (2020: 2) says, "Crucially, the last two combinations in Table 1 [=(5e) and (5f) here] are not attested in my sample."

20. Sohn (1999: 265).

21. For the Bantu language Ichindali see (ia), and for the Sino-Tibetan language Daai Chin (ib):

(i) a. umwana gwangu umwisa ngani (Kibona 2019: 907)
child my beautiful very
'the very beautiful child of mine'
b. aang-ki boo:k sa: (So-Hartmann 2009: 113).
shirt white INTNS
'a very white shirt'

22. For Italian see *un uomo molto alto* lit. 'a man very tall'. For Apatani see Abraham (1985: 124–125).

23. For the Turkic language Sakha, see (i), and for the Portuguese-based creole Korlai see *The Atlas of Pidgin and Creole Language Structures Online,* https://apics-online.info/valuesets/40-8, example 40-14. The Mongolic language Monguor, whose DP-internal order is Dem Num A N, also appears to display the order [[A INTNS] N] (see Chuluu 1994: 29, example 259).

(i) bu kïrakïj baɣajï deriebine-tten (Stapert 2013: 244)
this tiny INTNS village-ABL
'from this very tiny village.'

24. Yareba (Papuan) and Shupamem (Bantoid) appear to display the unexpected orders A N degree adverb ((6)e) and degree adverb N A ((6)f), respectively, alongside the neutral orders N A degree adverb ((6)b) for Yareba (see Weimer and Weimer 1975: section 4.12), and degree adverb A N ((6)a) for Shupamem (see Nchare 2012: 187). This recalls the case of Bulgarian *Mnogo beše visok* lit. 'Very he was tall', which when compared to the neutral *Beše* [*mnogo visok*] 'He was very tall') is felt as involving focalization of *mnogo* (Iliyana Krapova, pers. comm., January 17, 2021). Perhaps the Yareba and the Shupamem orders (6e) and (6f) involve a similar focus fronting of the degree adverb. More complex is the case of Basque, which has the order degree adverb N A.art ((6f)) in definite DPs and N degree adverb A art ((6c)) in indefinite ones. The former may involve a remnant movement derivation (I thank Richard Kayne for raising the case of Basque and for relevant discussion).

25. See *a six inch(*es) long pencil* (Matushansky 2008a: 33n15), and the Bulgarian example in (ib) of note 26.

26. See (1a), and (ia′), which is possible alongside (ib):

(i) a. un uomo alto due metri (Italian)
lit. a man tall two meters
a′. edin čovek visok dva metra (Bulgarian [Iliyana Krapova, pers. comm., January 17, 2021)
lit. a man tall two meters
b. edin dva metra visok čovek (Bulgarian [Iliyana Krapova, pers. comm., January 17, 2021])
lit. a two meters tall man
'a two meter tall man'

27. See the order in (i) (Ivana Jovović, pers. comm., February 20, 2020). Her Bosnian also allows the alternatives (iia) and (iib) (namely, the orders in (7a) and (7b), respectively). Boban Arsenijević (pers. comm., April 29, 2021) judges the order in (iib) as the most neutral in Serbian:

(i) čovjek dva metra visok
lit. man two meters tall

(ii) a. dva metra visok čovjek
lit. two meters tall man
b. čovjek visok dva metra
lit. man tall two meters
'a two meter tall man'

28. Alongside (ib), which conforms to the order (7a), Chinese also allows the order (ia), which however implies some contrast either on 'tall' or on 'two meters' (Shengyun Gu and Yangyu Sun, pers. comm., February 16, 2020):

(i) a. gao liang mi de ren
lit. tall two meter DE person
b. liang mi gao de ren
lit. two meter tall DE person
'a two meter tall man'

29. See Schwarzschild (2005) for further discussion. If the cardinal modifying the measure Head is itself complex (comprising a multiplier and a base), and if the color or size AP modifies a common noun 'color'/'size', as argued in section 2.7, the overall structure would be:

(i) a. [$_{NP}$ [$_{NPsize}$ [$_{APsize}$ [$_{DegreeP}$ [$_{MeasureP}$ [$_{CardinalP}$ multiplier base] measure] degree] AP] NP] N(P)]

b. ein hundert Meter zu hohes SIZE Gebäude
one hundred meter too tall SIZE building

Also see note 26 of chapter 3.

30. Perhaps this is true even in languages that apparently (Wierzbicka 1999: 274) have no word for 'color'. Andrew Radford observes that while the noun *color* may be redundant in English with adjectives of color such as *red*, it is not redundant, hence more natural, with modifiers that are not intrinsically color modifiers, such as *steel* (*a steel color pen*), though Ian Roberts would only accept *a steel-coloured pen.*

31. See the Mandarin example in (ia) (Zhang 2015: 388), the Nanning Cantonese example (ib) (de Sousa 2011: 32), and the Bulgarian example in (ic) (Iliyana Krapova, pers. comm., January 17, 2021).

(i) a. na si ge hong yanse de panzi
that four CL red color DE plate
'those/the four red plates'

b. wɔŋ^{21} ʃek^{5} tʃi^{55} pɐt^{5}
yellow color CLF pen
'the yellow pen'

c. červen cvyat kosa
red color hair
'red hair'

32. For Niuean (Oceanic) see (i):

(i) Ne fai fle lanu moana a ia (Massam 2001: 159)
PST have house color blue ABS he
'He had a blue house.'

For Lao (Tai-Kadai) see Enfield (2004: section 4.8) and for Vietnamese (Austroasiatic, Viet-Muong) see Nguyen (2004: 51fn33) and Clark (1989: 187). This order is also possible in Bulgarian (alongside the orders in (9a) and (9c) [Iliyana Krapova, pers. comm., January 17, 2021]), in Pnar (Austroasiatic, Khasic) (Sutradhar 2006: section 3), as well as in Hmong (Miao-Yao) and Khmer (Austroasiatic, Mon-Khmer) (see the examples in Clark [1989: 187]).

33. For the Mayan language Mocho' see (ia). For Bulgarian see (ib):

(i) a. we mis saq chi:nh (Palosaari 2011: 156)
DEF cat white color
'the white cat'

b. kosa červen cvyat
hair red color
'red hair'

34. See (i), which is acceptable, but somewhat emphatic, for Shengyun Gu (Yangyu Sun would instead use a relative clause: *yi liang yanse shi hongse de che*). As Audrey Li (pers. comm., July 16, 2020) points out, even (i) may actually involve a relative clause, where *yanse* is the subject and *hong* the predicate, as also shown by modification by *hen*, which is obligatory for her, as in predicate contexts:

(i) yi liang yanse (hen) hong de che
one CLF color red DE car
'one/a red car'

Yuri Lander (pers. comm., Augut 3, 2020) finds the order [['color'-GEN A_{color}-GEN] N] acceptable in Russian, in poetic style.

35. "There are many indications that in the tripartite construction consisting of quantifier (Q), classifier (Cl), and head noun (N), Q is in direct construction with Cl and this complex construction, which will be called the classifier phrase, is in turn in construction with N" (Greenberg 1975: 29). For the plausibility of assuming that all languages are "numeral classifier languages" (pace Ionin and Matushansky 2018: section 3.5.1), see Krifka (1995: section 3), Muromatsu (1998: section 3.3.3), Kayne (2003b), Wągiel and Caha (2020), and Cinque (2006a)· based in part on the impossibility for certain nouns with measure interpretation to be modified by an adjective, as is the case with Chinese sortal classifiers (cf. Cheng and Sybesma 1998: section 2.2, 1999: section 2.2.1). See, for example, the Italian cases in (i):

(i) a. E' tornato tre anni (*difficili) fa. 'He came back three (hard) years ago.'
b. L'ho rivisto due giorni (*brutti) dopo. 'I saw him again two (ugly) days later.'
c. L'ho incontrata solo tre volte (*bellissime). 'I met her only three (beautiful) times.' (cf. Moltmann 2021: section 3.2)

The English translations sound only marginal (or even possible, to some speakers), just as counterparts of (i) with pre- rather than postnominal adjectives sound better, but still odd, in Italian too, for reasons that remain to be understood.

36. On the distinction between individual and kind classifiers in Chinese, and its underlying partitive structure see Liao and Wang (2011). Also see Huang and Ochi (2014); and, for Japanese, Tatsumi (2017). Classifiers in Kana have been claimed to form a constituent with the noun rather than with the numeral (Ikoro 1994: section 3), but this is dubious. See Isaac (2016: section 3.1) for evidence that in the closely related language Gokana the classifier clearly forms a constituent with the numeral. Also see Aikhenvald (2000: 111fn7).

37. For critical discussion, also with respect to proposals assuming the existence of both constituencies, like those of Huang and Ochi (2011), Zhang (2011, 2013) and Li (2014), see Her and Tsai (2020). The existence of a second type of 'sortal' classifier forming a constituent with the noun rather than with the numeral, and overtly co-occurring in certain languages with the one forming a constituent with the numeral (Cinque 2022b), raises a potential problem for Greenberg's generalization seen in (3) above; and may require banning a landing site (for N) between the numeral and the classifier, and one (for [CLF [N]]) above Num in the structure [Num [CLF [N]]].

Chapter 3

1. Recall that with "Head" (capital H) I refer to the (minimal) phrasal constituent that heads a certain (sub)projection, indicated as X(P). See the text preceding (2) of chapter 2.

2. Each pair in (3) illustrates the case of the CLF following the (cardinal) numeral or the case of the CLF preceding it. Hall (2019: 29fn28) documents 10 of the 28 orders of (3).

3. For Upper Necaxa Totonac (Totonacan) see Beck (2004: section 2.2) and for (Eastern) Tamang (Sino-Tibetan) see (i):

(i)	cu	gor	som	lha:nan	grhen	wala	dim-gade	(Lee 2011: section 5.2)
	this	CLF	three	very	big	red	house-PL	

'these three very big red houses'

4. See Caron (1987: 155), where also the following example is given as an illustration:

(i)	n^{55}əy-t^{15}əy	py^{33}ee	t^{51}aw	c^{55}uu	c^{5}iə^{ʔ}
	these	four	CLF	dog	black

'these four black dogs'

5. For the order Dem Num N A see Ruhlen (2008: 1252) and for the order Num-CLF see Benton (1968: section 1).

6. On these Oceanic languages, which also display other orders, see Bril (2002: sections 7 and 9.1.3.2, 2014: section 8.2.2). Dem CLF Num N A is also an alternative order of Upper Necaxa Totonac (David Beck, pers. comm., March 12, 2021).

7. In Lahu (Sino-Tibetan) classifiers follow the Numeral. If the order Dem N Num A given in Croft and Deligianni (2001: 7) for Lahu (alongside Dem N A Num) is a possible order in addition to the one given in Caron (1987: 155) (N A Dem Num CLF), then Lahu shows the overall order in (3c). This is also a possible order of Shiwilu (Jebero—Kawapanan) alongside Dem Num N A. See (i), from Valenzuela (2016: 362).

(i) asu' ker' katu'-dan a'llupi-dan-t-a'su'
this manioc two-CLF.MANIOC large-CFL.MANIOC-V
'these two large maniocs'

8. Wamsley (2019: 13) gives the following order for the Hakha Chin noun phrase: [Dem [head N] classifier numeral adjective case Dem], where the rightmost demonstrative is plausibly a demonstrative reinforcer; a conjecture supported by the glosses in many of the examples in Danaher (2019).

9. For Stiêng see Bon (2014: part III, section 2.5). This order is also an alternative order of the Sinitic language Bai (whose canonical order is A N Dem Num) if one considers the following two examples, from Fitzgerald (1941) and Xu and Zhao (1984), reported in Dryer (2008: 25):

(i) a. sur a kuai ga (Fitzgerald 1941: 233)
mountain one CLF high
'a high mountain'
b. ke^{42} lɯ^{55} ŋɤ^{33} pe^{31} (Xu and Zhao 1984: 24)
bowl this five CLF
'these five bowls'

10. Lawton (1980: section 2.1, 1993: section 5.2.1) attributes to Kiriwina (Kilivila) the unmarked order N Dem Num A, saying that "when a noun is introduced as a theme in conversation, the order of NP constituents is as stated above ((head noun) (deictic) (number) (adjective)). The order is significant only for the basic NP; otherwise the order of NP constituents is free, being subject only to the constituent which is semantically prominent being placed first" (Lawton 1993: 150). The numeral classifier is

prefixed to the numeral (Lawton 1980: section 2.3.2). While Senft (1986: 105) gives an example with the order Num N Dem A (cf. Dryer 2018: 821), he also gives an example with the order Dem Num A N (69). Following the judgment of one of the editors of Lawton (1993) (Malcolm Ross on page v of the preface) I take Lawton's description to be the more accurate one.

11. For Yunnan Bai see Wiersma (2003: section 5.1); for Puxi Qiang see Huang (2004: 216), where the following illustrative example is given:

(i) tshumpa phu the χsi-la (220)
blue clothing that three-CLF
'those three pieces of blue clothing'

12. For Kayan Lahta, see Ywar (2013: section 4.1), who gives the illustrative example in (i), and for Yao`an Lolo, see Merrifield (2010: section 4.1).

(i) ɲa˧ ʃaʔ˥ pi˥ do˩ shu˩ ba˩ (Ywar 2013: 62)
1s chicken small that six clf
'those six small chickens of mine'

13. On the order N A Dem Num in Awara see Quigley (2002: section 3.7). For the position of classifiers she says: "Demonstratives are phonologically bound to the left of the classifier, and quantifiers are phonologically bound to the right of the classifier"(17). On the order N A Dem CLF-Num in West Makian, see Voorhoeve (1982: sections 2.2.10 and 2.3.2.1) and Asplund (2015: section 5.4.2). Jingp(h)o may be another case. Kurabe (2012: section 4.2) gives the following as the overall order of its nominal phrase REL-DEM-GEN-NOUN-ADJ-DEM-PL-[CLF-NUM]-NOMINAL PARTICLE, saying that demonstratives can simultaneously precede and follow the head noun.

14. For Mising see Doley and Post (2012: section 2.1), and for Nyishi, see Abraham (2005: sections 2.5.1 and 4.3). Also see Hall (2019: 29fn28).

15. This is also a possible order of Dulong (LaPolla 2017: 136).

16. Tongan shows the order N Dem A Num with deictic demonstratives and N A Num Dem with anaphoric demonstratives) (Macdonald 2014: chapter 1). The numeral classifier *toko* obligatorily precedes numerals (Macdonald 2014: section 4.3.4).

17. For the order N Dem A Num see Sapir (1976: 145), and for the order CLF Num see Sapir (1965: section 9.113).

18. On Coast Tsimshian (Tsimshianic) see Hall (2019: 29fn28); on Tojolabal (Mayan) see Curiel Ramírez Del Prado (2017: section 5.4).

19. For Kavalan (Austronesian) see Lee (2016: section 2.4.1) and for Q'anjob'al (Mayan) see Mateo Toledo (2017: section 5), who gives the example in (i):

(i)	heb'	naq	ka-wan	yalixh	winaq	tu	la
	PL	CLF	two-CLF:human	small	man	Dem	EVID:mirative

'those two small men'

20. For Chrau Thomas (1971: 127) gives the order Num CLF N Modifier, and Thomas (1976: 135) gives the order N A Dem. For Vietnamese (and Nung) see Hall (2019: 29fn28).

21. This is also an alternative order of Rongga:

(i) esa zhua mbo ito ndau (Arka 2008: 2)
CLF two house small that
'those two small houses'

22. For Kele see Ross (2011: section 2.6) and example (i). For Lele see Boettger (2015: section 4.7.4, 244).

(i) pihin ha-mow il tóti (Ross 2011: 132)
woman one-CLF old this
'this old woman'

23. This is the order given by Quesada (2012: 126) for Buglere. See the example in (i):

(i)	niumbada	bido-bu	jlene	je	
	vestido	CLFropa-dos	azul	Dem	
	dress	CLF- two	azure	that	['those two azure dresses']

This is also a possible order in Teribe, alternative to N A CLF Num Dem (Quesada 2000: 127).

24. For the orders A N Num Dem and CLF-Num of Galo, see Post (2007: sections 6.1.2.1 and 8.2.1). This is also one of the alternative orders of Mising. See Doley and Post (2012: section 2.1), who give the example in (i):

(i)	bɨɨ-kə	bottə-nə	okum-ikii	dor-kon	də-m
	3.SG-GEN	big-NZR:SUB	house-dog	CLF:ANIM-one	Dem

'that one big house-dog of his'

25. For Abun (West Papuan) see Berry and Berry (1999: section 5.2); for Sudest (Oceanic) see Anderson and Ross (2011: section 2.6). Also see the case of the alternative order of Tongan (note 16).

26. I will not try to document these orders, nor the 64 orders computed by multiplying 2 six times (given that each of the six Heads of the subprojections of (i) of note 29 of chapter 2, repeated here, can either precede or follow its modifier, depending on the language—(ib) and (ic) represent the order in German and English, in which all the Heads follow their modifiers).

(i) a. $[_{\text{NP}}\ [_{\text{NPsize}}\ [_{\text{APsize}}\ [_{\text{DegreeP}}\ [_{\text{MeasureP}}\ [_{\text{CardinalP}}$ multiplier base] measure] degree] AP] NP] N(P)]
b. ein hundert Meter zu hohes SIZE Gebäude
c. one hundred meter too tall SIZE building

Capitals in (ib) and (ic) indicate the nonpronunciation of the common noun corresponding to the adjective of size, which can be pronounced in languages other than German or English; e.g., Chinese (Shengyun Gu, pers. comm., February 27, 2020).

Note that this drastically reduces the orders that would be expected from the combinations of 7 elements (factorial 7 = 5,040) if the right constituencies and the restriction (1) on movement were not considered.

27. *Un(o)* 'one' is very plausibly silent in Italian also in *questo libro* 'this book' (cf. the analogous case of Mandarin Chinese [Her et al. 2015: section 3; Zhang 2019: section 2.2]), and *il primo libro* 'the first book' (and in their English equivalents), if we compare them with *questi due/tre/* etc. *libri* 'these two/three/etc. books', *i primi due/tre/*etc. *libri* 'the first two/three/etc. books'.

28. https://apics-online.info/surveys/63.

29. On the multiple possibilities found in German see Ionin and Matushansky (2018: section 5.3.4).

30. It remains to be seen whether the construct state Semitic numerals and the Slavic numerals governing genitive Case on the noun can be given a unified analysis with the clear cases of numerals as phrases in specifier position. The possibility of the presence of a silent head NUMBER/AMOUNT argued for in Kayne (2003b, 2007), Zweig (2006), and Tatsumi (2018) for the latter case may provide one such unification. For further general discussion see Shlonsky (2004), Danon (2012), Caha (2015), and references cited in these works. On the system of Irish (Celtic, more generally, and other VSO languages) discontinuous complex numerals, see Duffield (1995a: Chapter 5, Appendix, and 1995b).

31. See, for example, the different distribution of English *all* and *every* with respect to the definite article or a possessive adjective: *<*the> all <the> whims of Mrs. Thatcher* vs. *<the> every <*the> whim of Mrs. Thatcher*; *<*her> all <her> whims* vs. *her every <*her> whim* (examples originally due to Andrew Radford). In other languages 'all' and 'every' are expressed by the same morpheme, once above, and once below, determiners/demonstratives. See, for example, the case of Japanese in (i), provided by Hiromi Sato (pers. comm., February 27, 2000 date):

(i) <subete no> korera no <subete no> (?san-satu no) subarasii hon
<all GEN> these GEN <all GEN> (?three-CLF GEN) nice book
'<all> these <every> (three) nice books'

32. Also see West Polesian (Slavic [Roncero Toledo 2019: 174]) for the co-occurrence of indefinite quantifiers and cardinals, which arguably occupy a distinct position from multal/paucal quantifiers, as shown in Italian by their different positioning with respect to *altro* 'other' in its "additional token" interpretation: *Dammi <altri> due <*altri> minuti* 'Give me two more minutes' vs. *Mi diede <molti/pochi> altri <*molti/pochi> esempi* 'He/she gave me many/few other examples'. Cf. Cinque (2015).

33. As distinct from numeral classifiers (and akin to Gender, on which see Picallo's [2008] "Class functional projection"). Nominal classifiers are closer to the noun than the numeral classifiers and can co-occur with the numeral classifiers, as in Akatek Maya (ia) and Thai (ib).

(i) a. kaa-(e)b' xoyan 'ixim paat (Zavala 2000: 125)
two-CLF $\text{CLF}_{\text{numeral}}$ (for round objects) $\text{CLF}_{\text{nominal}}$ tortilla
'two tortillas'
b. mǎ tua lé g sǒ·ŋ tua nán (Haas 1942: section 3)
dog $\text{CLF}_{\text{nominal}}$ little two $\text{CLF}_{\text{numeral}}$ that
'those two little dogs'

34. (Integrated) nonrestrictive, kind-defining, finite restrictive, finite maximalizing, infinitival, and participial relative clauses appear to be merged at different heights of the nominal extended projection, and they too appear, like PPs, to be able to move independently of the NP (like the "extraposed" relative clauses of English and the derived predemonstrative relative clauses of Chinese and several head-final languages). See Cinque (2005: 327fn34) on PPs and Cinque (2020: sections 3.5 and 3.6) on relative clauses.

35. While the primary interest here lies in a system that may characterize the possible vs. impossible orders, the tendencies of the Greenbergian

tradition should also find some place in it. For some tentative general discussion, in addition to the present section, see section 4.2.

36. It remains to be seen whether the same proportions are found in attributive contexts (namely in [[degree word adjective] N], which is more typical of [more harmonic with] rigid head-final languages, and with [N [adjective degree word]], which is more typical of [more harmonic with] rigid head-initial ones, as well as with the less harmonic [N [$_{AP}$ degree word adjective]] and [[$_{AP}$ adjective degree word] N]; cf. (6) of chapter 2). Predicative and attributive usages do not always go together. In K'iche' (Mayan), for example, a degree word precedes the adjective in predicative position but follows, in suffix form, in attributive position (see Can Pixabaj 2017: section 3.5.1). "Harmonic" here means involving movements of the same kind at every level of embedding (see sections 3.2, 4.2, and 4.3).

37. See Greenberg (1972: 10–11) for the idea that a classifier is akin to a base with value '1' (plus some further classificatory value). For further discussion see (Allassonnière-)Tang and Her (2020) and references cited there.

38. For Uab Meto see (i):

(i) tui nono m-bo nua' (Yakob Metboki, pers. comm., February 20, 2020)
[pen [CLF [ten two]]]
'twenty pens'

39. (Allassonnière-)Tang and Her (2020: 511, section 6) report that their "detailed statistical analysis of a geographically and phylogenetically weighted set of 400 languages shows that the harmonization of word order between numeral bases, classifiers, and nouns is statistically highly significant, as only 8.25% (33/400) of the languages display violations."

40. I thank Yoshio Endo for this and the other Japanese data reported here. Korean behaves like Japanese (see (ia)) and so do Hungarian and Basque (Hackstein 2010: 39–40). German instead displays a head-initial ordering, like that of Italian (see (ib)).

(i) a. Kim Jhølsu kyosu nim (Hwang 1991: 121)
family name given name professor Mr.
b. Herr Professor Wolfgang Ulrich Dressler
Mr. professor given name(s) family name

For a more fine-grained classification of what I referred to here as "occupational title" see Acquaviva (2019: sections 2.2 and 3). Also see

Acquaviva's article and Matushansky (2008b) for discussion concerning complex names and for the different structures taken to underlie them. We differ here from Ionin and Matushansky (2018: 121–122), who do not believe that the different orders of English and Japanese names "have any deep linguistic significance" (122).

41. In its honorific usage the final *-e* of *signore* is obligatorily truncated (v. **Il signore professore/capitano Folena*), unless it enters a coordination of honorific titles (*il signore e la signora Folena* 'Mr. and Mrs. Folena').

42. For the silent (functional) N(P) ('person') heading the projection in (8a) and (8b) see immediately after these examples. For the Head status of the given name and the modifier/genitive-like relation of the family name to the given name see Krifka (1985: 85–86), and the interesting confirmation coming from Persian (Matushansky 2008b: 606fn22). The occupational title (which alternates [in Italian] with kinship terms: *la signora zia* lit.'the Mrs. aunt') can itself be a subprojection when it contains an occupational subspecification, like Italian [*un* [*medico*$_i$ [*virologo* t$_i$]]], or the English of at least some speakers [*a* [*virologist doctor*]$_i$ t$_i$], and the same holds of given names and family names when these are complex, each constituting a subprojection.

43. Basque and Hungarian are like Japanese for the order of family name > occupational title > honorific title (Hackstein 2010: 40). Head-final Bangla is mixed, having the order given name > family name, like Italian and German, but given name/family name > honorific title, like Japanese and Korean (Tsunoda 1994: 6; also see Tsunoda 1990). Japanese itself can have the order given name > family name with foreign names (e.g., Noam Chomsky [Yoshio Endo, pers. comm. October 10, 2021).

44. This is just a tendency as there are many inconsistencies. See for example that of SOV Yidiny:

(i) bama:l yabuɽuŋgu miɲa gangu:l wawa:l (Dixon 1977: 480)
person.ERG girl.ERG animal.ABS wallaby.ABS see.PST
'the girl saw the wallaby' (lit. 'person girl saw animal wallaby')

Generic nouns are attested in several other Australian languages.

45. "Generic nouns," such as 'thing', 'person', 'animal', are also present in Seri (language isolate [Moser 1977: 18]), and in the Malayo-Polynesian languages Acehnese (Durie 1985: section 5.8) and Taba (Bowden 1997: section 7.2.2.2), among other languages.

46. As noted in chapter 2, n3, I use PL instead of Number to avoid confusion with the silent or overt number/amount Head selecting numerals (as discussed in the text before (8) of section 2.7). Plural, dual, singular, etc., may well head different subprojections. See, for example, the case of the Papuan language Yele, where plural and dual morphemes co-occur (in compliance with Kayne's [2005b: 15] Principle of Decompositionality):

(i) [U kpâm dê y:oo] (Henderson 1995: 73)
his wife DU PL
'his two wives'

In some languages diminutive particles too appear as Heads, in prenominal position in head-initial languages (as in Teop—Oceanic (iia)) and in postnominal position in head-final languages (as in Kokama—Tupi-Guaraní (iib)). They appear closer to the noun than PL.

(ii) a. a maa si mono iana (Teop [Mosel with Thiesen 2007, section 7.6, example (1)])
DET PL DIM parcel fish
'little fish parcels'
b. ca+ yawara kɨra +nu (Kokama [Cabral 1995: 336])
1 dog DIM PL
'my little dogs'

On the functional heads that in some languages are required to license adnominal modification (often called "linkers"), see Manzini (2021) for discussion.

47. For a different derivation of head-initial/head-final languages see Moro and Roberts (2021).

48. As discussed in note 16, the order of postnominal modifiers in Tongan is N Dem A Num with deictic demonstratives and N A Num Dem with anaphoric demonstratives (Macdonald 2014: chapter 1).

49. The order of postnominal modifiers in East Uvean (Wallisian) (Polynesian) is N A Dem Num (Livingston 2016: 34).

50. The prenominal order of modifiers in both Laz and Argobba is Dem Num A N.

51. Here I will not be concerned with DP/PP complements. For the nominal domain of head-initial/-medial languages I will simply adopt Kayne's (2002, 2004b) idea that DP complements are attracted by (a Case and) a

preposition merged higher up in the structure, followed, in head-initial/-medial languages, by remnant movement, which locates the PPs after the Head (but see Adger 2013 and Baggio 2021 for a direct merger of PPs high up in the structure). Cinque (2005: 237fn34) notes that head-final languages, which show the PPs before demonstratives in the nominal domain, can be taken to lack the remnant movement part of the derivation present in head-initial/-medial ones.

52. A similar situation is found in Iraqw (South Cushitic), where nouns can be followed by number, determiner, possessive, and Case suffixes (Mous 1992: 84). One example with a possessive suffix given in Mous (2007: 13) is (i):

(i) hiikwa-'ée' kudá koo'an ló'wa hhoo' i amá
cattle-1SG.POSS DEM4 five very nice BE where
'Where are those five nice cows of mine?'

53. Kipsigis has the rare possibility of demonstrative (rather than determiner) spreading.

54. Also see the case of the Kordofanian language Moro. Jenks's (2014) discussion can be rendered compatible with phrasal movement rather than head-noun movement if all "arguments" and "adjuncts" of the noun are merged above NP, as argued for in chapter 1 and in chapter 4 (section 4.3: 73).

55. The differences between the other mirror-image pairs are more difficult to assess because they involve special conditions (see Abels and Neeleman 2007: section 4.2, 2012: 29fn4).

56. "In any well-formed constituent structure tree, for any nodes x and y, if x precedes y, then all nodes dominated by x precede all nodes dominated by y." (Partee et al. 1990: 442, cited in Abels 2016a: 180fn2).

57. Cf. Abels (2011: 4). For critical discussion and for an approach altogether different from the present one, and from Abels and Neeleman's (2012), see Medeiros (2017, 2018), and the discussion in Abels (2016b).

58. On the SOV nature of Dutch (partly obscured by the raising of the finite verb to CP in main clauses) see Koster (1975, 2000) and many other works since (pace Zwart 1997: III).

59. I report here Barbiers's (1995: section 4.3) rendition of Koster's (1974) findings. Instead of *door 'n stuurfout* 'by/because of a steering error', Koster (1974: 612) had *door gás te geven* 'by giving gas'.

60. On the characteristic mirror-image order of circumstantial PPs in head-final and head-initial/-medial languages see Bartsch and Venneman (1972: section 6.2), Boisson (1981, 1993: 106–107), Hinterhölzl (2002: 132), Cinque (2002: section 2.2), Schweikert (2005: 102), Sabel (2011: section 7), and Lu (no date). Focus-sensitive operations may conceal the existence of a strict order of circumstantial PPs, but the order becomes visible whenever some factor makes the focus-sensitive operations unavailable. See Schweikert (2005) and Cinque (2002) for discussion.

61. The derivations suggested in the remainder of the section are a particular implementation within the present framework of Barbiers's analysis and derivations. Also see Hinterhölzl (2009: section 3.3). The (partially) symmetric external merge of Abels and Neeleman's (2012) account could also accommodate these orders by base-generating the PPs directly to the left or to the right of the V(P), thereby abandoning the strict head-final nature of Dutch (though arguments and AdverbPs would necessarily have to be base-generated to the left).

62. It remains to be seen how best to capture the distribution of focus particles that Barbiers (1995) also discusses.

Chapter 4

1. See Roberts (2019: 359–364) on the behavior of these adverbs in double-object and verb-particle constructions.

2. On the partial raising of the lexical verb in English also see Johnson (1991) and Blight (2004: section 2.2.1).

3. The hierarchical/linear representation of (6), as a product of Merge, with V(P), Asp(P), T(P), and other Heads as final Heads (if linear order is part of narrow syntax) has something in common with Haider's (1992, 2000, 2013, 2015) and Fukui and Takano's (1998, 2000) approaches, except that these Heads not only move in the derivation of head-initial languages (here via the *whose-pictures* pied piping mode) but also in the derivation of head-final ones, via the *pictures-of-whom* pied piping mode. As noted in section 3.3, the fact that they select their complements in their specifiers is compatible with antisymmetry.

4. On the general order in (7) see sections 1 and 2 of Rackowski and Travis (2000) on Malagasy (VOS) and Niuean (VSO): "there . . . seems to be a correlation between preverbal elements which appear in their

hierarchical order and postverbal elements which are in the reverse order" (127). Also see Massam (2000, 2010). On what is found preverbally in "verb-initial languages" see the first part of Greenberg's (1963) Universal 16: "In languages with dominant order VSO, an inflected auxiliary always precedes the main verb." Carnie and Guilfoyle (2000a: 10) also state that a trait of VSO languages is represented by "preverbal tense, mood/aspect, question, and negation particles." Also see Pearson (2000: 359), the Konstanz Universals Archive (https://typo.uni-konstanz.de/rara/category/universals-archive/) numbers 501 and 1553, Dryer (1992: sections 4.3 and 4.5), Hendrick (2000), Chung (2017), and Clemens and Polinsky (2017), among others.

5. In Tangsa in embedded contexts the complementizer follows the modal/tense/aspect morphemes:

(i) [anɤ́a lôpô tʰîŋ ŋâləmə] cʰàm m-aʔ (Boro 2017: 505)
[here play should COMP] know NEG-3
'(They) did not know that (they) should have sex here.'

6. In a sense, the only difference between Turkish (see (11a)) and Italian (see (12)) resides in the pied piping mode of the (copula+)*miş* in Turkish and of the 3rd plural person auxiliary *hanno* in Italian. If Italian, like Turkish, utilized the *pictures-of-whom* pied piping, (12) would appear as (i), like Turkish (11a):

(i) Loro [[mangia-to] e [bevu-to-]](ha)-nno
they eat-PST.PART and drink-PST.PART-(have)-3rdPL
'They have eaten and drunk.'

7. What remains to be clarified are inflectional suffixes, and their derivation, which in the Morphology as Syntax approach (Collins and Kayne 2021; see also Manzini and Savoia 2007) are taken to be built in narrow syntax.

8. The VOS languages, in Hammarström's sample of 5,230 languages (see Hammarström 2015), are around 3.3% of the totality of languages and the VSO languages around 9.5%, VOS and VSO languages thus reaching together at most 13% of the total number of languages (also see Greenberg 1963: 76–77; Cinque 2013b: 70, 2017: 340fn42 and references cited there). The rigid head-final languages are apparently also a minority among the SOV languages. Greenberg's (1963: 109) rigid subtype of SOV languages (his group 23.III/PO/GN/AN) also lists

languages that are not as rigid as Japanese, Korean, or the Dravidian languages: with Hindi, Bengali, and Burushaski having initial complementizers and postverbal complement clauses; with Modern Armenian having different postverbal constituents; with Burmese having postnominal adjectives and numerals; with Nama Hottentot having postnominal possessives and postverbal objects; with Quechua having certain postverbal infinitival complements and adjuncts; among others. See Cinque (2017: section 4.1) for further discussion and references. Greenberg's notion of rigid SOV languages is "languages in which the verb is always at the end" (79), rather than languages in which all the Heads are always at the end.

9. In terms of the proposals in Roberts (2019: 173–174) these would represent mesoparameters.

10. See Cinque (2013b: 50fn8).

11. Sabel (2011) reports that among the Oceanic VOS languages, Kiribati and North-West Fijian have the inverse order of manner and frequency AdverbPs but the direct order of DP_{IO} DP_{DO}, whose overall derivation needs to be worked out in the present context.

12. Given that DPs/PPs (like possessive adjectives, relative clauses, and PPs in the nominal extended projection [cf. note 2 of chapter 2 and note 51 of chapter 3]) can also move independently to different Case/scope/specificity positions, they may appear in more than one place with respect to adverbs. See, for example, (i), from Rackowski and Travis (2000: section 1.3):

(i) Tsy manasa tsara foana <ny lamba> intsony <ny lamba> mihitsy <ny lamba> Rakoto
Neg PRES.AT.wash well always <DET clothes> anymore <DET clothes>at.all<DET clothes> Rakoto
'Rakoto does not wash at all any longer always well the clothes.'

In Malagasy the predicate appears to raise very high as even topics are after the subject (VOXSTopic). See Pearson (2001: section 3.1.2, 2007: section 3.1), and in particular Pearson (2007: 10) for evidence that such topics display weak crossover and reconstruction effects, suggesting the presence of movement. As to the left peripheral topic of Malagasy, Paul (2002: section 8) claims that it "is probably not generated via movement as almost any element may appear in the topic position and islands are not respected." This description seems to qualify it as a "Hanging Topic" (Cinque 1977, 1990: chapter 2), which arguably is never found clause-finally (see Kayne

2020a: section 3). The overall linear order of Malagasy thus seems to be HangingTopicVOXS(movement)Topic. The Mayan VOS language Ch'ol (which, like Niuean, alternates this order with VSO) has instead the order TopicFocusVOS (Coon 2010: 223).

13. In languages, like most of Mayan, where VOS alternates with VSO, VOS is only possible if the direct object is a bare NP. With full DP objects the order is obligatorily VSO. See for example Clemens and Coon (2018: 247). If bare NPs are closer to the V(P) than DPs, which are presumably raised to a higher position of specificity, the alternation could be analysed as movement of the V(P) to an initial position pied piping a smaller portion of the V(P) extended projection, the one containing the lower NP, though not the higher DP. For a different analysis see Clemens and Coon (2018).

14. In more rigid head-initial languages even high adverbs may appear post-verbally in the mirror-image order of that of head-final and many head-medial languages. See for example the case of VSO Peñoles Mixtec:

(i) ní šitu ba?a na?i -dě (cf. Daly 1973: 15)
PST plow well probably -he
'He probably plowed well'

This suggests that the VP raises with the *whose-pictures* pied piping mode across the lower adverb *ba?a* 'well', after which the T(P) morpheme also raises with the same pied piping mode (dragging along the VP) above the epistemic adverb and the (pronominal) subject, whereas in, say, English V(P) raises above the lower adverb without pied piping, arguably followed by the possible raising of T(P) with the *pictures-of-whom* pied piping mode.

15. On the syntax of verb clusters there is a substantial literature. In addition to Abels' works just cited, see, for data, different analyses, and further references, Haegeman (1992, 1994), Zwart (1995, 1996), Koopman and Szabolcsi (2000), Wurmbrand (2004, 2017), Barbiers (2005), Hinterhölzl (2006b, 2009), Svenonius (2007), Salzmann (2013b), Hendriks (2018), Barbiers et al. (2018), Haider (2020b: section 2.3), Van Craenenbroeck et al. (2019), and Roberts (2019: section 2.3.1).

16. But see Hinterhölzl (2006b: section 5.1) for the important observation that some apparent verb clusters involving 'want' may still be biclausal, as evidenced by the order of a lower adverb before a higher one, something impossible in a single clause (*volere* 'want' also enters

mono- and biclausal structures in Italian [Cinque 2006b: 61fn54, section 7.1]).

17. Let me quote from Abels (2011: 7, section 3.1) (see also Wurmbrand 2017: section 2, table 2): "For Aux>Mod>V clusters she [Wurmbrand (2004)] reports 1-2-3 order for Dutch and Swiss German, 1-3-2 orders for Standard German, the Allemanic Vorarlberg dialect, and certain Swiss German speakers, 3-1-2 orders for various German and Swiss German dialects, as well as the Allemanic Vorarlberg dialect, 2-3-1 orders for Afrikaans and, under certain circumstances West Flemish, 3-2-1 orders for some German dialects and the Allemanic Vorarlberg dialect, and no 2-1-3 orders." The systematic absence of 2-1-3 orders is also reported in Barbiers (2005: 233), Svenonius (2007: section 4), and Hendriks (2018: 55). As for the claim of its existence in Swiss German varieties (Salzmann 2013a, 2013b), see the critical discussion in Wurmbrand (2017: table 2 note f, section 3.1). Abels (2016a: section 3.1) also has a careful discussion of some apparent counterexamples, including 2-1-3 orders, which he shows are not genuine problems for a theory of neutral word order. For Dutch varieties see in particular Barbiers (2005), Barbiers et al. (2018), Hendriks (2018), and Van Craenenbroeck et al. (2019). The possibility of the orders in (26a′)–(26e′) and the impossibility of (26f′) is clearly illustrated by the Modern Greek determiner spreading paradigm (19) of Sichel (2002: 306), from Androutsopoulou (1994).

18. Different types of constructions (Aux Mod V, Mod Mod V, Mod Aux V, e.g., do not necessarily allow all the five orders nor the same range of orders. The determination of the possible and impossible orders in different constructions (and different languages, dialects, and geographical areas) is out of the question here. See Barbiers (2005) for dialects of the Dutch language area and Wurmbrand (2004, 2017) for Germanic in general and references cited there. As shown in Abels (2016a) the same pattern is found in clusters of four elements. Equally outside the scope of the present work is the phenomenon known as Verb Projection Raising (Haegeman and Riemsdijk 1986; Haegeman 1992, 1994; Wurmbrand 2017: section 3.2.3), where phrasal material is found interspersed between the verbs of the cluster. Haegeman (1992: chapter 3, 1994) argues that Verb Raising and Verb Projection Raising should be analyzed as two separate constructions.

19. For the idea, which I do not adopt, that PPs, DPs, and AdvPs should be formed on separate planes, see the last paragraph of section 4.4 for some critical discussion.

20. The analysis is closer to the VP movement analysis of Barbiers (2005: sections 3 and 4) than to Barbiers et al.'s (2018) approach, where a nonmovement derivation is proposed for the verb cluster (through external Merge) on the basis of the possible nominalized nature of the main verb in the orders 3-1-2, 2-3-1, 1-3-2. Hinterhölzl (2006b: 85) also takes the IPP complements in the 2-3-1 order to be nominalized. So the question whether a generalized movement approach to verb clusters is correct will have to remain open.

21. For problems with a head-movement derivation of Germanic verb clusters, which used to be the early standard analysis, see Barbiers (2005: 248) and Wurmbrand (2017: section 3.2.1.1).

22. I ignore here questions of antilocality, which can be circumvented by adding an additional projection.

23. This order requires movement even in a symmetric approach to word order that assumes that dependents are linearized either to the left or to the right of the Head in compliance with their different height of Merge and relative scope (à la Abels and Neeleman 2009, 2012), or that linearization only targets sister nodes (cf. Wurmbrand 2017: section 3.1). Here I assume, as in section 3.5, that all orders are derived by movement. Even if the main argument for verb cluster reordering taking place postsyntactically rather than via syntactic movement is that such a reordering has no semantic effect (cf. Wurmbrand 2017: section 3.1), I take this not to be a sufficient reason. There might be other requirements that force movement; for example, a requirement to endow every phrase on the main projection path of the sentence with a "verbal" feature. Also see Kayne (2020a).

24. Their different orders appear to be determined by the different ways the Head of the extended projection they belong to moves: the V(P) for AdverbPs (see Cinque 1999: chapter 2), and for PPs (see Schweikert 2004, 2005; Takamine 2010). Unlike what I assumed in Cinque (1999), I would now take the neutral order of complement DPs (bare indirect object and direct object) to also be a function of the movement of the V(P). As noted in Abels (2016a: 190) Pearson (2000: §2.4) reports that when we look at double object constructions across languages, there is only one unmarked order in OV languages and two in VO languages:

(i) a. IO DO V (OV languages)
    b. V IO DO ("direct" VO languages)
    c. V DO IO ("inverse" VO languages)

25. The same claim is made concerning the English paradigm (ia)–(id) in Svenonius (2002: section 3.1):

(i) a. Howard foolishly may have been trying to impress us.
b. Howard may foolishly have been trying to impress us.
c. Howard may have foolishly been trying to impress us.
d. Howard may have been foolishly trying to impress us.

"A head movement account is inadequate, since heads generally cannot cross other head positions. If all the auxiliaries in [(i)] occupy lower positions, and if they are all taken to have moved in [(id))], then each one will have to have crossed at least two other head positions" (210). Also see Nilsen (2003: chapter 4).

26. This version of Rizzi's (1990) Relativized Minimality which extends to Ā-chains Chomsky's (2000: section 6; 2001: (17)) insight that links of A-chains do not count as interveners was proposed in Krapova and Cinque (2008: section VII) to capture the fact that the order of *wh*-phrases in Bulgarian multiple *wh*-fronting reflects, up to the finest degree, their pre–*wh*-movement order. This version may subsume Haegeman's (1993a: 71) "Relation preservation on A-chains," which ensures order preservation of Subject, Indirect Object and Direct Object in West Flemish scrambling. Also see Haegeman (1993b, 1996a, 1996b).

27. Incidentally it is unclear whether the Head-Movement Constraint should still be held, especially if head-movement is abandoned in favor of XP-movement. Its effects appear to fall squarely under (the previous interpretation of) Relativized Minimality. This is true even if head-movement (X° adjunction to X°) is retained. See Roberts (2010, chapter 5).

28. See Chomsky (2019: 268, 278) for a critique of multidimensional phrase structure.

29. On the putative transitivity failures of adverb order raised in Nilsen (2003: sections 1.3 and 1.5) and after him in Zwart (2007a) see the discussion in Cinque (2006b: 139fn22).

30. This section follows in essence sections 4.2 and 4.3 of Cinque (2017).

31. On the role of generalizations (and related exceptions) in language acquisition see Yang (2015, 2016).

32. In Biberauer and Roberts's (2017) terminology these cases are "nanoparameters."

33. For some such cases in the Tibeto-Burman family see Dryer (2008: section 5.5).

34. The *enough* that modifies nouns and prepositions appears instead to have a [*pictures-of-whom* pied-piping] feature as it (preferably) precedes NPs and PPs (see Maling 1983: section 1.4).

35. "Direct modification" adjectives are attributive adjectives that cannot have a relative clause source because they are nonpredicative (some adjectives are ambiguous between a predicative and nonpredicative usage and thus can be used either as direct modifiers or as indirect ones, in Sproat and Shih's [1990] and Cinque's [2010b] sense).

36. The fact that their origin may ultimately be responsible for the different pied piping features of the different adjectival classes in Cypriot Maronite Arabic and Istro-Romanian is irrelevant. A child has to determine the feature responsible for the correct order without necessarily knowing from which grammars the adjectives were borrowed.

37. In Italian, provenance and classificatory adjectives, which are in direct modification of the noun, force the noun to move with the *whose-pictures* pied piping mode, while color, shape, size, and quality adjectives, which can be direct or indirect modifiers, allow either mode (see Cinque 2010b: chapter 6, for more detailed discussion) with the consequence that only the former adjectives are necessarily postnominal. Also see the case of classificatory adjectives in Polish, the only class of adjectives that can be postnominal, thus apparently triggering overt raising of the N(P) (Rutkowski and Progovac 2005). For finer distinctions among direct modification adjectives see Morita (2011).

38. In Biberauer and Roberts's (2017) terminology these cases are "microparameters."

39. The same is true of Maltese, whose adjectives are otherwise postnominal (Borg 1996: section 3.12). Those in the superlative form precede the numeral in prenominal position (Winchester 2019: 17). Also see the English case mentioned in Kayne (2008b: note 15), and reported in section 2.1 of this monograph: *The black*(est) two dogs that I've (ever) seen.*

40. In Biberauer and Roberts's (2017) terminology these cases are "mesoparameters."

41. In Biberauer and Roberts's (2017) terminology these cases are "macroparameters." Also see the discussion in Roberts (2019: section 2.5).

42. That both the attractor and the attractee may share features is also suggested in Rizzi (2016: section 6).

43. Raising further, in the case of Swedish APs, above any adverbial modifiers of the adjective, as shown in (i), from Platzack (2014: section 5):

(i) Han var [[sina motståndare]$_i$ mycket t_i överlägsen].
he was his.REFL opponents very superior
'He was quite superior to his opponents'

44. That the AP plausibly moves in this case without pied piping (the third case of movement assumed here) can be inferred from the fact that whenever an adjective takes two DP complements (like *skyldig* 'owing'), attraction is possible (in fact necessary) above the lower one (cf. (ia)), but when it takes place above both, the order is the direct one, not the mirror image one (cf. (ib)) (Platzack 2014: section 2):

(i) a. Han var sin son skyldig en ursäkt.
He was his.REFL son owing an excuse
b. Han var skyldig sin son en ursäkt.
He was owing his.REFL son an excuse

Modulo phrasal instead of head movement is similar to what Platzack (2014) proposes. Also see Platzack (2014: section 1) for arguments that the DP complements are not preceded by a silent preposition, and Platzack (1982).

45. As Ian Roberts (pers. comm., November 18, 2019) observed street names are to be distinguished from road names. They are compounds (despite the orthography) as the stress pattern reveals: "OXford Street" vs. "Oxford rOAd".

46. The latter order is quite strongly preferred in British English (Ian Roberts, pers. comm., November 18, 2019): *the River Thames/Avon/Humber* vs. **the Thames/Avon/Humber River*. As also noted in sections 2.7 and 3.2, the order of proper noun and common noun appears to correlate typically with the order of the genitive and the noun, as noted in Greenberg (1963: 89–90, and more generally with the other correlations pairs of the head-initial and head-final word order types. See Cinque (2011).

47. Also see the case of Vanimo (Papuan), which has the order N Num A Dem with human nouns and either the same order or the alternative order N A Num Dem with nonhuman nouns (Ross 1980: section 2.1).

48. I am not concerned here with axial part (or relator) "prepositions," such as 'under', 'behind', 'next to', and so on, which can follow the DP even in head-initial languages, possibly in correlation with the position of the genitive (for discussion see Cinque 2010a and references cited there).

49. These are often called "ambipositions," among other terms. See Libert (2006) for discussion, and for distinctions to be made within this class of adpositions.

50. I thank Alireza Soleimani (pers. comm., January 11, 2017) for corrections in Goldberg's examples and glosses.

51. In old Swedish one could have OVinf with objects whose D is not filled and VO otherwise (Holmberg and Platzack 2005: 449f), but here the difference depends on the object (whose associated FP may consequently be marked with a [*whose-pictures* pied piping] feature or a [*pictures-of-whom* pied piping] feature), not on the verb.

Chapter 5

1. Other left-right asymmetries are discussed in Kayne (2013).

2. "A head-final phrase αP cannot immediately dominate a head-initial phrase βP, if α and β are members of the same extended projection."(p. 1)

3. I thank Richard Kayne, Andrew Radford, Ian Roberts, and Peter Svenonius for sharing their judgments on the two types of pied piping. For Peter Svenonius (3b) is unacceptable rather than marginal. As seen in chapter 1, example (6), the contrast between the two types is neutralized, or is much weaker, in nonrestrictive relative clauses (also see (i)), although it remains robust in restrictives. See (ii):

(i) a. John, whose pictures have never appealed to anyone, . . . (ok)
    b. John, pictures of whom have never appealed to anyone,.. (ok; perhaps more natural in writing)
(ii) a. Here is someone whose pictures have always appealed to her.
    b. *?Here is someone pictures of whom have always appealed to her.

4. Movement of the Head by itself (without pied piping) also appears to be quite marked, perhaps even more marked than the *pictures-of-whom* pied piping, at least to judge from the cross-linguistic rarity of the N Dem Num A order (Greenberg's 1963: 52 "less popular" order) vis à vis the Dem Num A N order, and the relative rarity of V2 languages,

where the V(P) raises to CP without pied piping, thus not reversing the order of clausal arguments and modifiers.

5. This order was also claimed not to exist by Steele (1978: 42) and Haider (1992: section 5.2, 2000). Also see Dryer (1996: 1059), Kayne (2003a: section 9.3.2), and the Konstanz Universals Archive (numbers 1382 and 1553). On the apparent nonexistence of another FOFC-violating structure ($[_{CP}[_{VP}$ V O] C]), see Dryer (1992: section 4.3, 2009: section 5), but also the exceptions noted in this section and those mentioned in Abels (2013: section 4.2).

6. The fact that auxiliaries inflected for agreement are so rare when they are not contiguous to the subject (as opposed to invariant particles, which are not FOFC-compliant [Biberauer 2017]) might have to do with the virtual necessity for them to enter a Spec-head relation with the preverbal subject. For alternative ways to derive the FOFC see Zwart (2011: 110–111), Haider (2013: 132–135, 2020a), Hinterhölzl (2016: section 7), Sheehan (2017), Roberts (2019: chapter 2), and references cited there.

7. Table (i) gives the percentages reported by a number of authors, (ii) the language numbers given in WALS, and (iii) the language numbers given in Hammarström 2015: 10):

Table (i)

	SOV	SVO	VSO	VOS	OVS	OSV
Ruhlen (1975)	51.5%	35.6%	10.5%	2.1%	0.0%	0.2%
Tomlin (1979)	45.8%	41.5%	11.0%	1.5%	0.3%	0.0%
Mallinson and Blake (1981)	41.0%	35.0%	9.0%	2.0%	1.1%	1.0%
Cysouw (2008)	47.1%	41.2%	8.0%	2.4%	0.8%	0.4%
Hammarström (2015)	43.3%	40.3%	9.5%	3.3%	0.7%	0.3%

Table (ii)

SOV	SVO	VSO	VOS	OVS	OSV
497	435	85	26	9	4

Table (iii)

SOV	SVO	VSO	VOS	OVS	OSV
2267	2107	502	174	38	19

This distribution of "head-final" and "head-initial" languages, close to 50-50, makes it plausible to take the currently existing languages to be a fairly representative sample (for word order) of all possible languages (despite the often noted fact that the currently existing ones are a tiny fraction of all the languages that were and are no longer spoken, that will be spoken in the future, and that will never be spoken). Tables (i), (ii), and (iii) actually show a slight predominance of VO over OV languages ((ii) totals 546 languages for VO and 510 for OV and (iii) 2783 for VO and 2324 for OV), and the order of modifiers in the nominal phrase shows an even clearer skewing of the head-initial order N A Num Dem over the head-final Dem Num A N order in the number of languages and genera (see (6a) and (6b) of chapter 3), though one could have expected a much wider difference. Perhaps, consistency in the movement options when the more marked ones are involved is only mildly sanctioned, while what is more severely sanctioned is changing mode from the less marked pied piping to the more marked one.

8. As already noted, Greenberg (1990) states that the order of the multiplier (M) and the base (B) tends to correspond to that of the numeral (Q) and the noun (N), proposing a universal implication BM → NQ or, equivalently, MB → QN (Universal 28 of Greenberg 1990). Also see Greenberg (1989: 105–106). These harmonic orders involve movement of the Heads base and noun with the same pied piping mode.

9. For the similar case found in Quechua, Cole (1982: 74–75) says that "in instances in which an adjective, an adverbial and an (accusative) argument of the adjective are present in the same sentence, the accusative argument normally precedes the adverbial, which itself precedes the adjective. The marked order adverb, accusative argument, adjective is also possible:

[(i)] a. Marya-ta ashta llaki-mi ka-ni
María-ACC very sad-validator be-1
b. ashta marya-ta llaki-mi ka-ni
very María-ACC sad-validator be-1
'I'm very sad about María'"

10. Cf. Chomsky (2021: 13): Internal Merge is "the most economical subcase of Merge . . . , the case that involves least search by a huge margin."

11. Although, as Ian Roberts notes, many OV languages are very stable, Tamil, Korean, and Japanese seem to show no sign of major word order change over their 1,000+ year histories.

12. For a similar idea, within a somewhat different system, see Roberts (2017: section 3.4) and his Input Generalization.

References

Abels, Klaus. 2003. *Successive Cyclicity, Anti-locality, and Adposition Stranding.* PhD Dissertation, University of Connecticut. https://opencommons.uconn.edu/dissertations/AAI3104085/.

Abels, Klaus. 2011. Hierarchy-order relations in the Germanic verb cluster and in the noun phrase. *Groninger Arbeiten zur germanistischen Linguistik* 53 (2): 1–28 https://ugp.rug.nl/GAGL/article/view/30520/27820.

Abels, Klaus. 2013. On 2-3-1. *UCL Working Papers in Linguistics* 25: 67–101

Abels, Klaus. 2016a. The fundamental left–right asymmetry in the Germanic verb cluster. *Journal of Comparative Germanic Linguistics* 19: 179–220. https://discovery.ucl.ac.uk/id/eprint/1478207/2/art%253A10.1007%252Fs10828-016-9082-9.pdf.

Abels, Klaus. 2016b. Neutral word order and stack sorting. Ms., University College, London. https://www.academia.edu/29828395/Neutral_word_order_and_stack_sorting.

Abels, Klaus, and Ad Neeleman. 2007. Universal 20 without the LCA. Ms., University of Tromsø and University College London. https://ling.auf.net/lingbuzz/000279.

Abels, Klaus, and Ad Neeleman. 2009. Universal 20 without the LCA. In J. M. Brucart, A. Gavarró, and J. Solà, eds., *Merging Features: Computation, Interpretation and Acquisition.* 60–80. Oxford: Oxford University Press.

Abels, Klaus, and Ad Neeleman. 2012. Linear asymmetries and the LCA. *Syntax* 15 (1): 25–74.

Abraham, P. T. 1985. *Apatani Grammar.* Manasagangotri: Central Institute of Indian Languages.

Abraham, P. T. 2005. *A Grammar of Nyishi Language.* Delhi: Farsight Publishers and Distributors. http://www.rogerblench.info/Language/NEI/Tani/Nishi/Linguistics/Nyishi%20grammar%20Abraham%202005.pdf.

Acquaviva, Paolo. 2019. Two studies on the internal syntax of complex names. *Italian Journal of Linguistics* 32 (2): 3–36. http://www.italian-journal-linguistics.com/app/uploads/2021/05/1_Acquaviva.pdf.

Adams, Karen L., and Nancy Faires Conklin. 1973. Toward a theory of natural classification. *Papers from the 9th Regional Meeting of the Chicago Linguistic Society.* 1–10. Chicago: Chicago Linguistic Society.

Adell, Eric James. 2019. *The Phonetics, Phonology, and Morphology of Chajul Ixil (Mayan).* PhD Dissertation, The University of Texas at Austin. https://repositories.lib.utexas.edu/handle/2152/78376.

Adger, David. 2013. *A Syntax of Substance.* Cambridge, MA: MIT Press.

Ahland, Colleen Anne. 2012. *A Grammar of Northern and Southern Gumuz.* PhD Dissertation, University of Oregon. https://scholarsbank.uoregon.edu/xmlui/handle/1794/12559.

Aikhenvald, Alexandra Y. 2000. *Classifiers: A Typology of Noun Categorization Devices.* Oxford: Oxford University Press.

Aissen, Judith, Nora C. England, and Roberto Zavala Maldonado, eds. 2017. *The Mayan Languages.* Abingdon, United Kingdom: Routledge.

Ajíbóyè, Ọládiípọ̀ Jacob. 2005. *Topics in Yoruba Nominal Expressions.* PhD Dissertation, University of British Columbia. https://open.library.ubc.ca/media/download/pdf/831/1.0092961/2.

Alexiadou, Artemis, Elena Anagnostopoulou, Sjef Barbiers, and Hans-Martin Gärtner, eds. 2002. *Dimensions of Movement: From Features to Remnants.* 151–189. Amsterdam: Benjamins.

(Allassonière-)Tang, Marc, and One-Soon Her. 2020. Numeral base, numeral classifier, and noun: word order harmonization. *Language and Linguistics* 22 (4): 511–556. https://www.jbe-platform.com/docserver/fulltext/lali.00069.all.pdf?expires=1653139445&id=id&accname=guest&checksum=77494E0AAECC35F635CB9D5B354C3B51.

Allassonnière-Tang, Marc, Ying-Chun Chen, Nai-Shing Yen, and One-Soon Her. 2020. Investigating the branching of Chinese classifier phrases: Evidence from speech perception and production. In *Journal of East Asian Linguistics* 23 (4): 361–392. http://www3.nccu.edu.tw/~osh/T3%20paper-JCL-Post-Print.pdf.

Amha, Azeb. 2001. *The Maale Language*. Leiden, Netherlands: CNWS Publications. https://scholarlypublications.universiteitleiden.nl/access/item%3A2871399/view.

An, Duk-Ho. 2014. Genitive Case in Korean and its implications for noun phrase structure. *Journal of East Asian Linguistics* 23 (4): 361–392.

Anderson, Mike, and Malcolm Ross. 2011. Sudest. In Lynch et al., *Oceanic Languages*. 322–346.

Androutsopoulou, Antonia. 1994. The distribution of the definite determiner and the syntax of Greek DPs. In K. Beals, J. Denton, R. Knippen, L. Melnar, H. and E. Zeinfeld, eds., *Proceedings of the 30th Regional Meeting of the Chicago Linguistic Society*. 16–29. Chicago: University of Chicago Press.

Arka, I Wayan. 2008. Classifiers in Rongga. *Studies in Philippine Languages and Cultures* 18: 1–17. https://www.sil.org/system/files/reapdata/13/59/13/135913778944838096119610787285170940952/1_Arka.pdf.

Asplund, Leif. 2015. *Noun Categorisation in North Halmahera*. Honours Thesis, Stockholm University. http://su.diva-portal.org/smash/get/diva2:825519/FULLTEXT02.pdf.

Baggio, Pietro. 2021. Introducing arguments and modifiers in the noun phrase. *Linguistic Inquiry* 52 (2): 393–407.

Baker, Mark C. 1988. *Incorporation: A Theory of Grammatical Function Changing*. Chicago: University of Chicago Press.

Bakker, Peter. 1997. *A Language of Our Own: The Genesis of Michif, the Mixed Cree-French Language of the Canadian Métis*. New York: Oxford University Press.

Bale, Alan, and Jessica Coon. 2014. Classifiers are for numerals, not for nouns: Consequences for the mass/count distinction. *Linguistic Inquiry* 45: 695–707. https://citeseerx.ist.psu.edu/viewdoc/download?doi=10.

Bale, Alan, Jessica Coon, and Nicolás Arcos López. 2019. Classifiers, partitions, and measurements: Exploring the syntax and semantics of sortal classifiers. *Glossa: A Journal of General Linguistics* 4 (1): 77. 1–30. DOI: https://doi.org/10.5334/gjgl.752.

Ball, Douglas L. 2009. *Clause Structure and Argument Realization in Tongan*. PhD Dissertation, Stanford University.

Balle, Misriani, and Stuart Cameron. 2014. The interplay of quantifiers and number in Helong grammar. In Klamer and Kratochvíl, *Number and Quantity in East Nusantara.* 43–59. https://openresearch-repository.anu.edu.au/handle/1885/11917.

Barbiers, Sjef. 1995. *The Syntax of Interpretation.* Den Haag: HAG. https://www.researchgate.net/publication/243646889_The_syntax_of_interpretation.

Barbiers, Sjef. 2005. Word order variation in three-verb clusters and the division of labour between generative linguistics and sociolinguistics. In L.Cornips and K.Corrigan, eds., *Syntax and Variation. Reconciling the Biological and the Social.* 233–264. Amsterdam: Benjamins.

Barbiers Sjef, Hans Bennis, and Lotte Dros-Hendriks. 2018. Merging verb cluster variation. *Linguistic Variation* 18 (1): 144–196. https://openaccess.leidenuniv.nl/bitstream/handle/1887/67652/Merging_Verb_Clusters.pdf?sequence=1.

Barnes, Malone. 2000. El tuyuca. In M. S. González de Pérez, ed., *Lenguas Indígenas de Colombia. Una Visión Descriptiva.* 437–452. Santafé, Bogotá: Instituto Caro y Cuervo.

Bartsch, Renate, and Theo Vennemann. 1972. *Semantic Structures: A Study in the Relation between Semantics and Syntax.* Frankfurt am Main, Germany: Athenäum Verlag.

Bassene, Mamadou. 2012. *Morphophonology of Joola Eegimaa.* PhD Dissertation, University of Minnesota. https://conservancy.umn.edu/handle/11299/136031

Bayer, Josef. 1996. *Directionality and Logical Form: On the Scope of Focussing Particles and Wh-in-situ.* Dordrecht, Netherlands: Kluwer.

Beck, David. 2004. *Upper Necaxa Totonac.* Munich: Lincom Europa. An earlier version is available at https://sites.ualberta.ca/~dbeck/PDF/UNT.pdf.

Beckwith, Christopher I. 1998. Noun specification and classification in Uzbek. *Anthropological Linguistics* 40: 124–140.

Belletti, A. ed. 2004. *Structures and Beyond: The Cartography of Syntactic Structures, Volume 3.* New York: Oxford University Press.

Benton, Richard A. 1968. Numeral and attributive classifiers in Trukese. *Oceanic Linguistics* 7: 104–146.

Berry, Keith, and Christine Berry. 1999. *A Description of Abun: A West Papuan Language of Irian Jaya.* Canberra: Pacific Linguistics (The

Australian National University). http://sealang.net/archives/pl/pdf/PL-B115.pdf.

Bhatia, Tej K. 1993. *Punjabi*. London: Routledge.

Biberauer, Theresa. 2017. The Final-over-Final Condition and particles. In Sheehan et al., *Final-over-Final Condition*. 187–296.

Biberauer, Theresa, Anders Holmberg, and Ian Roberts. 2009. Linearization and the architecture of grammar: A view from the Final-over-Final Constraint. In V. Moscati and E. Servidio, eds., *Proceedings of the XXXV Incontro di Grammatica Generativa (Studies in Linguistics)* 3: 77–89. http://www.ciscl.unisi.it/doc/doc_pub/STiL-2009-vol3-special-IGG.pdf.

Biberauer, Theresa, Anders Holmberg, and Ian Roberts. 2014. A syntactic universal and its consequences. *Linguistic Inquiry* 45 (2): 169–225. https://eprints.ncl.ac.uk/file_store/production/177510/2DEDF827-5A07-410C-A7B7-EB999072748E.pdf.

Biberauer, Theresa, Anders Holmberg, Ian Roberts, and Michelle Sheehan. 2017. Empirical evidence for the Final-over-Final Condition. In Sheehan et al., *Final-over-Final Condition*. 11–25.

Biberauer, Theresa, and Ian Roberts. 2017. Parameter setting. In A. Ledgeway and I. Roberts, eds., *The Cambridge Handbook of Historical Syntax*. 134–162. Cambridge: Cambridge University Press.

Biberauer, Theresa, and Michelle Sheehan, eds. 2013. *Theoretical Approaches to Disharmonic Word Orders*. Oxford: Oxford University Press.

Blight, Ralph Charles. 2004. *Head Movement, Passive, and Antipassive in English*. PhD Dissertation, The University of Texas at Austin. https://repositories.lib.utexas.edu/handle/2152/1480.

Bobaljik, Jonathan David. 1999. Adverbs: The hierarchy paradox. *Glot International* 4 (9/10): 27–28. https://citeseerx.ist.psu.edu/viewdoc/download?doi=10.1.1.496.4421&rep=rep1&type=pdf.

Boechat de Medeiros, Alessandro. 2017. Interview with Noam Chomsky. In Generative Grammar: Celebrating the 60th Anniversary of Syntactic Structures (1957–2017). Special issue, *Revista Linguística* 13 (2): 15–21. https://revistas.ufrj.br/index.php/rl/article/view/14025.

Boettger, Juliane. 2015. *Topics in the Grammar of Lele: A Language of Manus Island, Papua New Guinea*. PhD Dissertation, James Cook University. http://researchonline.jcu.edu.au/41204/1/41204-boettger-2015-thesis.pdf.

Boisson, Claude Pierre. 1981. Hiérarchie universelle des spécifications de temps, de lieu, et de manière. *Confluents* (Centre d'études Anglaises et Nord-américaines, Université Lyon 2) 7 (2): 69–126.

Boisson, Claude Pierre. 1993. La linéarité: Iconicité et arbitraire. In *L'ordre des Mots II. Domaine Anglais.* 85–124. Lyon: Université de Saint-Etienne.

Bon, Noëllie. 2014. *Une Grammaire de la Langue Stieng. Langue en Danger du Cambodge et du Vietnam.* Thèse de Doctorat, Université Lumière Lyon 2. https://www.academia.edu/6680660/Une_grammaire_de_la_langue_stieng_langue_en_danger_du_Cambodge_et_du_Vietnam.

Borer, Hagit. 2005. *Structuring Sense.* Vol. 1 of *In Name Only.* Oxford: Oxford University Press.

Borg, Albert J. 1996. The structure of the noun phrase in Maltese. *Italian Journal of Linguistics/Rivista di Linguistica* 8: 5–28. https://www.italian-journal-linguistics.com/app/uploads/2021/06/2_Borg-structure.pdf.

Boro, Krishna. 2017. *A Grammar of Hakhun Tangsa.* PhD Dissertation, University of Oregon. https://scholarsbank.uoregon.edu/xmlui/handle/1794/22739.

Bowden, John. 1997. *Taba (Makian Dalam): description of an Austronesian language from Eastern Indonesia.* PhD Dissertation, University of Melbourne. https://minerva-access.unimelb.edu.au/handle/11343/35661.

Bril, Isabelle. 2002. *Le Nêlêmwa (Nouvelle-Calédonie). Analyse Syntaxique et Sémantique.* Paris: Peeters. https://www.academia.edu/3070909/Le_n%C3%AAl%C3%AAmwa_Nouvelle_Cal%C3%A9donie_Analyse_syntaxique_et_s%C3%A9mantique_.

Bril, Isabelle. 2014. Number and numeration in Nêlêmwa and Zuanga (New Caledonia): Ontologies, definiteness and pragmatics. In G. Dimmendaal and A. Storch, eds., *Number: Constructions and Semantics. Case Studies from Africa, Amazonia, India and Oceania.* 167–198. Amsterdam: Benjamins. https://hal.archives-ouvertes.fr/hal-00994177/document.

Brown, Lea. 2001. *A Grammar of Nias Selatan.* PhD Dissertation, University of Sydney. https://ses.library.usyd.edu.au/handle/2123/12669.

Cabral, Ana Suelly de Arruda Camara. 1995. *Contact-Induced Language Change in the Western Amazon: The Non-genetic Origin of the Kokama Language.* PhD Dissertation, University of Pittsburgh.

http://etnolinguistica.wdfiles.com/local--files/tese:cabral-1995/cabral_kokama1995.pdf.

Caha, Pavel. 2015. Czech numerals and no bundling. In U. Shlonsky, ed., *Beyond Functional Sequence: The Cartography of Syntactic Structures, Volume 10.* 173–195. New York: Oxford University Press. https://is.muni.cz/do/rect/metodika/VaV/evaluace/2019-ff_filologie/fulltext/9_Caha-Czech_Numerals.pdf.

Can Pixabaj, Telma A. 2017. K'iche'. In Aissen et al., *Mayan Languages.* 461–499.

Carnie, Andrew, and Eithne Guilfoyle. 2000a. Introduction. In Carnie and Guilfoyle, *Syntax of Verb Initial Languages.* 3–11.

Carnie, Andrew, and Eithne Guilfoyle, eds. 2000b. *The Syntax of Verb Initial Languages.* New York: Oxford University Press.

Caron, Bruce R. 1987. A comparative look at Yao numerical classifiers. *Linguistics of the Tibeto-Burman Area* 10 (2): 151–168. http://sealang.net/sala/archives/pdf8/caron1987comparative.pdf.

Cheng, Lisa Lai-Shen, and Rint Sybesma. 1998. Yi-wan tang, yi-ge tang: Classifiers and massifiers. *Tsing Hua Journal of Chinese Studies, New Series* 28: 385–412. https://citeseerx.ist.psu.edu/viewdoc/download?doi=10.1.1.726.6003&rep=rep1&type=pdf.

Cheng, Lisa Lai-Shen, and Rint Sybesma. 1999. Bare and not-so-bare nouns and the structure of NP. *Linguistic Inquiry* 30 (4): 509–542. https://scholarlypublications.universiteitleiden.nl/access/item%3A2860296/view.

Cheung, Chi-Hang. 2003. *An Investigation of the Jingpo Nominal Structure.* MA Thesis, The Chinese University of Hong Kong. https://repository.lib.cuhk.edu.hk/sc/item/cuhk-324928

Chomsky, Noam. 1965. *Aspects of the Theory of Syntax.* Cambridge, MA: MIT Press.

Chomsky, Noam. 1994. *Bare Phrase Structure.* MIT Occasional Papers in Linguistics 5. Cambridge, MA: MIT, Department of Linguistics and Philosophy, MITWPL.

Chomsky, Noam. 1995. *The Minimalist Program.* Cambridge, MA: MIT Press.

Chomsky, Noam. 2000. Minimalist inquiries: The framework. In R. Martin, D. Michaels, and J. Uriagereka, eds., *Step by Step. Essays on*

Minimalist Syntax in Honor of Howard Lasnik. 89–155. Cambridge, MA: MIT Press.

Chomsky, Noam. 2001. Derivation by phase. In M. Kenstowicz, ed., *Ken Hale: A Life in Language*. 1–52. Cambridge, MA: MIT Press.

Chomsky, Noam. 2004. Beyond explanatory adequacy. In Belletti, *Structures and Beyond*. 104–131.

Chomsky, Noam. 2013. Problems of projection. *Lingua* 130: 33–49.

Chomsky, Noam. 2015. Problems of projection: Extensions. In E. Di Domenico, C. Hamann, and S. Matteini, eds., *Structures, Strategies and Beyond: Studies in Honour of Adriana Belletti*. 3–16. Amsterdam: Benjamins.

Chomsky, Noam. 2019. Some puzzling foundational issues: The Reading program. In Á. J. Gallego and D. Ott, eds., Generative Syntax. Questions, Crossroads, and Challenges. Special issue, *Catalan Journal of Linguistics* 263–285. https://revistes.uab.cat/catJL/article/view/sp2019-chomsky/287-pdf-en.

Chomsky, Noam. 2020. *The UCLA Lectures (April 29—May 2, 2019) with an Introduction by Robert Freidin*. https://ling.auf.net/lingbuzz/005485.

Chomsky, Noam. 2021. Minimalism: Where are we now, and where can we hope to go? Ms., University of Arizona. https://www.ls-japan.org/modules/documents/LSJpapers/journals/160_chomsky.pdf.

Chomsky, Noam, Ángel J. Gallego, and Dennis Ott. (2017) 2019. Generative grammar and the faculty of language: Insights, questions, and challenges. Ms., MIT, Universitat Autònoma de Barcelona and University of Ottawa. https://ling.auf.net/lingbuzz/003507.

Chuluu, Üjiyediin. 1994. Introduction, Grammar, and Sample Sentences for Monguor. *Sino-Platonic Papers* (Department of East Asian Languages and Civilizations, University of Pennsylvania) 57: 1–31 http://sino-platonic.org/complete/spp057_monguor_language.pdf

Chung, Sandra. 2017. VOS languages: Some of their properties. In Everaert and van Riemsdijk, *Wiley Blackwell Companion to Syntax*. 1–36.

Cinque, Guglielmo. 1977. The movement nature of left dislocation. *Linguistic Inquiry* 8 (2): 397–412. https://iris.unive.it/handle/10278/5000711.

Cinque, Guglielmo. 1990. *Types of Ā-Dependencies*. Cambridge, MA: MIT Press.

Cinque, Guglielmo. 1999. *Adverbs and Functional Heads: A Cross-Linguistic Perspective.* New York: Oxford University Press.

Cinque, Guglielmo. 2002. Complement and adverbial PPs: Implications for clause structure. Paper presented at the 25th Generative Linguistics in the Old World (GLOW) Colloquium, Amsterdam. (Published in Cinque, *Restructuring and Functional Heads.* 145–166.) https://iris.unive.it/handle/10278/5000731.

Cinque, Guglielmo. 2005. Deriving Greenberg's Universal 20 and its exceptions. *Linguistic Inquiry* 36: 315–332. (Reprinted in Cinque 2013a, *Typological Studies.* 57–67.) https://www.academia.edu/3577370/Deriving_Greenberg_s_Universal_20_and_Its_Exceptions.

Cinque, Guglielmo. 2006a. Are all languages 'numeral classifier languages'? *Rivista di Grammatica Generativa* 31: 119–122. (Reprinted in Cinque 2013a, *Typological Studies.* 107–109.) https://lingbuzz.com/j/rgg/2006/cinque_rivista_2006.pdf.

Cinque, Guglielmo. 2006b. *Restructuring and Functional Heads.* New York: Oxford University Press.

Cinque, Guglielmo. 2009. The fundamental left-right asymmetry of natural languages. In S. Scalise, E. Magni, and A. Bisetto, eds., *Universals of Language Today.* 165–184. Dordrecht, Netherlands: Springer. (Reprinted in Cinque 2013a, *Typological Studies.* 96–106.) https://www.academia.edu/2557014/The_Fundamental_Left_Right_Asymmetry_of_Natural_Languages.

Cinque, Guglielmo. 2010a. Mapping spatial PPs: An introduction. In G. Cinque and L. Rizzi, eds., *Mapping Spatial PPs: The Cartography of Syntactic Structures, Volume 6.* 3–25. New York: Oxford University Press. (Reprinted in Cinque 2013a, *Typological Studies.* 86–95.) https://www.academia.edu/27093999/Mapping_Spatial_PPs_The_Cartography_of_Syntactic_Structures_Volume_6 .

Cinque, Guglielmo. 2010b. *The Syntax of Adjectives: A Comparative Study.* Cambridge, MA: MIT Press.

Cinque, Guglielmo. 2011. Greenberg's Universal 23 and SVO languages. In M. Frascarelli, ed., *Structures and Meanings: Cross-Theoretical Perspectives.* 75–80. Paris: L'Harmattan. (Reprinted in Cinque 2013a, *Typological Studies.* 110–113.) https://www.academia.edu/27094000/Greenberg_s_Universal_23_and_SVO_languages.

Cinque, Guglielmo. 2012. A generalization concerning DP-internal ellipsis. *Iberia: An International Journal of Theoretical Linguistics* 4: 174–193. https://revistascientificas.us.es/index.php/iberia/article/view/232/232.

Cinque, Guglielmo. 2013a. *Typological Studies: Word Order and Relative Clauses*. London: Routledge.

Cinque, Guglielmo. 2013b. Word-order typology: A change of perspective. In Biberauer and Sheehan, *Theoretical Approaches to Disharmonic Word Orders*. 47–73. (Reprinted in Cinque 2013a, *Typological Studies*. 13–33.) https://www.academia.edu/8406312/_Word_Order_Typology_A_Change_of_Perspective_in_Biberauer_T_M_Sheehan_eds_Theoretical_Approaches_to_Disharmonic_Word_Orders_47_73_Oxford_Oxford_University_Press_2013._

Cinque, Guglielmo. 2015. A note on 'other'. In E. Brandner, A. Czypionka, C. Freitag, and A. Trotzke, eds., *Charting the Landscape of Linguistics: Webschrift for Josef Bayer*. 22–27. Konstanz, Germany: Universität Konstanz. http://ling.uni-konstanz.de/pages/WebschriftBayer/2015/title.html.

Cinque, Guglielmo. 2017. A microparametric approach to the head-initial/head-final parameter. *Linguistic Analysis* 41 (3–4): 309–366. https://iris.unive.it/retrieve/handle/10278/3702027/134636/MicroparametersWordOrder%28LA%29.pdf.

Cinque, Guglielmo. 2020. *The Syntax of Relative Clauses: A Unified Analysis*. Cambridge: Cambridge University Press.

Cinque, Guglielmo. 2021. Some notes on externalization and meaningless movement. To appear in D. Ott and Á. Gallego, eds., *Cartography and Explanatory Adequacy*. Oxford: Oxford University Press.

Cinque, Guglielmo. 2022a. A (Universal 20) movement approach to DP-internal ellipsis. Talk presented at the 'You're on mute' NYU ellipsis seminar series 2021–2022, April 15 2022. https://nyu.zoom.us/rec/share/cP6j75NoGCl2XCdENoVxcQeAaq95LKaDTHfgwvIGqiH8v9MQKod7hXG7RurK_OnT.11s8MhvtFTObkyXM

Cinque, Guglielmo. 2022b. Two types of sortal classifiers and their co-occurrence. To appear in a Festschrift.

Cinque, Guglielmo. 2022c. On two sub-projections of the nominal extended projection: some Romance evidence. To appear in *Probus*.

Cinque, Guglielmo. In preparation. Again on the order of demonstrative, numeral, adjective, and noun.

Cinque, Guglielmo, and Richard S.Kayne, eds., 2005. *The Oxford Handbook of Comparative Syntax*. New York: Oxford University Press.

Clark, Marybeth. 1989. Hmong and Areal South-East Asia. In D. Bradley, ed., *Papers in South-East Asian Linguistics* 11. 175–230. Canberra: Pacific Linguistics (The Australian National University). http://nickenfield.org/files/clark_1989.pdf.

Clem, Emily. 2018. Disharmony and the Final-over-Final Condition in Amahuaca. Paper presented at the 41st GLOW Colloquium, Budapest. https://pages.ucsd.edu/~eclem/clem-2018-fofc-glow41.pdf

Clem, Emily. 2020. Disharmony and the Final-over-Final Condition in Amahuaca. Ms., University of California, San Diego. https://pages.ucsd.edu/~eclem/clem-2020-fofc-ms.pdf.

Clemens, Lauren, and Jessica Coon. 2018. Deriving verb-initial word order in Mayan. *Language* 94 (2): 237–280.

Clemens, Lauren, and Maria Polinsky. 2017. Verb-initial word orders, primarily in Austronesian and Mayan Languages. In Everaert and van Riemsdijk, *Wiley Blackwell Companion to Syntax*. 1–50. http://www.mariapolinsky.com/wp-content/uploads/2018/03/clemensEtAl_17_Verb-Initi.6.pdf.

Cole, Peter. 1982. *Imbabura Quechua*. Amsterdam: North Holland.

Cole, Peter, and Gabriella Hermon. 2008. VP raising in a VOS language. *Syntax* 11: 144–197.

Collins, Chris, and Richard Kayne. 2021. Towards a theory of morphology as syntax. Ms., New York University. https://ling.auf.net/lingbuzz/005693.

Comrie, Bernard. 1997. Some problems in the theory and typology of numeral systems. In B. Palek, ed., *Proceedings of Linguistics and Phonetics 1996*. 41–56. Prague: Charles University Press.

Comrie, Bernard. 2016. Numeral bases. In M.S. Dryer and M. Haspelmath, eds., *The World Atlas of Language Structures Online*. Chapter 131. https://wals.info/chapter/131.

Conklin, Nancy Faires. 1981. *The Semantics and Syntax of Numeral Classification in Tai and Austronesian*. PhD Dissertation, The University of Michigan.

Coon, Jessica. 2010. *Complementation in Chol (Mayan): A Theory of Split Ergativity*. PhD Dissertation, MIT. http://ling.auf.net/lingbuzz/001072.

Corver, Norbert and Yuta Tatsumi. 2021. Number names: internal structure and morphological marking. Ms., Utrecht University and Meikai University. http://norbert.abelcorver.com/wp-content/uploads/2021/08/24June2021CorverTatsumiNumberNames.pdf

Craenenbroeck, Jeroen Van, Marjo van Koppen, and Antal van den Bosch. 2019. A quantitative-theoretical analysis of syntactic microvariation: Word order in Dutch verb clusters. *Language* 95 (2): 333–370. https://static1.squarespace.com/static/5217e223e4b090faa01f8f2d/t/5e134f6df8000d4096373c04/1578323894708/published-version.pdf.

Croft, William and Efrosini Deligianni. 2001. Asymmetry in NP word order. Paper presented at the International Symposium on Deictic Systems and Quantification in Languages Spoken in Europe and Northern and Central Asia, Udmurt State University, Izhevsk, Russia, May 2001.

Cuonzo, Clara. 2019. On the syntax of the negative adverb angorə in Abruzzese. *Rivista di Grammatica Generativa—Research in Generative Grammar* 41: 1–29. https://lingbuzz.com/j/rgg/2019/2019.03/cuonzo_angore-in-abruzzese_RGG-2019-03.pdf.

Curiel Ramírez Del Prado, Alejandro. 2017. Tojolabal. In Aissen et al., *Mayan Languages*. 570–609.

Curry, Haskell Brooks. 1961. Some logical aspects of grammatical structure. In R. Jakobson, ed., *Structure of Language and Its Mathematical Aspects*. 56–68. Providence, RI: American Mathematical Society.

Cysouw, Michael. 2008. Linear Order as a Predictor of Word Order Regularities. *Advances in Complex Systems* 11: 411–415.

Daly, John P. 1973. *A Generative Syntax of Peñoles Mixtec*. Norman: University of Oklahoma and Summer Institute of Linguistics. https://www.sil.org/resources/archives/8830.

Danaher, Jillian Grace. 2019. Verbal characteristics of adjectives in Hakha Chin. *Indiana Working Papers in South Asian Languages and Cultures* (*IWPSALC*) 1 (1): 1–11. https://scholarworks.iu.edu/journals/index.php/iwpsalc/article/view/27457/32774.

Danon, Gabi. 2012. Two structures for numeral-noun constructions. *Lingua* 122: 1282–1307. https://faculty.georgetown.edu/rtk8/Danon%202012%20two%20structures%20for%20numeral-noun%20constructions.pdf.

Dayley, Jon Philip. 1981. *Tzutujil Grammar*. PhD Dissertation, University of California, Berkeley. https://escholarship.org/content/qt4cx9t9b1/qt4cx9t9b1_noSplash_aa75d270aef86e270815c99e2bf9ede2.pdf

Dékány, Éva. 2021. *The Hungarian nominal functional sequence*. Dordrecht, Netherlands: Springer. https://sites.google.com/site/dekany linguistics/publications.

Denning, Keith, and Suzanne Kemmer, eds., 1990. *On Language: Selected Writings of Joseph H. Greenberg*. Stanford, CA: Stanford University Press.

de Sousa, Hilário. 2011. Nanning Cantonese and Nanning Pinghua—their Tai-ness and non-Tai-ness. Paper presented at 21st Conference of Southeast Asian Linguistics Society, Kasetsart University, Bangkok, May 11–13. http://jseals.org/seals21/desousa11nanningp.pdf

Dixon, Robert M.W. 1977. *A Grammar of Yidiny*. Cambridge: Cambridge University Press.

Doble, Marion. 1987. A description of some features of Ekari language structure. *Oceanic Linguistics* 26 (1/2): 55–113.

Doley, Sarat Kumar, and Mark W. Post. 2012. Classifiers in Mising. In G. Hyslop, S. Morey, and M. W. Post, eds., *North East Indian Linguistics Volume 4*. 243–266. New Delhi: Cambridge University Press India. https://www.academia.edu/197857/Classifiers_in_Mising.

Dryer, Matthew S. 1992. The Greenbergian word order correlations. *Language* 68: 81–138. http://www.acsu.buffalo.edu/~dryer/DryerGreenbergian .pdf.

Dryer, Matthew S. 1996. Word order typology. In J. Jacobs, ed., *Handbook of Syntax*. Vol. 2. 1050–1065. Berlin: Mouton de Gruyter http:// www.acsu.buffalo.edu/~dryer/jacobs.pdf.

Dryer, Matthew S. 2008. Word order in Tibeto-Burman languages. *Linguistics of the Tibeto-Burman Area* 31 (1): 1–83. http://sealang.net /archives/ltba/pdf/LTBA-31.1.1.pdf.

Dryer, Matthew S. 2009. The Branching Direction Theory of Word Order Correlations Revisited. In S.Scalise, E.Magni and A.Bisetto, (as in Cinque 2009), eds., *Universals of Language Today*. 185–207. Dordrecht, Netherlands: Springer. http://www.acsu.buffalo.edu/~dryer /DryerBDTrevisited.pdf

Dryer, Matthew S. 2012. On the position of interrogative phrases and the order of complementizer and clause. In T. Graf, D. Paperno, A. Szabolcsi, and J. Tellings, eds., Theories of Everything: In Honor of Ed Keenan. Special issue, *UCLA Working Papers in Linguistics* 17: 72–79. http://phonetics.linguistics.ucla.edu/wpl/issues/wpl17/papers/11_dryer .pdf.

Dryer, Matthew S. 2018. On the order of demonstrative, numeral, adjective, and noun. *Language* 94 (4): 798–833. https://www.linguisticsociety.org/sites/default/files/05_94.4Dryer.pdf.

Dryer, Matthew S. 2019. The position of pronominal possessive words relative to other modifiers of nouns. Paper presented at ALT 13, the 13th Conference of the Association for Linguistic Typology, Pavia, September 4–6. ALT Book of Abstracts, 62–63. https://drive.google.com/file/d/1Mos92cIc_9rFSXk7jfFuX-lDAgrYcROC/view.

Duarte, Fábio Bonfim. 2019. The particle 'ke' as a differential object and subject marker in Ka'apor. *Boletim do Museu Paraense Emílio Goeldi: Ciências Humanas* 14 (3): 805–825. http://editora.museu-goeldi.br/bh/artigos/chv14n3_2019/particle(duarte).pdf.

Duffield, Nigel. 1995a. *Particles and projections in Irish syntax.* Dordrecht, Netherlands: Springer.

Duffield Nigel. 1995b. On the Number of Numeral Projections. Paper presented at the 1995 Conference of the Canadian Linguistic Association.

Duffield, Nigel. 1999. Final modals, adverbs and antisymmetry in Vietnamese. *Revue Québécoise de Linguistique* 27: 92–129. https://www.erudit.org/fr/revues/rql/1999-v27-n2-rql2949/603177ar.pdf.

Durie, Mark. 1985. *A Grammar of Acehnese on the Basis of a Dialect of North Aceh.* Dordrecht, Netherlands: Foris Publications.

Eguren, Luis, Olga Fernández-Soriano, and Amaya Mendikoetxea, eds., 2016. *Rethinking Parameters.* Oxford: Oxford University Press.

Enfield, Nick J. 2004. Adjectives in Lao. In R. M. W. Dixon and A. Aikhenvald, eds., *Adjective Classes: A Cross-linguistic Typology.* 323–347. Oxford: Oxford University Press.

Epps, Patience, Claire Bowern, Cynthia A. Hansen, Jane H. Hill, and Jason Zentz. 2012. On numeral complexity in hunter-gatherer languages. *Linguistic Typology* 16 (1): 41–109. https://jasonzentz.files.wordpress.com/2014/08/epps_et_al2012-lt.pdf.

Everaert, Martin, and Henk van Riemsdijk, eds. 2017. *The Wiley Blackwell Companion to Syntax.* 2nd ed. Hoboken, NJ: Wiley-Blackwell.

Ezard, Bryan. 1984. *The Tawala Language.* Vol. 1. Ukarumpa: Summer Institute of Linguistics. https://www.sil.org/resources/archives/31157.

Fan, Wenjia. 2019. *A Grammar of Lakkja, South China.* PhD Dissertation, University of Melbourne.

Fenger, Paula. 2020. *Words within Words: The Internal Syntax of Verbs*. PhD Dissertation, University of Connecticut. https://lingbuzz.net/lingbuzz/005431.

Fitzgerald, Charles Patrick. 1941. *The Tower of Five Glories; a Study of the Min Chia of Ta Li, Yunnan*. London: Cresset Press.

Forker, Diana. 2020. *A Grammar of Sanzhi Dargwa*. Berlin: Language Science Press. https://langsci-press.org/catalog/book/250.

Fukui, Naoki, and Yuji Takano. 1998. Symmetry in Syntax: Merge and Demerge. *Journal of East Asian Linguistics* 7: 27–86.

Fukui, Naoki, and Yuji Takano. 2000. Nominal structure: An extension of the symmetry principle. In Svenonius, *Derivation of VO and OV*. 219–254.

García-Vega, Michelle. 2018. Functions and uses of numeral classifiers in Upper Necaxa Totonac. *Anthropological Linguistics* 60 (4): 346–385.

Garzonio, Jacopo, and Cecilia Poletto. 2012. Sulla posizione degli avverbi nella struttura frasale in alcune varietà delle Marche. *Quaderni di Lavoro ASIt* 15: 23–43. http://asit.maldura.unipd.it/documenti/ql15/ASIt15_garzonio_poletto.pdf.

Gaved, Timothy J. D. 2020. *A Grammar of Mankanya: An Atlantic Language of Guinea-Bissau, Senegal and the Gambia*. PhD Dissertation, Rijksuniversiteit te Leiden. https://www.lotpublications.nl/Documents/561_fulltext.pdf.

Gell-Mann, Murray, and Merritt Ruhlen. 2011. The origin and evolution of word order. *PNAS* 108 (42): 17290–17295. https://authors.library.caltech.edu/59840/.

Getachew, Anteneh Yigzaw. 2014. *Grammatical Description and Documentation of Majang*. PhD Dissertation, Addis Ababa University. http://213.55.95.56/handle/123456789/16341

Getahun, Amare. 2018. The structure of Argobba nominal phrase. *Journal of African Languages and Linguistics* 39 (2): 127–151.

Goldberg, Adele. 2002. Persian auxiliaries. Ms., Princeton University.

Goral, D. R. 1978. Numeral classifier systems: A Southeast Asian cross-linguistic analysis. *Linguistics of the Tibeto-Burman Area* 4: 1–72.

Greenberg, Joseph H., 1963. Some universals of grammar with particular reference to the order of meaningful elements. In J. H. Greenberg, ed., *Universals of Language*. 73–113. Cambridge, MA: MIT Press.

Greenberg, Joseph H. 1972. Numeral classifiers and substantival number: Problems in the genesis of a linguistic type. *Working Papers on Language Universals* 9: 1–39. (Reprinted in Denning and Kemmer, *On Language*. 166–193.)

Greenberg, Joseph H. 1975. Dynamic aspects of word order in the numeral classifier. In C. N. Li, ed., *Word Order and Word Order Change*. 28–45. Austin: University of Texas Press.

Greenberg, Joseph H. 1989. The internal and external syntax of numerical expressions: Explaining language specific rules. *Belgian Journal of Linguistics* 4: 105–118.

Greenberg, Joseph H. 1990. Generalizations about numeral systems. In Denning and Kemmer, *On Language*. 271–309. (Originally in Greenberg et al., *Universals of Human Language*. 249–295)

Greenberg, Joseph H., Charles A. Ferguson, and Edith A. Moravcsik, eds. 1978. *Universals of Human Language, Volume 3: Word Structure*. Stanford, CA: Stanford University Press.

Guérois, Rozenn. 2015. *A Grammar of Cuwabo* (*Mozambique, Bantu P34*). Thèse de doctorat, Université Lumière Lyon 2. https://biblio.ugent.be/publication/8561497/file/8561498.pdf.

Guha, Ambalika. 2017. Focus and nominal ellipsis in the Bangla DP. In M. Y. Erlewine, ed., *Proceedings of GLOW in ASIA XI, Volume* 2. 73–86. MIT Working Papers in Linguistics 85. https://glowlinguistics.org/asia11/wp-content/uploads/sites/3/2017/11/v2-guha.pdf.

Güldemann, Tom. 2004. Linear order as a basic morphosyntactic factor in Non-Khoe Khoisan. Handout of a paper given at the Syntax of the World's Languages, Leipzig, August 8.

Haan, Johnson Welem. 2001. *The Grammar of Adang: A Papuan Language Spoken on the Island of Alor East Nusa Tenggara—Indonesia*. PhD Dissertation, University of Sydney. https://ses.library.usyd.edu.au/handle/2123/6413.

Haas, Mary. 1942. The use of numeral classifiers in Thai. *Language* 18: 201–205.

Hackstein, Olav. 2010. *Apposition and Nominal Classification in Indo-European and Beyond*. Vienna: Verlag der Österreichischen Akademie der Wissenschaften. https://www.academia.edu/14251053/Apposition_and_Nominal_Classification_in_Indo-European_and_Beyond.

Haegeman, Liliane. 1992. *Theory and Description in Generative Syntax. A Case Study in West Flemish.* Cambridge: Cambridge University Press.

Haegeman, Liliane. 1993a. The morphology and distribution of object clitics in West Flemish. *Studia Linguistica* (NS) 47: 57–94.

Haegeman, Liliane. 1993b. Some speculations on argument shift, clitics and crossing in West Flemish. In W. Abraham and J. Bayer, eds., *Linguistische Berichte: Dialektsyntax.* 131–160. Opladen: Westdeutscher Verlag.

Haegeman, Liliane. 1994. Verb raising as verb projection raising: Some empirical problems. *Linguistic Inquiry* 25: 509–522.

Haegeman, Liliane. 1996a. Object clitics in West Flemish. In A. Halpern and A. Zwicky, eds., *Second Position Clitics and Related Phenomena.* 135–164. Stanford, CA: CSLI Press.

Haegeman, Liliane. 1996b. The typology of syntactic positions: L-relatedness and the A/A' distinction. In W. Abraham, S. Epstein and J.-W. Zwart, eds., *Minimal Ideas.* 141–165. Amsterdam: Benjamins.

Haegeman, Liliane, and Henk C. van Riemsdijk. 1986. Verb projection raising and the typology of rules affecting verbs. *Linguistic Inquiry* 17: 417–466.

Haider, Hubert. 1992. Branching and discharge. *Arbeitspapiere des SFB 340, Nr. 23.* Stuttgart, Germany: University of Stuttgart.

Haider, Hubert. 2000. OV is more basic than VO. In Svenonius, *Derivation of VO and OV.* 45–67.

Haider, Hubert. 2013. *Symmetry Breaking in Syntax.* Cambridge: Cambridge University Press.

Haider, Hubert. 2015. Head directionality—in syntax and morphology. In A. Fábregas, J. Mateu, M. Putnam, eds., *Contemporary Linguistic Parameters.* 73–97. London: Bloomsbury.

Haider, Hubert. 2020a. *Final-over-Final—*Initial-over-Final—the universal asymmetry of functional projections. Ms., University of Salzburg. https://ling.auf.net/lingbuzz/005598.

Haider, Hubert. 2020b. VO-/OV-Base Ordering. Chapter 15 of *The Cambridge Handbook of German Linguistics.* 339–364. Cambridge: Cambridge University Press.

Hall, Barbara. 1964. Review of Šaumjan and Soboleva (1963). *Language* 40: 397–410.

Hall, David. 2015. *Spelling Out the Noun Phrase: Interpretation, Word Order, and the Problem of "Meaningless Movement."* PhD Dissertation, Queen Mary, University of London. https://qmro.qmul.ac.uk/xmlui/handle/123456789/12824.

Hall, David. 2019. Licensing D in classifier languages and "numeral blocking." In A. Aguilar-Guevara, J. Pozas Loyo, and V. Vásquez-Rojas Maldonado, eds., *Definiteness across Languages*. 221–257. Berlin: Language Science Press. https://drive.google.com/file/d/1xz8Ladp8vuT0J9KBKFlO44GqN6TqE0sh/view.

Hammarström, Harald. 2015. The basic word order typology: An exhaustive study. Slides of a paper presented in Leipzig, March 3. http://www.eva.mpg.de/fileadmin/content_files/linguistics/conferences/2015-diversity-linguistics/Hammarstroem_slides.pdf.

Hanna, William J. 1995. Relative clauses in Tai Lue. Research Report 119. Chiang Mai, Thailand: Payap Research and Development Institute, Payap University and Summer Institute of Linguistics. https://www.academia.edu/21721788/Relative_Clauses_in_Tai_Lue.

Harrison, Sheldon P. 1976. *Mokilese Reference Grammar*. Honolulu: The University Press of Hawai'i.

Harro, Gretchen, and Nancy Haynes. 1991. *Grammar Sketch of Yemba*. Yaoundé, Cameroon: SIL International. https://www.sil.org/resources/publications/entry/47892.

He, Chuansheng. 2015. Complex numerals in Mandarin Chinese are constituents. *Lingua* 164: 189–214.

Henderson, James. 1995. *Phonology and Grammar of Yele, Papua New Guinea*. Canberra: Pacific Linguistics. https://www.sil.org/resources/archives/22998.

Henderson, Mara. 2006. Between lexical and lexico-grammatical classification: Nominal classification in Sinhala. *Santa Barbara Papers in Linguistics* 17: 29–48. https://www.linguistics.ucsb.edu/sites/secure.lsit.ucsb.edu.ling.d7/files/sitefiles/research/papers/Working%20Papers%20Vol%2017.pdf.

Hendrick, Randall. 2000. Celtic initials. In Carnie and Guilfoyle, *Syntax of Verb Initial Languages*. 13–37.

Hendriks, Lotte Diana Herma. 2018. *Not Another Book on Verb Raising*. PhD Dissertation, University of Leiden. https://www.lotpublications.nl/Documents/487_fulltext.pdf.

Heny, Frank, and Barry Richards, eds. 1983. *Linguistic Categories: Auxiliaries and Related Puzzles. Volume One: Categories.* Dordrecht, Netherlands: Reidel.

Hepner, Mark. 2006. *Bargam Grammar Sketch.* Ukarumpa, Papua New Guinea: Summer Institute of Linguistics.

Her, One-Soon. 2017a. Deriving classifier word order typology, or Greenberg's Universal 20A, and Universal 20. *Linguistics* 55 (2): 265–303. http://www3.nccu.edu.tw/~osh/HER-Universal%2020A-POSTPRINT-LINGUISTICS.pdf.

Her, One-Soon. 2017b. Structure of numerals and numeral classifiers in Chinese: Historical and typological perspectives and cross-linguistic implications. *Language and Linguistics* 18 (1): 26–71. https://www.ling.sinica.edu.tw/item/en?act=journal&code=directory&volume=18&period=1.

Her, One-Soon, and Hui-Chin Tsai. 2020. Left is right, right is not: On the constituency of the classifier phrase in Chinese. *Language and Linguistics* 21 (1): 1–32. http://www3.nccu.edu.tw/~osh/publication/A50-Left%20is%20Right-L&L-Post-Print.pdf.

Her, One-Soon, Jing-Perng Chen, and Hui-Chin Tsai. 2015. Justifying silent elements in syntax: The case of a silent numeral, a silent classifier, and two silent nouns in Mandarin Chinese. *International Journal of Chinese Linguistics* 2 (2): 193–226. http://www3.nccu.edu.tw/~osh/justifying%20silent%20elements%20in%20syntax%20HER%20%EF%BC%86TSAI-post-print.pdf.

Heycock Caroline, and Roberto Zamparelli. 2005. Friends and colleagues: Plurality, coordination, and the structure of DP. *Natural Language Semantics* 13: 201–270.

Hinterhölzl, Roland. 2001. Event-related adjuncts and the OV/VO distinction. *Proceedings of the 20th West Coast Conference of Formal Linguistics (WCCFL)* 20: 276–289. https://arca.unive.it/retrieve/handle/10278/35986/26535/WCCFL2001paper.pdf.

Hinterhölzl, Roland. 2002. Parametric variation and scrambling in English. In W. Abraham and C. J-W. Zwart, eds., *Studies in Comparative Germanic Syntax.* 131–151. Amsterdam: Benjamins. https://core.ac.uk/download/pdf/53173786.pdf.

Hinterhölzl, Roland. 2006a. The phase condition and cyclic spell out: Evidence from VP-topicalization. In M. Frascarelli, ed., *Phases of*

Interpretation. 237–259. Berlin: Mouton de Gruyter. https://iris.unive.it/retrieve/handle/10278/28517/22176/Phasecondition%26cyclicspellout.pdf

Hinterhölzl, Roland. 2006b. *Scrambling, Remnant Movement and Restructuring in West Germanic.* Oxford: Oxford University Press.

Hinterhölzl, Roland. 2009. A phase-based comparative approach to modification and word order in Germanic. *Syntax* 12 (3): 242–284. https://iris.unive.it/retrieve/handle/10278/26525/22414/synt129.pdf.

Hinterhölzl, Roland. 2016. On the variable nature of head final effects in German and English: An interface account. In E. Bidese, F. Cognola and M. C. Moroni, eds., *Theoretical Approaches to Linguistic Variation.* 177–202. Amsterdam: Benjamins. https://iris.unive.it/retrieve/handle/10278/3680685/85736/07hin.pdf.

Hinterhölzl, Roland. 2018. Implications of displaced affixes for the analysis of non-finite morphology and the headedness of VP in German. *Zeitschrift für Dialektologie und Linguistik* 83 (3): 69–88. https://iris.unive.it/retrieve/handle/10278/3699256/127737/Displaced-Affixes-2018.pdf.

Hinterhölzl, Roland. 2020. V2 and topicalization in Germanic and Romance. Ms., Ca' Foscari University, Venice.

Holmberg, Anders. 2000. Deriving OV order in Finnish. In Svenonius, *Derivation of VO and OV.* 123–152.

Holmberg, Anders. 2017. The Final-over-Final Condition and linearization in generative grammar. In Sheehan et al., *Final-over-Final Condition.* 43–77.

Holmberg, Anders, and Christer Platzack. 2005. The Scandinavian languages. In Cinque and Kayne, *Oxford Handbook of Comparative Syntax.* 420–458.

Holmer, Arthur. 1996. *A Parametric Grammar of Seediq.* Lund, Sweden: Lund University Press.

Holmer, Arthur. 2005. Seediq—antisymmetry and final particles in a Formosan VOS language. In A. Carnie, H. Harley, S. A. Dooley, eds., *Verb First: On the Syntax of Verb-Initial Languages.* Amsterdam: Benjamins. https://portal.research.lu.se/portal/files/4585496/625666.pdf.

Holton, Gary. 2003. *Tobelo.* Munich: Lincom Europa.

Hopkins, Nicholas Arthur. 1967. *The Chuj Language.* PhD Dissertation, The University of Chicago.

Hsieh, Miao-Ling. 2008. *The Internal Structure of Noun Phrases in Chinese*. Taipei, Taiwan: Crane.

Huang, Chenglong. 2004. *A Reference Grammar of the Puxi Variety of Qiang*. PhD Dissertation, City University of Hong Kong.

Huang, C.-T. James. 1982. *Logical Relations in Chinese and the Theory of Grammar*. PhD Dissertation, MIT. https://dspace.mit.edu/handle/1721.1/15215.

Huang, C.-T. James, and Masao Ochi. 2011. Classifiers and nominal structure: A parametric approach and its consequences. In M.-L. Gao, ed., *Universals and Variation* (*Proceedings of GLOW in Asia VIII, 2010*). 191–197. Beijing: Beijing Language and Culture University Press.

Huang, C.-T. James, and Masao Ochi. 2014. Remarks on classifiers and nominal structure in East Asian. In C.-T. J. Huang and F.-H. Liu, eds., *Peaches and Plums*. 53–74. Taipei, Taiwan: Institute of Linguistics, Academia Sinica. https://scholar.harvard.edu/files/ctjhuang/files/2014_haungochi.pdf?m=1443108945.

Huang, C.-T. James, Y.-H. Audrey Li, and Yafei Li. 2009. *The Syntax of Chinese*. Cambridge: Cambridge University Press.

Hudson, Grover. 1972. Is deep structure linear? *UCLA Papers in Syntax* 2: 51–77. (Reprinted in Meisel and Pam, *Linear Order and Generative Theory*. 23–69.)

Hurford, James R. 2003. The interaction between numerals and nouns. In Plank, *Noun Phrase Structure in the Languages of Europe*. 561–620.

Hwang, Shin Ja J. 1991. Terms of address in Korean and American cultures. *Intercultural Communication Studies* I (2): 117–134. https://web.uri.edu/iaics/files/08-Shin-Ja-J.-Hwang.pdf.

Ikoro, Suanu M. 1994. Numeral classifiers in Kana. *Journal of African Languages and Linguistics* 15: 7–28.

Inglis, Douglas. 2003. Conceptual structure of numeral classifiers in Thai. In E. H. Casad and G. B. Palmer, eds., *Cognitive Linguistics and Non-Indo European Languages*. 223–246. Berlin: Mouton de Gruyter. https://www.sil.org/resources/archives/63397.

Ionin, Tania, and Ora Matushansky. 2006. The composition of complex cardinals. *Journal of Semantics* 23 (4): 315–360. https://www.academia.edu/26118937/The_Composition_of_Complex_Cardinals

Ionin, Tania, and Ora Matushansky. 2018. *Cardinals: The Syntax and Semantics of Cardinal-Containing Expressions*. Cambridge, MA: MIT Press.

Isaac, Baridisi H. 2016. Numeral classifiers in Gokana and Kana. In O. Ndimele, E. S. L. Chan, eds., *The Numeral Systems of Nigerian Languages*. 267–277. Port Harcourt, Nigeria: M and J Grand Orbit Communications.

Jayaseelan, K. A. 2010. Stacking, stranding and pied piping: A proposal about word order. *Syntax* 13: 298–330. (Reprinted in K. A. Jayaseelan and R. Amritavalli. 2017. *Dravidian Syntax and Universal Grammar*. 93–125. New York: Oxford University Press.)

Jenks, Peter. 2014. Head movement in Moro DPs: Evidence for a unified theory of movement. *Proceedings of the 31st West Coast Conference on Formal Linguistics*. 248–257. Somerville, MA: Cascadilla. http://www.lingref.com/cpp/wccfl/31/paper3027.pdf.

Johnson, Kyle. 1991. Object positions. *Natural Language and Linguistic Theory* 9: 577–636.

Johnson, Kyle. 2001. What VP ellipsis can do, what it can't, but not why. In M. Baltin and C. Collins, eds., *The Handbook of Contemporary Syntactic Theory*. 439–479. Oxford: Blackwell.

Joswig, Andreas. 2019. *The Majang language*. PhD Dissertation, Rijksuniversiteit te Leiden. https://www.lotpublications.nl/Documents/536_fulltext.pdf.

Kane, Fatou Cisse. 2020. *Description Générale de l'Oniyan*. PhD Dissertation, Universität zu Köln. https://kups.ub.uni-koeln.de/10555/.

Kayne, Richard S. 1994. *The Antisymmetry of Syntax*. Cambridge, MA: MIT Press. https://as.nyu.edu/content/dam/nyu-as/linguistics/documents/richie/Kayne%200217%20-The%20Antisymmetry%20of%20Syntax.pdf.

Kayne, Richard S. 2002. On some prepositions that look DP-internal: English *of* and French *De*. *Catalan Journal of Linguistics* 1: 71–115. (Reprinted in Kayne, *Movement and Silence*. 136–175.)

Kayne, Richard S. 2003a. Antisymmetry and Japanese. *English Linguistics* 20: 1–40. (Reprinted Kayne, *Movement and Silence*. 215–240.)

Kayne, Richard S. 2003b. Silent years, silent hours. In L.-O. Delsing, C. Falk, G. Josefsson, and H. Sigurdsson, eds., *Grammar in Focus: Festschrift for Christer Platzack 18 November 2003. Volume II*. 209–226.

Lund, Sweden: Department of Scandinavian Languages, University of Lund. (Reprinted in Kayne, *Movement and Silence*. 241–260.)

Kayne, Richard S. 2004a. Here and there. In C. Leclère, E. Laporte, M. Piot, and M. Silberztein, eds., *Lexique Syntaxe, et Lexique-Grammaire/Syntax, Lexis and Lexicon Grammar: Papers in Honour of Maurice Gross*. 253–275. Amsterdam: Benjamins. (Reprinted in Kayne, *Movement and Silence*. 65–84.)

Kayne, Richard S. 2004b. Prepositions as probes. In Belletti, *Structures and Beyond*. 192–212. (Reprinted in Kayne, *Movement and Silence*. 85–104.)

Kayne, Richard S. 2005a. *Movement and Silence*. New York: Oxford University Press. https://as.nyu.edu/content/dam/nyu-as/linguistics/documents/richie/Kayne%200317%20Movement_and_Silence.pdf.

Kayne, Richard S. 2005b. Some notes on comparative syntax, with special reference to English and French. In Cinque and Kayne, *Oxford Handbook of Comparative Syntax*. 3–69. (Reprinted in Kayne, *Movement and Silence*. 277–333.)

Kayne, Richard S. 2006a. A note on the syntax of numerical bases. In Y. Suzuki, ed., *In Search of the Essence of Language Science: Festschrift for Professor Heizo Nakajima on the Occasion of His Sixtieth Birthday*. 21–41. Tokyo: Hituzi Syobo. (Reprinted in Kayne. 2010. *Comparison and Contrasts*. 57–72.) https://as.nyu.edu/content/dam/nyu-as/linguistics/documents/kayne-publications/Kayne0705NumericalBases.pdf.

Kayne, Richard S. 2006b. On parameters and on principles of pronunciation. In H. Broekhuis, N. Corver, R. Huybregts, U. Kleinhenz, and J. Koster, eds., *Organizing Grammar: Linguistic Studies in Honor of Henk van Riemsdijk*. 289–299. Berlin: Mouton de Gruyter. (Reprinted in Kayne, *Comparison and Contrasts*. 73–81.)

Kayne, Richard S. 2007. On the syntax of quantity in English. In J. Bayer, T. Bhattacharya, and M. T. H. Babu, eds., *Linguistic Theory and South Asian Languages: Essays in Honour of K. A. Jayaseelan*. 73–105. Amsterdam: Benjamins. (Originally "A Note on the Syntax of Quantity in English" in Kayne, *Movement and Silence*. 176–214.)

Kayne, Richard S. 2008a. Antisymmetry and the lexicon. *Linguistic Variation Yearbook* 8: 1–31. (Reprinted in Kayne, *Comparison and Contrasts*. 165–189.) https://as.nyu.edu/content/dam/nyu-as/linguistics/documents/kayne-publications/Kayne0208AntisymmetryLexicon.pdf.

Kayne, Richard S. 2008b. Some preliminary comparative remarks on French and Italian definite articles. In R. Freidin, C. P. Otero, and M. L. Zubizarreta, eds., *Foundational Issues in Linguistic Theory: Essays in Honor of Jean-Roger Vergnaud*. 291–321. Cambridge, MA: MIT Press. (Reprinted in Kayne, *Comparison and Contrasts*. 3–28.) https://as.nyu.edu/content/dam/nyu-as/linguistics/documents/kayne-publications/Kayne1004DefiniteArticles.pdf.

Kayne, Richard S. 2010. *Comparison and Contrasts*. New York: Oxford University Press.

Kayne, Richard S. 2012. A note on *Grand* and its silent entourage. *Studies in Chinese Linguistics* 33 (2):71–85. (Reprinted in Kayne, *Questions of Syntax*. 258–271.) http://www.cuhk.edu.hk/ics/clrc/scl_33_2/kayne.pdf

Kayne, Richard S. 2013. Why are there no directionality parameters? In Biberauer and Sheehan, *Theoretical Approaches to Disharmonic Word Order*. 219–244. (Reprinted in Kayne, *Questions of Syntax*. 275–303.) https://as.nyu.edu/content/dam/nyu-as/linguistics/documents/kayne-publications/Kayne0810WhyAreThereNoDirectionalityParameters.pdf.

Kayne, Richard S. 2016. The silence of heads. *Studies in Chinese Linguistics* 37: 1–37. (Reprinted in Kayne, *Questions of Syntax*. 95–126.) https://content.sciendo.com/view/journals/scl/37/1/scl.37.issue-1.xml.

Kayne, Richard S. 2017. English *one* and *ones* as complex determiners. In G. Sengupta, S. Sircar, M. G. Raman, and R. Balusu, eds., *Perspectives on the Architecture and Acquisition of Syntax: Essays in Honor of R. Amritavalli*. 77–114. Singapore: Springer. (Reprinted in Kayne, *Questions of Syntax*. 199–238.) https://as.nyu.edu/content/dam/nyu-as/linguistics/documents/kayne-publications/Kayne0615One.pdf.

Kayne, Richard S. 2018. The place of linear order in the language faculty. Paper presented at the University of Venice, January 16. (Printed in *Linguistic Analysis* 42 (2019–2020): 441–471.) https://as.nyu.edu/content/dam/nyu-as/linguistics/documents/Kayne%200118%20Venice%20The%20Place%20of%20Linear%20Order%20in%20the%20Language%20Faculty.pdf.

Kayne, Richard S. 2019. *Questions of Syntax*. New York: Oxford University Press.

Kayne, Richard S. 2020a. Antisymmetry and externalization. Ms. New York University. https://ling.auf.net/lingbuzz/005554.

Kayne, Richard S. 2020b. Some thoughts on *one* and *two* and other numerals. In L. Franco and P. Lorusso, eds., *Linguistic Variation: Structure and Interpretation.* 335–356. Berlin: Mouton de Gruyter. (Reprinted in Kayne, *Questions of Syntax.* 181–198.) https://as.nyu.edu/content/dam/nyu-as/linguistics/documents/kayne-publications/Kayne0516Numeral.pdf.

Keenan, Edward L. 1978. The syntax of subject-final languages. In Lehmann, *Syntactic Typology.* 267–328.

Kerr, Harland B. 1988. Cotabato Manobo grammar. *Studies in Philippine Linguistics* 7 (1): 1–123. https://www.sil.org/resources/archives/25582.

Kibona, Neema Jangstony. 2019. An analysis of a noun phrase in Ichindali. *Journal of Language Teaching and Research* 10 (5): 906–913. http://www.academypublication.com/issues2/jltr/vol10/05/02.pdf.

Kießling, Roland. 2018. Niger-Congo numeral classifiers in a diachronic perspective. In W. B. McGregor and S. Wichmann, eds., *The Diachrony of Classification Systems.* 33–75. Amsterdam: Benjamins.

Kim, Alan Hyun-Oak. 1995. Word order at the noun phrase level in Japanese: Quantifier constructions and discourse functions. In P. Downing and M. Noonan, eds., *Word Order in Discourse.* 199–246. Amsterdam: Benjamins.

Klamer, Marian, and František Kratochvíl, eds., 2014. *Number and Quantity in East Nusantara: Papers from 12-ICAL, Volume 1.* Canberra, Australia: Asia-Pacific Linguistics. https://openresearch-repository.anu.edu.au/handle/1885/11917.

Koopman, Hilda. 2002. Derivations and complexity filters. In Alexiadou et al., *Dimensions of Movement.* 151–189. https://linguistics.ucla.edu/wp-content/uploads/2017/04/Derivations-and-complexity-%EF%AC%81lters.pdf.

Koopman, Hilda. 2005. Korean (and Japanese) morphology from a syntactic perspective. *Linguistic Inquiry* 36: 601–633.

Koopman, Hilda, and Anna Szabolcsi. 2000. *Verbal Complexes.* Cambridge, MA: MIT Press.

Kornfilt, Jaklin. 1996. On copular clitic forms in Turkish. *ZAS Papers in Linguistics* 6: 96–114. https://www.academia.edu/30792139/On_Copular_Clitic_Forms_in_Turkish.

Kornfilt, Jaklin. 2012. Revisiting "suspended affixation" and other coordinate mysteries. In L. Brugè et al., eds., *Functional Heads. The Cartography of Syntactic Structures, Volume 7.* 181–196. New York: Oxford University Press.

Koster, Jan. 1974. Het werkwoord als spiegelcentrum. *Spektator* 3: 601–618. https://www.dbnl.org/tekst/kost007werk01_01/kost007werk01_01.pdf.

Koster, Jan. 1975. Dutch as an SOV language. *Linguistic Analysis* 1: 111–136. https://www.dbnl.org/tekst/kost007dutc01_01/kost007dutc01_01_0001.php.

Koster, Jan. 2000. Pied piping and the word orders of English and Dutch. In M. Hirotani, A. Coetzee, N. Hall, and J.-Y.Kim, eds., *NELS 30: Proceedings of the North East Linguistic Society.* 415–426. Amherst, MA: GLSA. http://www.let.rug.nl/koster/papers/koster.pdf.

Kouneli, Maria. 2019. *The Syntax of Number and Modification: An Investigation of the Kipsigis DP.* PhD Dissertation, New York University. https://ling.auf.net/lingbuzz/004599.

Krapova, Iliyana, and Guglielmo Cinque. 2008. On the order of wh-phrases in Bulgarian multiple wh-fronting. In G. Zybatow, L. Szucsich, U. Junghanns, and R. Meyer, eds., *Formal Description of Slavic Languages: The Fifth Conference, Leipzig 2003.* 318–336. Frankfurt am Main, Germany: Peter Lang. https://citeseerx.ist.psu.edu/viewdoc/download?doi=10.1.1.528.4215&rep=rep1&type=pdf.

Krifka, Manfred. 1985. Harmony or consistency? Review of John A. Hawkins, *Word Order Universals. Theoretical Linguistics* 12: 73–94. https://amor.cms.hu-berlin.de/~h2816i3x/Publications/Krifka%201985%20Harmony.PDF.

Krifka, Manfred. 1995. Common nouns: A contrastive analysis of Chinese and English. In G. N. Carlson and F. J. Pelletier, eds., *The Generic Book.* 398–411. Chicago: University of Chicago Press. https://amor.cms.hu-berlin.de/~h2816i3x/Publications/Krifka%20Common%20Nouns.PDF.

Kung, Susan S. 2007a. *A Descriptive Grammar of Huehuetla Tepehua.* PhD Dissertation, The University of Texas at Austin. http://repositories.lib.utexas.edu/handle/2152/3137.

Kung, Susan S. 2007b. Numeral classifiers in Lhiimaqalhqama'. In F. Hoyt, N. Seifert, A. Teodorescu, and J.White, eds., *Morphosyntax of*

Underrepresented Languages. 185–201. Texas Linguistics Society 9. Stanford, CA: CSLI Publications. http://web.stanford.edu/group/cslipublications/cslipublications/TLS/TLS9-2005/TLS9_Kung_Susan.pdf.

Kurabe, Keita. 2012. Jingpho dialogue texts with grammatical notes. *Asian and African Languages and Linguistics* 7: 121–153. http://repository.tufs.ac.jp/bitstream/10108/73109/1/aall7_8.pdf.

Kutscher, Silvia. 2001. *Nomen und Nominales Syntagma im Lasischen: Eine Descriptive Analyse des Dialekts von Ardeşen.* Munich: Lincom Europa.

LaPolla, Randy J. 2017. Dúlóng 獨龍 Language. In R.Sybesma, ed., *Encyclopedia of Chinese Language and Linguistics, vol.2.* Leiden: Brill.

Larson, Richard K. 1988. On the double object construction. *Linguistic Inquiry* 21: 589–632.

Lawton, Ralph S. 1980. *The Kiriwinan Classifiers.* MA Thesis, The Australian National University. https://openresearch-repository.anu.edu.au/handle/1885/132948.

Lawton, Ralph S. 1993. *Topics in the Description of Kiriwina.* Edited by Malcolm Ross and Janet Ezard. Canberra: Pacific Linguistics (The Australian National University). https://openresearch-repository.anu.edu.au/bitstream/1885/145793/1/PL-D84.pdf.

Lee, Sung-Woo. 2011. *Eastern Tamang Grammar Sketch.* MA Thesis. Graduate Institute of Applied Linguistics, Dallas. https://www.sil.org/resources/archives/42567

Lee, Wei-Wei. 2016. *The Expression and Conceptualization of Time in Kavalan (Austronesian, Taiwan).* MA Thesis, Rijksuniversiteit te Leiden. https://openaccess.leidenuniv.nl/handle/1887/45363.

Lehmann, Winfred P. 1978a. The great underlying ground-plans. In Lehmann, *Syntactic Typology.* 3–56. https://liberalarts.utexas.edu/lrc/resources/books/typology/1-ground-plans.php.

Lehmann, Winifred P., ed. 1978b. *Syntactic Typology: Studies in the Phenomenology of Language.* Austin: University of Texas Press.

Leu, Thomas. 2008. *The Internal Syntax of Determiners.* PhD Dissertation, New York University. Published in Special issue, *Groninger Arbeiten zur Germanistischen Linguistik* 47: 1–224. https://ugp.rug.nl/GAGL/article/view/30489/27789.

Li, Yen-hui Audrey. 2013. P-insertion and ellipsis. *Studies in Chinese Linguistics* 34: 99–128. http://www.cuhk.edu.hk/ics/clrc/scl_34_2/li.pdf.

Li, Yen-hui Audrey. 2014. Structure of noun phrases: Left or right? *Taiwan Journal of Linguistics* 12 (2): 1–32. http://tjl.nccu.edu.tw/main/uploads/0805a_12.2__.1_1_.pdf.

Liao, Wei-wen Roger, and Yuyun Iris Wang. 2011. Multiple-classifier constructions and nominal expressions in Chinese. *Journal of East Asian Linguistics* 20: 145–168.

Libert, Alan. 2006. *Ambipositions*. Munich: Lincom Europa.

Lin, Hsiu-hsu. 2005. The grammaticalization of tense/aspect auxiliaries in Seediq. *Concentric: Studies in Linguistics* 31: 111–132. http://ir.lib.cyut.edu.tw:8080/bitstream/310901800/9734/1/sdq_musa_concentric_final_draft.pdf.

Lin, Jo-Wang. 1997. Chinese noun phrase structure: DP or NP?. In F.-f. Tsao and H. S. Wang eds., *Chinese Language and Linguistics III: Morphology and Lexicon*. 401–434. Taipei, Taiwan: Academia Sinica.

Livingston, Andrew. 2016. *East Uvean. A Condensed Grammar.* MA Thesis, University of Washington. https://digital.lib.washington.edu/researchworks/bitstream/handle/1773/37169/Livingston_washington_0250O_16252.pdf?sequence=1.

Lu, Bingfu. No date. Ordering of time, duration, location, instrument, manner. Ms., University of Southern California.

Lynch, John Malcolm Ross, and Terry Crowley, eds. 2011. *The Oceanic Languages.* London: Routledge.

Macdonald, Catherine Marie. 2014. *Functional Projections and Non-Local Relations in Tongan Nominal Phrases*. PhD Dissertation, University of Toronto. https://tspace.library.utoronto.ca/bitstream/1807/68305/1/Macdonald_Catherine_M_201411_PhD_thesis.pdf.

Maling, Joan. 1983. Transitive adjectives: A case of categorial reanalysis. In Heny and Richards, *Linguistic Categories*. 253–289.

Mallinson, Graham and Barry J. Blake. 1981. *Language Typology: cross-linguistic studies in syntax*. Amsterdam: North-Holland.

Manzini, M. Rita. 2021. Chomsky's (2020) Links and linker phenomena. *Quaderni di Linguistica e Studi Orientali (Qulso)* 7: 89–102. https://oaj.fupress.net/index.php/bsfm-qulso/article/view/12004/10228.

Manzini, M. Rita and Leonardo M. Savoia. 2007. *A Unification of Morphology and Syntax. Investigations into Romance and Albanian Dialects.* London: Routledge.

Massam, Diane. 2000. VSO and VOS: Aspects of Niuean word order. In Carnie and Guilfoyle, *Syntax of Verb Initial Languages.* 97–116.

Massam, Diane. 2001. Pseudo noun incorporation in Niuean. *Natural Language and Linguistic Theory* 19: 153–197.

Massam, Diane. 2010. Deriving inverse order. In R. Mercado, E. Potsdam, and L. D. Travis, eds., *Austronesian and Theoretical Linguistics.* 271–296. Amsterdam: Benjamins.

Mateo Toledo, Eladio. 2017. Q'anjob'al. In Aissen et al., *Mayan Languages.* 533–569.

Matushansky, Ora. 2008a. On the attributive nature of superlatives. *Syntax* 11: 26–90.

Matushansky, Ora. 2008b. On the linguistic complexity of proper names. *Linguistics and Philosophy* 21: 573–627.

Mbuvi, Martha Mungai Katunga. 2005. *The Syntax of Kikamba Noun Modification.* MA Thesis, University of Nairobi. http://erepository.uonbi.ac.ke/handle/11295/17849.

Medeiros, David P. 2017. Stack-sorting: Universal 20 and beyond. Ms., University of Arizona. Paper presented at the POL Symposium, Tokyo, 2016. http://davidpmedeiros.com/wp-content/uploads/2017/02/Stack-sorting-Universal-20-and-beyond.pdf.

Medeiros, David P. 2018. ULTRA: Universal grammar as a universal parser. *Frontiers of Psychology* 9: 155. https://www.frontiersin.org/articles/10.3389/fpsyg.2018.00155/full.

Meinunger, André. 2015. Complex numeral expressions: A plea for grafts. *Syntax* 18 (2): 103–123.

Meisel, Jürgen M. and Martin D. Pam, eds. 1979. *Linear Order and Generative Theory.* Amsterdam: Benjamins.

Mekonnen, Assefa. 2010. *Relative Clause in Gawwada.* MA Thesis, Addis Ababa University. http://213.55.95.56/handle/123456789/16261.

Merrifield, Judith Thomas. 2010. *Yao'an Lolo Grammar Sketch.* MA Thesis, Graduate Institute of Applied Linguistics, Dallas. https://studylib.net/doc/18725547/yao-an-lolo-grammar-sketch.

Metboki, Yakob, and Kate Bellamy. 2014. Expressions of quantity in the Amanuban dialect of Uab Meto. In Klamer and Kratochvíl, *Number and Quantity in East Nusantara*. 60–78.

Miller, Vera Grace. 1976. *An Overview of Stiêng Grammar*. MA Thesis, University of North Dakota. (Also in *Work Papers of the Summer Institute of Linguistics, University of North Dakota Session* 20: article 7.) https://commons.und.edu/sil-work-papers/vol20/iss1/7/.

Moltmann, Friederike. 2021. The mass-count distinction and Davidsonian events: A truthmaker-based approach. Ms., Ca' Foscari University, Venice.

Moodie, Jonathan Paul. 2019. *A Grammar of the Lopit Language*. PhD Dissertation, The University of Melbourne. https://minerva-access.unimelb.edu.au/handle/11343/227686.

Morita, Chigusa. 2011. Three types of direct modification APs. *Linguistic Research* 27: 89–102. https://www.academia.edu/21084980/Three_Types_of_Direct_Modification_Aps.

Moro, Andrea, and Ian Roberts. 2021. Unstable structures and labelling algorithm. Paper presented at the 46th Incontro di Grammatica Generativa, Siena, February 23–26. *IGG46 Book of Abstracts*. 61–62. http://www.ciscl.unisi.it/igg46/book_of_abstracts-IGG46.pdf.

Mosel, Ulrike (with Yvonne Thiesen). 2007. *The Teop Sketch Grammar*. Ms., University of Kiel. https://www.smg.surrey.ac.uk/media/1147/teop_sketch_grammar_may07.pdf

Moser, Mary B. 1977. Articles in Seri. *Work Papers of the Summer Institute of Linguistics, University of North Dakota Session* 21: article 10. https://commons.und.edu/cgi/viewcontent.cgi?article=1229&context=sil-work-papers.

Mous, Maarten. 1992. *A Grammar of Iraqw*. PhD Dissertation, Rijksuniversiteit te Leiden. https://www.academia.edu/825349/A_grammar_of_Iraqw.

Mous, Maarten. 2007. *A Sketch of Iraqw Grammar*. Ms. Leiden: Leiden University. https://www.academia.edu/3507742/A_Sketch_of_Iraqw_Grammar.

Muromatsu, Keiko. 1998. *On the Syntax of Classifiers*. PhD Dissertation, University of Maryland.

Nchare, Abdoulaye Laziz. 2012. *The Grammar of Shupamem*. PhD Dissertation, New York University. http://www.laziz.hasmandesign.com/images/NAL%20Dissertation%202012.pdf.

Neeleman, Ad, and Fred Weerman. 1993. The balance between syntax and morphology: Dutch particles and resultatives. *Natural Language and Linguistic Theory* 11: 433–475.

Nekitel, Otto. 1985. *Sociolinguistic Aspects of Abu': A Papuan Language of the Sepik Area, Papua New Guinea*. PhD Dissertation, Australian National University, Canberra. https://openresearch-repository.anu.edu.au/handle/1885/132442.

Nguyen, Tuong Hung. 2004. *The Structure of the Vietnamese Noun Phrase*. PhD Dissertation, Boston University.

Niederer, Barbara. 2011. La langue hmong. In E. Bonvini, J. Busuttil, and A. Peyraube, eds., *Dictionnaire des Langues*. 1285–1299. Paris: Presses Universitaires de France.

Nilsen, Øystein. 2003. *Eliminating Positions: Syntax and Semantics of Sentence Modification*. PhD Dissertation, Universiteit Utrecht.

Ntelitheos, Dimitrios. 2004. *Syntax of Elliptical and Discontinuous Nominals*. MA Thesis, UCLA. https://linguistics.ucla.edu/general/matheses/Ntelitheos_UCLA_MA_2004.pdf.

Olsen, Neil Hayes. 2014. *A Descriptive Grammar of Kơho-Sre: A Mon-Khmer Language*. PhD Dissertation, The University of Utah, Salt Lake City. https://collections.lib.utah.edu/dl_files/05/bd/05bd65d92245f7554dd76a8f6895678da3adab44.pdf.

Ouwayda, Sarah, and Ur Shlonsky. 2015. Order in the DP! On word order and the structure of the DP. *LSA Annual Meeting Extended Abstracts*. 18: 1–5. https://journals.linguisticsociety.org/proceedings/index.php/ExtendedAbs/article/view/3019.

Ouwayda, Sarah, and Ur Shlonsky. 2017. Word order variation in Lebanese Arabic DPs: In support of low numerals. *Linguistic Inquiry* 48 (1): 181–193.

Palmer, Bill. 2009. *Kokota Grammar*. Honolulu: University of Hawai'i Press.

Palosaari, Naomi Elizabeth. 2011. *Topics in Mocho' Phonology and Morphology*. PhD Dissertation, The University of Utah, Salt Lake City. https://collections.lib.utah.edu/dl_files/1c/e5/1ce544ddd9a66d8d2afda0406d75166934c90889.pdf.

Panayidou, Fryni. 2013. *(In)flexibility in Adjective Ordering*. PhD Dissertation, Queen Mary College, London. https://www.qmul.ac.uk/sllf/media/sllf-new/department-of-linguistics/30-QMOPAL-Panayidou.pdf.

Partee, Barbara Hall, Alice G. B. ter Meulen, and Robert E. Wall. 1990. *Mathematical Methods in Linguistics*. Dordrecht, Netherlands: Kluwer.

Paul, Ileana M. 2002. The syntactic encoding of topic and focus. *Georgetown Working Papers in Formal Linguistics* 2: 247–261. https://ir.lib.uwo.ca/frenchpub/83.

Pearson, Matthew. 2000. Two types of VO languages. In Svenonius, *Derivation of VO and OV*. 327–363.

Pearson, Matthew. 2001. *The Clause Structure of Malagasy: A Minimalist Approach*. PhD Dissertation, University of California, Los Angeles. https://linguistics.ucla.edu/images/stories/pearson.%202000.pdf.

Pearson, Matthew. 2007. Predicate fronting and constituent order in Malagasy. Ms. Reed College. https://www.reed.edu/linguistics/pearson/papers/VOSpaper.pdf.

Philip, Joy N. 2010. Harmonic word order constraints are not created equal: The Final-over-Final Constraint as an epiphenomenon. Paper presented at the 5th Newcastle Postgraduate Conference in Linguistics, March 23. https://discovery.ucl.ac.uk/id/eprint/88638/1/2010_Harmonic.pdf.

Philip, Joy N. 2012. *Subordinating and Coordinating Linkers*. PhD Dissertation, University College, London. https://discovery.ucl.ac.uk/id/eprint/1349441/1/Philip_Thesis.pdf.

Picallo, M. Carme. 2008. Gender and number in Romance. *Lingue e Linguaggio* 7: 47–66. https://clt.uab.cat/publicacions_clt/GenderandNumber.pdf.

Plank, Frans. 2003a. Double articulation. In Plank, *Noun Phrase Structure in the Languages of Europe*. 337–395.

Plank, Frans, ed. 2003b. *Noun Phrase Structure in the Languages of Europe*. Berlin: Mouton de Gruyter.

Platzack, Christer. 1982. Transitive adjectives in Swedish. A phenomeon with implications for the theory of abstract case. *Linguistic Review* 2: 39–56.

Platzack, Christer. 2014. Predicative adjectives with NP complement(s): A case of optional head movement. In K. Helgesson et al., eds., *Fint språk/Good Language: Festskrift till Lars-Gunnar Andersson*. 129–142. Gothenburg, Sweden: Meijerbergs arkiv för svensk ordforskning. https://gupea.ub.gu.se/handle/2077/54761.

Polinsky, Maria. 1997. Dominance in precedence: SO/OS languages. In K. Singer, R. Eggbert, and G. Anderson, eds., *CLS 33: Papers from tThe Panels*. 253–269. Chicago: Chicago

Polinsky, Maria, and Lilla Magyar. 2020. Headedness and the lexicon: The case of verb-to-noun ratios. *Languages* 5: 9. doi:10.3390/languages 5010009.

Pollock, Jean-Yves. 1989. Verb movement, universal grammar, and the structure of IP. *Linguistic Inquiry* 10: 365–424.

Post, Mark William. 2007. *A Grammar of Galo*. PhD Dissertation, La Trobe University. https://www.academia.edu/197280/A_Grammar_of_Galo.

Prisecaru, Luminiţa. 2015. *A Brief Grammar of the Ale Language*. Addis Ababa: Comprehensive Plan for Ethiopia (C.P.) and Summer Institute of Linguistics, Ethiopia.

Quesada, Juan Diego. 1999. Chibchan, with special reference to participant-highlighting. *Linguistic Typology* 3: 209–258.

Quesada, Juan Diego. 2000. *A Grammar of Teribe*. Munich: Lincom Europa.

Quesada, Juan Diego. 2012. *Gramática del Buglere*. Quito, Ecuador: Editorial Abya-Yala.

Quigley, Susan R. 2002. *The Awara Verbal System*. MA Thesis, University of North Dakota, Grand Forks.

Rackowski, Andrea. 1998. Malagasy adverbs. In I. Paul, ed., *The Structure of Malagasy, Volume II*. 11–33. UCLA Occasional Papers in Linguistics 20. Los Angeles: Department of Linguistics, UCLA. https://linguistics.ucla.edu/general/WorkingPapers/Occasional_Papers20_TheStructureofMalagasy.pdf.

Rackowski, Andrea, and Lisa Travis. 2000. V-initial languages: X or XP movement and adverbial placement. In Carnie and Guilfoyle, *Syntax of Verb Initial Languages*. 117–141.

Riemsdijk, Henk van. 1983. The case of German adjectives. In Heny and Richards, *Linguistic Categories*. 223–252.

Rizzi, Luigi. 1990. *Relativized Minimality*. Cambridge, MA: MIT Press.

Rizzi, Luigi. 1997. The fine structure of the left periphery. In L. Haegeman, ed., *Elements of Grammar: A Handbook of Generative Syntax*. 281–337. Dordrecht, Netherlands: Kluwer.

Rizzi, Luigi. 2004. Locality and left periphery. In Belletti, *Structures and Beyond*. 223–251.

Rizzi, Luigi. 2016. Labeling, maximality and the head-phrase distinction. *Linguistic Review* 33: 103–127.

Rizzi, Luigi. 2017. Comparing extractions from *wh*-islands and superiority effects. In C. Mayr and E. Williams, eds., Festschrift für Martin Prinzhorn. Special issue, *Wiener Linguistische Gazette* 82: 253–261. https://wlg.univie.ac.at/fileadmin/user_upload/p_wlg/822017/A_Festschrift_Prinzhorn.pdf.

Rizzi, Luigi. 2018. Intervention effects in grammar and language acquisition. *Probus* 30 (2): 339–367.

Rizzi, Luigi, and Giuliano Bocci. 2017. Left periphery of the clause: Primarily illustrated for Italian. In Everaert and van Riemsdijk, *Wiley Blackwell Companion to Syntax*. 1–33.

Roberts, Ian. 2010. *Agreement and Head Movement: Clitics, Incorporation, and Defective Goals*. Cambridge, MA: MIT Press.

Roberts, Ian. 2017. Harmony, symmetry and dominance in word order universals. In Sheehan et al., *Final-over-Final Condition*. 27–42.

Roberts, Ian. 2019. *Parameter Hierarchies and Universal Grammar*. Oxford: Oxford University Press.

Roncero Toledo, Kristian. 2019. *A Typological Approach to West Polesian Morphology and Syntax*. PhD Dissertation, University of Surrey. https://openresearch.surrey.ac.uk/esploro/outputs/doctoral/A-typological-approach-to-West-Polesian-morphology-and-syntax/99511010302346.

Ross, Malcolm. 1980. Some elements of Vanimo, a New Guinea tone language. *Papers in New Guinea Linguistics* 20: 77–109. https://openresearch-repository.anu.edu.au/bitstream/1885/254417/1/PL-A56.77.pdf.

Ross, Malcolm. 2011. Kele. In Lynch et al., *Oceanic Languages*. 123–147

Ruhlen, Merritt. 1975. *A Guide to the World's Languages*. Stanford: Language Universals Project, Stanford University.

Ruhlen, Merritt. 2008. *A Global Linguistic Database*. http://starling.rinet.ru/typology.pdf.

Rutkowski, Paweł, and Ljiljana Progovac. 2005. Classification projection in Polish and Serbian: The position and shape of classifying adjectives. In S. Franks, F. Y. Gladney, and M. Tasseva-Kurktchieva, eds., *Formal*

Approaches to Slavic Linguistics: The South Carolina Meeting 2004. 289–299. Ann Arbor: Michigan Slavic Publications.

Sabel, Joachim. 2011. Deriving linear order in OV/VO languages: Evidence from Oceanic languages. In C. Moyse-Faurie and J. Sabel, eds., *Topics in Oceanic Morphosyntax.* 27–64. Berlin: de Gruyter. https://www.academia.edu/40478993/Deriving_linear_order_in_OV_VO_languages_evidence_from_Oceanic_languages.

Salmond, Anne. 1974. *A Generative Syntax of Luangiua: A Polynesian Language.* The Hague: Mouton.

Salzmann, Martin. 2013a. New arguments for verb cluster formation at PF and a right-branching VP. *Linguistic Variation* 13: 81–132.

Salzmann, Martin. 2013b. New evidence for postsyntactic verb cluster formation and a rightbranching base order. In S. Keine and S. Sloggett, eds., *Proceedings of the North Eastern Linguistics Society Annual Meeting 42.* 135–148. Amherst: University of Massachusetts, GLSA.

Sanders, Gerald A. 1970. Constraints on constituent ordering. *Papers in Linguistics* 2: 460–502. (Reprinted in Meisel and Pam, *Linear Order and Generative Theory.* 71–98.)

Sanders, Gerald A. 1975. *Invariant Ordering.* The Hague: Mouton.

Šaumjan, Sebastian K. 1965. Outline of the Applicational Generative Model for the description of language. *Foundations of Language* 1: 189–222.

Šaumjan, Sebastian K., and Polina A. Soboleva. 1963. Applikativnaja poroždajuščaja model'i isčislenie transformacij v russkom jazyke [Applicational generative and transformational calculus as applied to the Russian language]. Moscow: Izdatel'stvo Akademii Nauk, SSSR.

Sapir, J. David. 1965. *A Grammar of Diola-Fogny.* London: Cambridge University Press.

Sapir, J. David. 1976. Diola. In M. E. Kropp Dakubu, ed., *West African Data Sheet. Volume I.* 143–149. Leiden: West African Linguistic Society.

Sato, Hiroko. 2013. *Grammar of Kove: An Austronesian Language of the West New Britain Province, Papua New Guinea.* PhD Dissertation, University of Hawai'i, Mānoa. http://www.ling.hawaii.edu/graduate/Dissertations/HirokoSatoFinal.pdf.

Schwarzschild, Roger. 2005. Measure phrases as modifiers of adjectives. *Recherches Linguistiques de Vincennes* 34: 207–228. https://journals.openedition.org/rlv/1401.

Schweikert, Walter. 2004. The order of prepositional phrases. *University of Venice Working Papers in Linguistics* 14: 195–216. http://citeseerx.ist.psu.edu/viewdoc/download;jsessionid=CD9D1A6ABC050500E20ADCA6CA216D71?doi=10.1.1.537.331&rep=rep1&type=pdf.

Schweikert, Walter. 2005. *The Order of Prepositional Phrases in the Structure of the Clause*. Amsterdam: Benjamins.

Scott, Gary-John. 2002. Stacked adjectival modification and the structure of nominal phrases. In G. Cinque, ed., *Functional Structure in DP and IP: The Cartography of Syntactic Structures, Volume 1*. 91–120. New York: Oxford University Press.

Senft, Gunter. 1986. *Kilivila. The Language of the Trobriand Islanders*. Berlin: Mouton de Gruyter.

Sharpe, Margaret C. 2005. *Grammar and Texts of the Yugambeh-Bundjalung Dialect Chain in Eastern Australia*. Munich: Lincom Europa.

Sheehan, Michelle. 2017. The Final-over-Final Condition and processing. In Sheehan et al., *Final-over-Final Condition*. 79–96.

Sheehan, Michelle, Theresa Biberauer, Ian Roberts, and Anders Holmberg. 2017. *The Final-over-Final Condition: A Syntactic Universal*. Cambridge, MA: MIT Press.

Shlonsky, Ur. 2004. The form of Semitic noun phrases. *Lingua* 114: 1465–1526. https://archive-ouverte.unige.ch/unige:83461.

Shlonsky, Ur, and Luigi Rizzi. 2018. Criterial freezing in small clauses and the cartography of copular constructions. In J. Hartmann et al., eds., *Freezing*. 29–65. Berlin: Mouton de Gruyter. https://library.oapen.org/handle/20.500.12657/23803.

Sichel, Ivy. 2002. Phrasal movement in Hebrew adjectives and possessives. In Alexiadou et al., *Dimensions of Movement*. 297–339.

So-Hartmann, Helga. 2009. *A Descriptive Grammar of Daai Chin*. STEDT Monograph 7. Berkeley: University of California. https://stedt.berkeley.edu/pubs_and_prods/STEDT_Monograph7_Daai-Chin.pdf.

Sohn, Ho-Min. 1999. *The Korean Language*. Cambridge: Cambridge University Press.

Sommer, Bruce Arthur. 1970. *Kunjen Syntax: A Generative View*. PhD Dissertation, University of Hawai'i, Mānoa.

Sonnenschein, Aaron Huey. 2004. *A descriptive grammar of San Bartolomé Soogocho Zapotec*. PhD Dissertation, University of Southern California.

Sperlich, Wolfgang B. 1991. *Namakir: A Description of a Central Vanuatu Language*. PhD Dissertation, University of Auckland. https://researchspace.auckland.ac.nz/handle/2292/2314.

Sproat, Richard, and Chinlin Shih. 1990. Prenominal adjectival ordering in English and Mandarin. In C. Georgopoulos and R. Ishihara, eds., *Interdisciplinary Approaches to Language: Essays in Honor of S.-Y. Kuroda*. 565–593. Dordrecht, Netherlands: Kluwer.

Staal. Johan F. 1967. *Word Order in Sanskrit and Universal Grammar*. Dordrecht, Netherlands: Reidel.

Stampe, David. 1976. Cardinal number systems. In S. S. Mufwene, C. A. Walker, and S. B. Steever, eds., *Papers from the Twelfth Regional Meeting of the Chicago Linguistic Society*. 594–609. Chicago: Chicago Linguistic Society.

Stapert, Eugénie. 2013. *Contact-Induced Change in Dolgan: An Investigation into the Role of Linguistic Data for the Reconstruction of a People's (Pre)History*. PhD Dissertation, Rijkuniversiteit te Leiden. https://www.lotpublications.nl/Documents/336_fulltext.pdf.

Steele, Susan. 1978. The category AUX as a language universal. In Greenberg et al., *Universals of Human Language*. 7–46.

Stirtz, Timothy M. 2012. *A Grammar of Gaahmg: A Nilo-Saharan Language of Sudan*. PhD Dissertation, Rijksuniversiteit te Leiden. https://scholarlypublications.universiteitleiden.nl/handle/1887/18452.

Sutradhar, Joyshree. 2006. Nominal modification in Pnar: A relativization strategy. Ms., Jawaharlal Nehru University. https://www.academia.edu/252111/Nominal_Modification_in_Pnar_A_Relativization_Strategy.

Svenonius, Peter, ed. 2000. *The Derivation of VO and OV*. Amsterdam: Benjamins.

Svenonius, Peter, 2002. Subject positions and the placement of adverbials. In P. Svenonius, ed., *Subjects, Expletives, and the EPP*. 201–242. New York: Oxford University Press.

Svenonius, Peter. 2007. 1 . . . 3-2. In G. Ramchand and C. Reiss, eds., *The Oxford Handbook of Linguistic Interfaces*. 239–288. Oxford: Oxford University Press. https://ling.auf.net/lingbuzz/000200.

Szabolcsi, Anna. 1994. The Noun Phrase. In Kiefer and Kiss, eds., *The Syntactic Structures of Hungarian* (Syntax and Semantics 27). 179–275. New York: Academic Press.

Takamine, Kaori. 2010. *The Postpositional Hierarchy and Its Mapping to Clause Structure in Japanese*. PhD Dissertation, University of Tromsø. https://munin.uit.no/handle/10037/2465.

Takano, Yuji. 2004. Coordination of verbs and two types of verbal inflections. *Linguistic Inquiry* 35: 168–178.

Tatsumi, Yuta. 2017. Classifiers of two kinds: Notes on the syntax and semantics of classifiers. *Gengo-Bunka Kyoodoo-Kenkyuu-Purozyekuto 2016: Sizen-Gengo-e-no Riron-Teki-Apuroochi* [Joint Project on Language and Culture 2016: Theoretical Approaches to Natural Language]. 39–48. https://drive.google.com/file/d/1eyMukyLNhshGDGgJh7q-MZCLCk1aL4ds/view.

Tatsumi, Yuta. 2018. The silent "number" in complex cardinals. *Proceedings of the 35th West Coast Conference on Formal Linguistics. WCCFL* 35: 382–390. http://www.lingref.com/cpp/wccfl/35/paper3411.pdf.

Tatsumi, Yuta. 2019. Making additive complex cardinals without coordination. *Proceedings of the 12th Generative Linguistics in the Old World in Asia and the 21st Seoul International Conference on Generative Grammar.* 574–583. Seoul: Korean Generative Grammar Circle. https://drive.google.com/file/d/1FrS9tvEjw1HkMRhffHQbrZnsKeKYpJoM/view.

Tatsumi, Yuta. 2020. (Im)possible constituent orders: nominals, numerals, classifiers and ordinal markers. *University of Pennsylvania Working Papers in Linguistics* 26 (1): article 25. https://repository.upenn.edu/pwpl/vol26/iss1/25.

Tatsumi, Yuta. 2021. *Linguistic Realization of Measuring and Counting in the Nominal Domain: A Cross-linguistic Study of Syntactic and Semantic Variations*. PhD Dissertation, University of Connecticut. https://ling.auf.net/lingbuzz/006098.

Thomas, David. 1971. *Chrau Grammar.* Honolulu: University Press of Hawai'i. https://www.sil.org/resources/archives/2776.

Thomas, David. 1976. A Chrau noun phrase battery. *The Mon-Khmer Studies Journal* 5: 135–138. https://www.sil.org/resources/archives/8171.

Thomas, Michael F. 2014. *A Grammar of Sakun (Sukur).* PhD Dissertation, University of Colorado, Boulder. https://scholar.colorado.edu/concern/graduate_thesis_or_dissertations/1c18dg03s.

Tomlin, Russell Schenck. 1979. *An Explanation of the Distribution of Basic Constituent Orders*. PhD Dissertation, University of Michigan.

Traill, Anthony. 1994. *A !Xóõ Dictionary.* Cologne, Germany: Rüdiger Köppe.

Tryon, Darrell T. 1970. *An Introduction to Maranungku (Northern Australia).* Canberra: Pacific Linguistics. B-15. The Australian National University.

Tsunoda, Tasaku. 1990. Typological study of word order in languages of the Pacific Region (6): Korean. *Department Bulletin Papers.* University of Tsukuba.

Tsunoda, Tasaku. 1994. Typological study of word order (18): Bengali. *Department Bulletin Papers.* University of Tsukuba.

Uzar, Henning. 1989. Studies in Gumuz: Sese phonology and TMA system. In M. L. Bender, ed., *Topics in Nilo-Saharan Linguistics.* 347–383. Hamburg, Germany: Helmut Buske Verlag.

Valenzuela, Pilar M. 2016. Classifiers in Shiwilu (Kawapanan) in Northewestern Amazonian Perspective. *Anthropological Linguistics* 58 (4): 333–380

Vallejos, Rosa. 2010. *A Grammar of Kokama-Kokamilla.* PhD, University of Oregon. http://etnolinguistica.wdfiles.com/local--files/tese%3Avallejos-2010/vallejos_2010_kokama.pdf

Voorhoeve, Clemens Lambertus, ed. 1982. The West Makian Language, North Moluccas, Indonesia: A field work report. In *The Makian Languages and Their Neighbours.* 1–74. Canberra, Australia: Pacific Linguistics. https://openresearch-repository.anu.edu.au/bitstream/1885/144389/1/PL-D46.pdf.

Vries, Lourens de. 2012. Some notes on the Tsaukambo language of West Papua. In H. Hammarström and W. van den Heuvel, eds., History, Contact and Classification of Papuan Languages. Special issue, part I, *Language and Linguistics in Melanesia* 2012: 165–193. https://research.vu.nl/en/publications/some-notes-on-the-tsaukambo-language-of-west-papua.

Wągiel, Marcin and Pavel Caha. 2020. Complex simplex numerals. *Acta Linguistica Academica* 68 (4): 470–515.

Wamsley, James C. 2019. Demonstratives in the noun phrase structure of Hakha Chin. *Indiana Working Papers in South Asian Languages and Cultures* (*IWPSALC*) 1(1). https://scholarworks.iu.edu/journals/index.php/iwpsalc/article/view/27454/32776.

Watanabe, Akira. 2006. Functional projections of nominals in Japanese: Syntax of classifiers. *Natural Language and Linguistic Theory* 24 (1): 241–306.

Webelhuth, Gert. 1992. *Principles and Parameters of Syntactic Saturation.* New York: Oxford University Press.

Wegener, Claudia Ursula. 2012. *A grammar of Savosavo.* Berlin: Mouton de Gruyter.

Wiersma, Grace. 2003. Yunnan Bai. In G. Thurgood and R. J. LaPolla, eds., *The Sino-Tibetan languages.* 651–673. London: Routledge. https://www.academia.edu/650582/The_Sino-Tibetan_Languages.

Wierzbicka, Anna. 1999. *Emotions across Languages and Cultures: Diversity and Universals.* Cambridge: Cambridge University Press.

Willer Gold, Jana, Boban Arsenijević, Mia Batinić, Michael Beckerd, Nermina Čordalija, Marijana Kresić, Nedžad Leko, Franc Lanko Marušič, Tanja Milićev, Nataša Milićević, Ivana Mitić, Anita Peti-Stantić, Branimir Stanković, Tina Šuligoj, Jelena Tušekh, and Andrew Nevins. 2018. When linearity prevails over hierarchy in syntax. *PNAS* 115 (3): 495–500. https://www.pnas.org/doi/epdf/10.1073/pnas.1712729115.

Williams-van Klinken, Catharina, John Hajek, and Rachel Nordlinger. 2002. *A Short Grammar of Tetun Dili.* Munich: Lincom Europa.

Winchester, Lindley. 2019. *The Morphosyntax of the Maltese Determiner Phrase.* PhD Dissertation, Georgetown University. https://repository.library.georgetown.edu/handle/10822/1054969.

Wurmbrand, Susi. 2004. West Germanic verb clusters: The empirical domain. In K. É. Kiss and H. van Riemsdijk, eds., *Verb Clusters: A Study of Hungarian, German and Dutch.* 43–85. Amsterdam: Benjamins.

Wurmbrand, Susi. 2017. Verb clusters, verb raising and restructuring. In Everaert and van Riemsdijk, *Wiley Blackwell Companion to Syntax.I* 1–110. https://ling.auf.net/lingbuzz/002433.

Xu, Lin, and Yansun Zhao. 1984. Baiyu Jianzhi [A brief description of the Bai language]. Beijing: Minzu Chubanshe.

Yang, Charles. 2015. Negative knowledge from positive evidence. *Language* 91: 938–953.

Yang, Charles. 2016. *The Price of Linguistic Productivity: How Children Learn to Break the Rules of Language.* Cambridge, MA: MIT Press.

Yoon, James H. 1994. Korean verbal inflection and checking theory. In H. Harley and C. Phillips, eds., *The Morphology-Syntax Connection.*

MIT Working Papers in Linguistics 22. Cambridge, MA: MIT Press. http://faculty.las.illinois.edu/jyoon/Papers/Korean_Infl_MITWPL_1994_Yoon.pdf.

Ywar, Naw Hsa Eh. 2013. *A Grammar of Kayan Lahta.* MA Thesis, Payap University. https://citeseerx.ist.psu.edu/viewdoc/download?doi=10.1.1.695.2171&rep=rep1&type=pdf.

Zavala, Roberto. 2000. Multiple classifier systems in Akatek (Mayan). In G. Senft, ed., *Systems of Nominal Classification.* 114–146. Cambridge: Cambridge University Press.

Zegrean, Iulia-Georgiana. 2012. *Balkan Romance: Aspects of the Syntax of Istro-Romanian.* PhD Dissertation, Ca' Foscari University, Venice. http://dspace.unive.it/bitstream/handle/10579/1166/Zegrean.pdf.

Zhang, Niina Ning. 2011. The constituency of classifier constructions in Mandarin Chinese. *Taiwan Journal of Linguistics* 9: 1–50. http://tjl.nccu.edu.tw/main/uploads/9.1-1Zhang__.pdf.

Zhang, Niina Ning. 2013. *Classifier Structures in Mandarin Chinese.* Berlin: De Gruyter Mouton.

Zhang, Niina Ning. 2015. Nominal-internal phrasal movement in Mandarin Chinese. *Linguistic Review* 32 (2): 375–425.

Zhang, Niina Ning. 2019. Complex indefinites and the projection of DP in Mandarin Chinese. *Journal of East Asian Linguistics* 28: 179–210.

Zompì, Stanislao. 2020. Distinctness effects in English nominals. Ms., MIT. http://www.mit.edu/~zompi/pdfs/zompi_distinctness.pdf.

Zwart, C. Jan-Wouter. 1995. A note on verb clusters in the Stellingwerf Dialect. In M. den Dikken and K. Hengeveld, eds., *Linguistics in the Netherlands.* 215–226. Amsterdam: Benjamins.

Zwart, C. Jan-Wouter. 1996. Verb clusters in continental West Germanic dialects. In J. R. Black and V. Motapanyane, eds., *Microparametric Syntax and Dialect Variation.* 229–258. Amsterdam: Benjamins.

Zwart, C. Jan-Wouter. 1997. *Morphosyntax of Verb Movement: A Minimalist Approach to the Syntax of Dutch.* Dordrecht, Netherlands: Kluwer.

Zwart, C. Jan-Wouter. 2007a. Some notes on the origin and distribution of the IPP-effect. *Groninger Arbeiten zur Germanistischen Linguistik* 45: 77–99. https://ugp.rug.nl/GAGL/article/view/30481.

Zwart, C. Jan-Wouter. 2007b. Uncharted territory? Towards a non-cartographic account of Germanic syntax. *Groninger Arbeiten zur*

Germanistischen Linguistik 45: 55–75. https://ugp.rug.nl/GAGL/article/view/30497/27797.

Zwart, C. Jan-Wouter. 2011. Structure and order: Asymmetric merge. In C. Boeckx, ed., *The Oxford Handbook of Linguistic Minimalism*. 96–118. Oxford: Oxford University Press.

Zweig, Eytan. 2006. Nouns and adjectives in numeral NPs. In L. Bateman and C. Ussery, eds., *Proceedings of the North Eastern Linguistics Society Annual Meeting 35*. 663–675. Amherst: University of Massachusetts, GLSA. https://www-users.york.ac.uk/~ez506/downloads/NELS35_numeral_phrases_proceedings.pdf.

Author Index

Language Index

Subject Index

Linguistic Inquiry Monographs

Samuel Jay Keyser, general editor

1. *Word Formation in Generative Grammar*, Mark Aronoff
2. *Syntax: A Study of Phrase Structure*, Ray Jackendoff
3. *Recent Transformational Studies in European Languages*, S. Jay Keyser, editor
4. *Studies in Abstract Phonology*, Edmund Gussmann
5. *An Encyclopedia of AUX: A Study of Cross-Linguistic Equivalence*, Susan Steele
6. *Some Concepts and Consequences of the Theory of Government and Binding*, Noam Chomsky
7. *The Syntax of Words*, Elisabeth O. Selkirk
8. *Syllable Structure and Stress in Spanish: A Nonlinear Analysis*, James W. Harris
9. *CV Phonology: A Generative Theory of the Syllable*, George N. Clements and Samuel Jay Keyser
10. *On the Nature of Grammatical Relations*, Alec P. Marantz
11. *A Grammar of Anaphora*, Joseph Aoun
12. *Logical Form: Its Structure and Derivation*, Robert May
13. *Barriers*, Noam Chomsky
14. *On the Definition of Word*, Anna-Maria Di Sciullo and Edwin Williams
15. *Japanese Tone Structure*, Janet Pierrehumbert and Mary E. Beckman
16. *Relativized Minimality*, Luigi Rizzi
17. *Types of Ā-Dependencies*, Guglielmo Cinque
18. *Argument Structure*, Jane Grimshaw
19. *Locality: A Theory and Some of Its Empirical Consequences*, Maria Rita Manzini
20. *Indefinites*, Molly Diesing
21. *Syntax of Scope*, Joseph Aoun and Yen-hui Audrey Li
22. *Morphology by Itself: Stems and Inflectional Classes*, Mark Aronoff
23. *Thematic Structure in Syntax*, Edwin Williams

24. *Indices and Identity*, Robert Fiengo and Robert May

25. *The Antisymmetry of Syntax*, Richard S. Kayne

26. *Unaccusativity: At the Syntax–Lexical Semantics Interface*, Beth Levin and Malka Rappaport Hovav

27. *Lexico-Logical Form: A Radically Minimalist Theory*, Michael Brody

28. *The Architecture of the Language Faculty*, Ray Jackendoff

29. *Local Economy*, Chris Collins

30. *Surface Structure and Interpretation*, Mark Steedman

31. *Elementary Operations and Optimal Derivations*, Hisatsugu Kitahara

32. *The Syntax of Nonfinite Complementation: An Economy Approach*, Željko Bošković

33. *Prosody, Focus, and Word Order*, Maria Luisa Zubizarreta

34. *The Dependencies of Objects*, Esther Torrego

35. *Economy and Semantic Interpretation*, Danny Fox

36. *What Counts: Focus and Quantification*, Elena Herburger

37. *Phrasal Movement and Its Kin*, David Pesetsky

38. *Dynamic Antisymmetry*, Andrea Moro

39. *Prolegomenon to a Theory of Argument Structure*, Ken Hale and Samuel Jay Keyser

40. *Essays on the Representational and Derivational Nature of Grammar: The Diversity of* Wh-*Constructions*, Joseph Aoun and Yen-hui Audrey Li

41. *Japanese Morphophonemics: Markedness and Word Structure*, Junko Ito and Armin Mester

42. *Restriction and Saturation*, Sandra Chung and William A. Ladusaw

43. *Linearization of Chains and Sideward Movement*, Jairo Nunes

44. *The Syntax of (In)dependence*, Ken Safir

45. *Interface Strategies: Optimal and Costly Computations*, Tanya Reinhart

46. *Asymmetry in Morphology*, Anna Maria Di Sciullo

47. *Relators and Linkers: The Syntax of Predication, Predicate Inversion, and Copulas*, Marcel den Dikken

48. *On the Syntactic Composition of Manner and Motion*, Maria Luisa Zubizarreta and Eunjeong Oh

49. *Introducing Arguments*, Liina Pylkkänen

50. *Where Does Binding Theory Apply?*, David Lebeaux

51. *Locality in Minimalist Syntax*, Thomas S. Stroik

52. *Distributed Reduplication*, John Frampton

53. *The Locative Syntax of Experiencers*, Idan Landau

54. *Why Agree? Why Move? Unifying Agreement-Based and Discourse-Configurational Languages*, Shigeru Miyagawa

55. *Locality in Vowel Harmony*, Andrew Nevins

56. *Uttering Trees*, Norvin Richards

57. *The Syntax of Adjectives*, Guglielmo Cinque

58. *Arguments as Relations*, John Bowers

59. *Agreement and Head Movement*, Ian Roberts

60. *Localism versus Globalism in Morphology and Phonology*, David Embick

61. *Provocative Syntax*, Phil Branigan

62. *Anaphora and Language Design*, Eric J. Reuland

63. *Indefinite Objects: Scrambling, Choice Functions, and Differential Marking*, Luis López

64. *A Syntax of Substance*, David Adger

65. *Subjunctive Conditionals*, Michela Ippolito

66. *Russian Case Morphology and the Syntactic Categories*, David Pesetsky

67. *Classical NEG Raising: An Essay on the Syntax of Negation*, Chris Collins and Paul M. Postal

68. *Agreement and Its Failures*, Omer Preminger

69. *Voice and v: Lessons from Acehnese*, Julie Anne Legate

70. *(Re)labeling*, Carlo Cecchetto and Caterina Donati

71. *A Two-Tiered Theory of Control*, Idan Landau

72. *Concepts, Syntax, and Their Interface: Tanya Reinhart's Theta System*, Martin Everaert, Marijana Marelj, and Eric Reuland, editors

73. *Contiguity Theory*, Norvin Richards

74. *Impossible Persons*, Daniel Harbour

75. *Agreement Beyond Phi*, Shigeru Miyagawa

76. *The Final-over-Final Condition: A Syntactic Universal*, Michelle Sheehan, Theresa Biberauer, Ian Roberts, and Anders Holmberg

77. *Situations and Syntactic Structures: Rethinking Auxiliaries and Order in English*, Gillian Ramchand

78. *Features of Person: From the Inventory of Persons to Their Morphological Realization*, Peter Ackema and Ad Neeleman

79. *Cardinals: The Syntax and Semantics of Cardinal-Containing Expressions*, Tania Ionin and Ora Matushansky

80. *Composing Questions*, Hadas Kotek

81. *Probes and Their Horizons*, Stefan Keine

82. *A Theory of Indexical Shift: Meaning, Grammar, and Crosslinguistic Variation*, Amy Rose Deal

83. *Merge: Binarity in (Multidominant) Syntax*, Barbara Citko and Martina Gračanin-Yüksek

84. *A Selectional Theory of Adjunct Control*, Idan Landau

85. *Syntax in the Treetops*, Shigeru Miyagawa

86. *On Linearization: Toward a Restrictive Theory*, Guglielmo Cinque